ANNALS OF THE SPANISH AMERICAN
NORMAL SCHOOL

THE FIRST 112 YEARS
OF NORTHERN NEW MEXICO COLLEGE

ANNALS OF THE SPANISH AMERICAN
NORMAL SCHOOL

THE FIRST 112 YEARS
OF NORTHERN NEW MEXICO COLLEGE

by

SIGFREDO MAESTAS

SANTA FE

NOTE: Information and facts as presented in this book by the author are accurate as of the date of the publication of this book. The publisher takes no responsibility for the accuracy of the content of this book.

© 2022 by Sigfredo Maestas
All Rights Reserved
No part of this book may be reproduced in any form or by any electronic or mechanical means including information storage and retrieval systems without permission in writing from the publisher, except by a reviewer who may quote brief passages in a review.

Sunstone books may be purchased for educational, business, or sales promotional use. For information please write: Special Markets Department, Sunstone Press, P.O. Box 2321, Santa Fe, New Mexico 87504-2321.
Printed on acid-free paper

Library of Congress Cataloging-in-Publication Data

Names: Maestas, Sigfredo, 1940- author.
Title: Annals of the Spanish American Normal School : the first 112 years
   of Northern New Mexico College / by Sigfredo Maestas.
Description: Santa Fe : Sunstone Press, [2022] | Summary: "A history of the
   Spanish American Normal School founded in El Rito, New Mexico,
   1909-2021"-- Provided by publisher.
Identifiers: LCCN 2022011859 | ISBN 9781632933638 (paperback)
Subjects: LCSH: Spanish American Normal School (El Rito, Rio Arriba County,
   N.M.)--History. | Teachers--Training of--New Mexico--History. | Teachers
   colleges--New Mexico--History.
Classification: LCC LB1918 .E47 2022 | DDC 370.71/10978952--dc23
   LC record available at https://lccn.loc.gov/2022011859

WWW.SUNSTONEPRESS.COM
SUNSTONE PRESS / POST OFFICE BOX 2321 / SANTA FE, NM 87504-2321 /USA
(505) 988-4418 / FAX (505) 988-1025

DEDICATIONS

This book is dedicated to the following students and all information is current at the time of publication of this book.

First, there is John A. Martin (whose middle name was an Irish name, Aloysius) who was born to George Martin and Margaret Allen Martin, who had charge of the school upon arrival in El Rito. He was the first president, and she later served on the Board of Regents of the Spanish American Normal School. John Martin, in later life, lived with his wife Barbara in Santa Fé. John and Barbara had two sons, Meade and Christopher and they also reside in Santa Fé. Meade appears elsewhere in this book; he explained in a school paper the need for the Spanish American Normal School at a time when no one was writing about the Normal School.

John resided in Santa Fé during the time that I knew him, although I knew that he had served with the U.S. government in San Salvador during developmental projects in said country, and I knew that he was fluent in Spanish.

John helped me get the Northern New Mexico Community College (NNMCC) Foundation on firm ground. It was then that I learned that John's memory took him back to 1927, as he remembered the Martins returning to El Rito and reestablishing George's family after an absence of years after the elder Martin had left the Normal School. The Martin family had resided in Pueblo, Colorado.

John knew then, as I do now, how difficult those days were. I'm certain that John was always the same friendly guy whom I knew almost 80 years later. And John knew that his parents had a new automobile, perhaps the first car in El Rito, and described roads in those days. Mere dirt paths.

John passed on to me impressions, which I hope to convey to readers, that are astounding and unique in their thoroughness.

A second student whom I got to know well is Jane Goddard, who married Fabián García and lived down the road, not far from the Community College (NNMCC). Jane was the daughter of Clarence and Augusta Goddard. Clarence was not fluent in Spanish, but Augusta spoke Spanish beautifully, she being from Mexico originally. Jane remembers that, in her childhood, she was given to learn language from friends, and the language was one spoken by compatriots, including this author.

Jane García remembers some things about the Normal School rather vividly. She was always interested in books, and the Normal School library had many from which to select. Jane Goddard graduated from the high school in May 1941 and soon met and married Fabián. (Not incidentally, because of Fabián's presence, the Garcías were unusually good neighbors for the Community College, both before and after I arrived on campus.) Fabián had been a student at St. Michael's High School in Santa Fé. Fabián is deceased.

I regret that Jane had a complaint about the Spanish American Normal School, under Joseph Grant at the time, that I have heard from students in El Rito many times. Jane felt that the Normal School had distinctly cold feelings toward students in El Rito, the old matter of a "town and gown" problem, which should not have existed. This problem—because it most definitely was a problem that had one remedy—even manifested itself in the manner that students were not afforded a place to eat at lunch time.

One of the photographs given to me by Jane García is of the graduating class of 1929. Present in the picture are Raymond Romero, Vadito; Pauline Goddard, El Rito; Richard Ortega, Chimayó; Olive Parker, El Rito; José M. Valdez, McPhee, Colorado; Simmie Atencio, Santa Cruz; and Cruz Trujillo, Chimayó. Sitting is Isabel Ward, class sponsor. There is a story concerning Olive Parker in the chapter "Sons and Daughters of the Normal School." The photograph is in *Children of the Normal School*, published in 2011, by Sunstone Press.

José Valdez lived in a village called Lyden and he happened to teach my mother in a village called Monero, also in Rio Arriba County.

And, as you would guess, I learned from Jane, as I did from John Martin, about the Normal School and its ambience.

A third student, Fabiola Lucero, has lived in Pueblo, Colorado for a long time. She is the aunt-by-marriage of Dr. Richard Bailey, the current president of Northern New Mexico College. Dr. Bailey used as a credential the fact that Fabiola had attended the Normal School beginning about 10th grade. I then contacted her, through Dr. Bailey, and he had been enthralled by her stories from those days at the Normal School. (The high school remained the Spanish American Normal School up to the 1950s when it became Northern New Mexico Normal School. This part of the story is about the older Normal School.)

Fabiola was willing to spend an entire afternoon with me discussing the Normal School. Fabiola arrived at the Normal School in the presence of Andres Lucero and Felicita Bachicha Lucero for 10th grade. Her grandfather was a man from the llano by the name of Bernabe Lucero, and according to Fabiola, "boy, he was a cool cookie." I read a lot into that statement. Bernabe was obviously handsome, probably, to her tall and slender. He would have been interested in cars, and probably had an automobile that he cared for a lot. But, there she was at the Spanish American Normal School at El Rito. She was not aggressive; she was what you called "shy."

Fabiola, shown in a photograph with a teacher named Pablo Mares, participated in a Orquesta Típica, which Mr. Mares sponsored. (Not incidentally, I met Pablo Mares and members of his family, and one can guess the direction of this tale.) Fabiola liked Mr. Mares very much, and he helped her to become more outgoing. She had felt abandoned when her parents dropped her off in El Rito. Mr. Mares, well liked by students at El Rito, eventually found a means by which Fabiola Lucero would "come out of her shell," as she put it.

Fabiola found other things to like at the Normal School. She thought the meals were "delicious" and she particularly liked piñón, which were a variety of nuts still popular in the high country where these nuts grow.

We spent a long afternoon, she telling me about the early 1940s at the Spanish American Normal School at El Rito.

A fourth student, Paul Romero, whom I (you and I, actually) owe a debt of gratitude to in our daily lives is a veteran of World War II. This is the only living individual whom I know was in the Pacific theater in the war, and who married my aunt Cecilia Valdez in Velarde about 1945. Paul graduated from the Spanish American Normal School in 1944, and was immediately inducted into the US Army. Paul, to whom I extend great reverence and respect to in our own way, is one of the fellows that Tom Brokaw, a news announcer with the ABC Network, declared a member of The Greatest Generation. These are individuals who survived the Great Depression and then went on to defeat either Emperor Hirohito's Japan or Hitler's Germany during World War II.

Paul, who is not very talkative about the war, told me that General MacArthur is famous for saying "I shall return," upon having to leave the Philippine Islands, and then "returned on the backs of United States Army infantrymen." Paul says this with no bitterness, having returned to recapture the island of Luzon from the Japanese soldiers. It was these same infantrymen who took prisoner-of-war camps and freed American soldiers who had seen Japan's prisons in the earlier part of the war.

Paul retired from Los Alamos National Laboratory after an adult life-time of service. Paul, an unusually sober individual, gained the respect of community, quietly, and probably has seen his name in print in these books more than usual.

Yes, this is an apt term as applied to Paul Romero and his generation of people, The Greatest Generation.

If you would like to read about Paul, please see pages 62 and 63 in *Children of the Normal School*.

CONTENTS

Preface ~ 10

1 / The Spanish American Normal School at El Rito ~ 14
2 / The Earliest Days ~ 22
3 / Uncertainty in the First Decade ~ 26
4 / The High School in the 1920s ~ 32
5 / 1933–1935, Years of Decision ~ 39
6 / A School to Build a Dream On ~ 50
7 / Final Years of the Spanish American Normal School ~ 88
8 / Sons and Daughters of the Normal School ~ 130

Photographs ~ 204

9 / The New Mexico Technical Vocational School ~ 228
10 / Northern New Mexico Community College: Growing Pains and Halcyon Days ~ 242
11 / Return to the Normal School's Original Mission ~ 268
12 / Northern New Mexico College ~ 283
13 / Northern New Mexico College Enters its Fifth Year ~ 296
14 / Northern New Mexico College Enters its Eleventh Year ~ 299
15 / Northern New Mexico College—Entering a New Saga ~ 304

Students Attending the Normal School During the Early Years ~ 308
Graduates of the Normal School ~ 312

Index of Principal Names ~ 333

PREFACE

In 2009, Northern New Mexico College celebrated 100 years of its founding as the Spanish American Normal School. This book is about the Normal School and what it became. Although a very small school in its early history, it served its students, the majority of them from this region of the Río Arriba, by adapting to their times and changing needs. Northern New Mexico College, as the school is known today, evolved from its origin in 1909 to become a source of pride for people here and a cause for hope for a better lives of residents. Its influence is known and felt by people in its service area, educationally, socially, culturally, and economically.

The book is celebratory, not profoundly analytical nor intentionally critical. I wrote it because, as many readers know, I have first-hand knowledge that I acquired about the institution as a student of the Northern New Mexico Normal School in the mid-1950s. My acquaintance with the present college grew in the latter part of the 20th century, and the turn of the new century, when I became a dean, then its seventeenth president. I have lived longer than any single individual on the Normal School's campus at El Rito, sixteen years. I have acquired a grasp of, and great appreciation for the social and cultural history of this region, aided by first-hand accounts of people who lived here. Our shared fondness for stories of times past have done much to sustain this modest effort, writing this book. Names of people, whom I have known here over the years thus figure prominently in this story. Correctly told, then, the book is not strictly history, for I am not a historian and make no pretense to be one. "Annals" seems like an apt title for these recollections and words.

Public and higher education in New Mexico have changed greatly since 1909 when the Spanish American Normal School was founded.

It follows that needs of people, potential students, have also changed. Many times the Normal School's adaptation was exactly what the populace demanded; but sometimes it was not. I have tried to point out, as honestly as the dim light of history permits, where the Normal School was successful in serving its people, and when it was less so. I should point out early in this discussion, however, that because the school at El Rito was a boarding campus serving people who were economically poor, someone's need was always met.

A word about style: the book is written primarily in the active voice, which I prefer. I try to relate a story unencumbered by my own thoughts and opinions, although occasionally they are inevitable and I try to be clear when my statements are opinion. Occasionally, when I feel detached from the story, I speak in the third person, such as, "The author goes on too long." I write Spanish names using diacritical marks, accents and tildes, in their proper places, although most readers will not be used to seeing them. I am guessing, in this instance, that the popular typewriters of the last century simply did not have them, but with the advent of modern word processors we have no excuse for perpetuating the error.

Also related to style, I have chosen to say "Normal School" frequently in referring to this school in its several eras. It is sort of what people would say a long time ago, "la escuela normal." Another usage is my reference to the Río Arriba, which was more than the present county; this was a region that encompassed all of north central New Mexico and the San Luis Valley in southern Colorado. Places south of Santa Fe and others on down the river were in the land of the Río Abajo.

In preparing to write this book, I consulted the usual sources: history books, memoirs, school records, minutes of meetings, old school catalogs, and the school yearbook *El Chamisal*. Archives of the State were useful, as was archival material available on the Internet. Staff of the archival departments of Notre Dame University and Regis College in Denver were wonderfully helpful. I remain most grateful to personnel at Notre Dame and Regis College, and to the tens of people who agreed to interviews with me for the purpose of illuminating a not-so-distant past.

A few books proved indispensable;"*Politics and Education in Hispanic New Mexico: From the Spanish American Normal School to Northern New Mexico Community College,* by Dr. Guillermo Lux and published in 1984, is the only book-length account of the school. I relied on Lux's book and in addition, brief papers by Meade Martin (1978) and Dr. Robert McGeagh (about 1992). Martin's paper, "A Question of Need: The Origin of the Spanish American Normal School" reviews the original purpose of the Normal School and its demonstration of an ability to adapt to meet needs of its students. In "Historical Facts concerning the Administration Building at the El Rito Campus of NNMCC to be included in the History Section of the Application to list the Building on the State Cultural Properties Register," McGeagh relates the most complete account of the origin and uses of the Delgado Hall building that has been written anywhere.

A very useful account, particularly about the State of New Mexico's financing of public education, was written in 1965 by Dr. Tom Wiley, now deceased, and carries the title, "Public School Education in New Mexico." I used Wiley's book and "Forgotten People", by Dr. George I. Sánchez, to assess the educational climate at the turn of the century, just prior to the founding of the Spanish American Normal School.

I chose to rely on oral history of the people in and around El Rito and the Río Arriba according to their memory beginning with the 20th century. A delightful brief memoir, *Romance of a Little Village Girl*, by Cleofas Martínez Jaramillo, added to my knowledge of her husband Venceslao Jaramillo, and to appreciation for the culture of the couple's social set. The older history of New Mexico, back to the time of the Mexican War, has been told by writers such as Territorial Governor L. Bradford Prince in *Historical Sketches of New Mexico* (1883); Ralph Emerson Twitchell in *The Military Occupation of the Territory of New Mexico from 1846 to 1851*(2007); and Bernard DeVoto's *The Year of Decision: 1846* (1942 and 1943). I have read these books, and winced with the latter two books, as would any nuevo mexicano of any age. I also read *The Spanish Redemption: Heritage, Power, and Loss on New Mexico's Upper Rio Grande* by Charles Montgomery and *Blood and Thunder: The Epic Story of Kit Carson and the Conquest of the American West* by Hampton Sides, newer books that show a greater understanding of people in these parts, but rely on many of the same sources nevertheless.

I felt it necessary often in writing these pages to help the reader create an image of life in New Mexico, particularly prior to World War II, and to contrast it with the rest of the United States. Two books that I consulted stand out as being useful to me in this regard: Only *Yesterday* (1931) by Frederick Lewis Allen and *Daily Life in the United States, 1920–1940* (2002), written by David Kyvig.

I invite you to examine the appendices. You will find the most complete list of names to be found anywhere of students who attended the high school, which was known widely as the El Rito Normal School, when state and school officials were going through the tiresome exercise of settling for the official name of the school. Because the term Normal School suggests teachers' college, I have also included the names of new graduates of Northern New Mexico College who have earned the bachelor's degree (in all fields.)

1

THE SPANISH AMERICAN NORMAL SCHOOL AT EL RITO

Founding of the Spanish-American Normal School resulted from perspicacity of Venceslao Jaramillo, native of El Rito, and his willingness to wait for the appropriate time to seek from the Territorial Legislature and Governor of the territory the support needed. His tenacity—he waited about six years after failing in his attempt to establish the teachers' college that he sought for the Río Arriba—paid off when the clamor for statehood, particularly at the Capitol in Santa Fe increased as a result of frustration, this time, from failed attempts by governmental officials to have the Territory of New Mexico gain full admission to the Union.

The history of New Mexico's quest for statehood is a lesson in how timing can serve in seeking the appropriate moment in which to achieve a political objective. In 1874 and again in 1876, New Mexico's non-voting representative in the Congress saw the territory's chances for statehood disappear in a bizarre sequence of events that I shan't recount here. Suffice it to say that readers who have an interest in the political process that ultimately resulted in New Mexico becoming the 47th state in the Union should read this bit of history. For our story, the need to be admitted to the USA as a state and New Mexico's ultimate success are what is important. Serious consideration of the issue had to be postponed, however, for over a quarter of a century to 1912.

Many reasons existed why New Mexico sought to be admitted. Commerce, and any fledgling industry, needed the law of the Nation in everything from finance to transportation, in addition to the ordinary protections that statehood provided. Although there was seldom unanimity on the issue of statehood, politicians' ability to hold office and govern in the territory were measured by their success or failure in achieving statehood for this one of few remaining territories. Health and education were considerations that still trailed in importance, but more forward-looking citizens in these fields of endeavor recognized benefits to be derived from statehood, also. Gaining admission to the Union had remained a vexing problem. A near-miss in 1876, when Colorado was admitted to the Union, was frequently discussed and blamed on congressional delegate Stephen B. Elkins. Discussions that pin blame on a single individual, as in this case, are speculative. What a former state historian, Robert J. Torres, stated in "Cuarto Centennial History of New Mexico" (See Chapter Seven: The Quest for Statehood) is closer to the truth of the matter, I believe.

Many reasons have been suggested why it took New Mexico so long to become a state. Early efforts were hampered, in part, by general ignorance about the territory and suspicion toward its people. Statehood was opposed by those who felt that New Mexico's predominantly Hispanic and Indian population was too foreign and too Catholic for admission to the American Union.

There was little that New Mexico could do to expedite the matter of statehood but to analyze useful strategy and remain patient. One thing that could be done was to educate its people in the English language, and that it had demonstrated willingness to do, albeit somewhat late.

To Venceslao Jaramillo, it must have seemed that everything was in order to reintroduce the proposal of a normal school in El Rito. The Territory was once again interested in statehood, and education of its people in English seemed imperative. More than this, he had great friends and supporters whom he could reliably count as January, 1909 approached, with the impending legislative session set to convene. Although he was no longer a representative in the Territorial House, he should act now. Chief among his allies was L. Bradford Prince, Councilman in the legislature, and former territorial Governor who lived downriver in Chamita (Governor Prince's address was listed in Española.) Another friend was Hermegildo Vigil, Representative in the House, who resided in Velarde. A very prominent member and Chairman of the Council was Charles Spiess from Las Vegas. All three gentlemen were Republican, members of Venceslao Jaramillo's party, and good personal friends. Speaker of the House was Epimenio A. Miera, who represented Sandoval county and was from Cuba, another Republican.

No longer in the legislature, but nevertheless influential friends, were T.D. Burns from Los Ojos and John Sargent from El Rito, still active in political circles.

The matter of timing in this instance cannot be overly emphasized. One has to remember that six years earlier, Venceslao had sought and obtained legislation and funds for the construction of a building in El Rito to house a boys' reformatory school. He was the designated chairman of a board to govern the reform school and directed construction of the bulding, which never opened its doors. This did not fit into his plans, to the good fortune of people whose primary interest was in education for people in north central New Mexico.

If English were to be taught in Rio Arriba county, as the area had come to be known, there was huge need for education and training of teachers, primarily for the public schools. Dr. Guillermo Lux, in his 1984 book, *Public Education in Hispanic New Mexico: From Spanish American Normal School to Northern New Mexico Community College*, has made this point amply. Every statistic extant from the first decade of the 1900s supports this. Even if one questions the accuracy of data available then, it is clear that there were very few teachers available for even the small number of pupils attending school. It was reported to the 38th session of the legislature that there were 93,815 students enrolled in New Mexico, assisted by 1065 teachers. There were 88 teachers per pupil? Astounding! It was noted that progress had been made in the previous two years, during which the number of teachers had increased by 185. Dr. Tom Wiley noted in his book, *Public Education in New Mexico*, (1965) that some teachers, in a slightly earlier time, not university trained, could not sign their name. Let there be no question, New Mexico needed teachers.

Venceslao Jaramillo saw an opening for fulfillment of an educational project for northern New Mexicans that had been shunted by indifferent legislators and governor in 1903. The state of affairs was not unusual then, nor is it now, in our state. Rural areas do not get much consideration from politicians at the State Capitol. But in 1909 the situation was slightly different. People of the north would be required, and benefited, by ability to speak, read and write in the English language; many more new teachers were needed for existing and new schools; perhaps statehood could be achieved, at last, for New Mexico if people "up there" spoke English; and, the legislature and Governor of the Territory were of Jaramillo's party. Now was the time to introduce new legislation to establish the Spanish-American Normal School.

In his address to the 38th Legislative Assembly in January, 2009, Governor George Curry spoke optimistically on several points on the state of the Territory:

> It was growing, approaching a population of 450,000.
>
> The financial condition of the Territory was good, having felt little ill effects of the country's financial panic of 1908.
>
> The total assessed value was growing, approaching $52 million in 1909.
>
> Then he spoke to the matter of his desires, and those of colleagues, for statehood: "We have every reason to believe that New Mexico at last is to be given her rights and statehood is very near at hand." He went on to say that older antagonisms of some Senators and representatives had diminished. He stated that President Theodore Roosevelt, "...has given and is giving his hearty support to our cause." He stated further that President-elect Taft had also given indication of his support.
>
> The Governor erred in stating that the New Mexico Reform School was located at El Rito, Rio Arriba county, but it was an understandable slip. He then correctly made mention of the new building at El Rito that he stated "...will be open for the reception and care of juvenile offenders of the territory in the near future..."
>
> He mentioned with pride the territory's institutions of higher education: University of New Mexico, New Mexico College of Agriculture and Mechanical Arts, New Mexico School of Mines, New Mexico Normal University in Las Vegas, New Mexico Normal School at Silver City, and New Mexico Military Institute.
>
> He spoke about the anti-gambling law which had been enacted in January, 1908. As a result, he said, "...New Mexico today is freer from the evils of gambling than any other commonwealth in the Union."
>
> Governor Curry spoke about the need for better roads to connect villages and cities.

He recommended that capital punishment be abolished.

The Governor went on to cover aspects of concern to legislators that are beyond the scope of this book. I point out the last three items above because these are issues that are germane yet one hundred years later. One thing is certain about Governor Curry and this speech: he was overly optimistic about the matter of statehood for New Mexico. It wasn't until a full three years later, in January, 1912, that President Howard H. Taft signed the proclamation that made New Mexico the 47th member of the American Union. This puts us ahead in the discussion of the Normal School, but this has dealt with an important point surrounding the founding of the Spanish-American Normal School.

Governor Prince introduced legislation to establish the Spanish-American Normal School at El Rito as had been envisaged years earlier by Venceslao Jaramillo and, no doubt, other close friends. This year was finally to be cause for celebration in bringing an old idea to fruition. Passage of a bill was not easy, however. It wasn't until March 18, 1909, during the last day of the legislative session, An Act to establish the Spanish-American Normal School at El Rito was approved. The preamble to the Act speaks more clearly, perhaps, to some of the points I have written here about need that resulted in this legislative and gubernatorial action. It is taken from Chapter 97, A.C.B. No. 69 which reads:

> Whereas, over 400 country schools in New Mexico are composed principally of scholars whose native language is Spanish, and who consequently can only be taught English and other studies effectively by teachers acquainted with the Spanish language;
>
> Whereas, The most pressing need of our country common schools in counties where the Spanish language is prevalent is a sufficient number of native Spanish-speaking teachers, in sympathy with their scholars, and with ample education and training in their profession to teach such schools in English;
>
> Whereas, The Territory of New Mexico posses a commodious and well-build edifice at El Rito, erected for the purpose of the Territorial Reform School, but which has never yet been occupied, and by its situation is not well adapted to the purpose for which it was constructed, but is centrally located to the counties having the

largest proportion of Spanish-speaking persons, and can easily be adapted to general education use; therefore,

Be it enacted by the Legislative Assembly of the Territory of New Mexico...

The first statement reveals the sensitivity of the writer for the need that students had for Spanish-speaking teachers to teach them in the new language. Second, one is impressed by the urgency expressed in the document, surrounding the need for more teachers at the time.

The Act was completed in language that set forth the purpose, mission and role which were intended for the Spanish-American Normal School.

Section 1. There is hereby constituted and established the New Mexico Spanish-American Normal School, the object of which shall be to educate Spanish speaking natives of New Mexico for the vocation of teachers in the public schools of the counties and districts where the Spanish language is prevalent.

Said Normal School is hereby located at El Rito, Rio Arriba county on the premises now occupied by the New Mexico Reform School; and said premises together with the buildings erected thereon, and all fixtures and equipment connected therewith are hereby transferred to the said normal school.

Sec. 2. The management and control of said Spanish-American Normal School, the appointment, qualification, powers and duties of its trustees shall be the same as provided for said Reform School and other Territorial institutions by Sections 6 and 7 of Chapter 2, of the laws of 1903; so far as applicable.

Sec. 3. The courses of instruction at said Normal School shall be particularly arranged for the training and qualification of teachers to give instructions in English in the ordinary rural public schools of the Territory, and especially those where the greater part of the scholars belong to Spanish-speaking families.

Every scholar admitted to said Normal School shall sign an obligation agreeing, in case he or she graduates, to teach at least two years in public schools of the Territory, unless excused for good cause by the Territorial Board of Education.

No scholar shall be received in said school who has not passed the fourth grade as established in the public schools of New Mexico in a satisfactory manner; or passes a satisfactory examination for entrance in the fifth grade; and the trustees of said school are directed to make regulations to insure compliance with this provision.

Sec. 4. The sum of $4,500 or so much of thereof as may be necessary, is hereby appropriated from money in the Territorial Treasury raised by taxation to the credit of the New Mexico Reform School, for obtaining necessary furniture and apparatus for the opening of said school and for expenses and maintenance of the same to July 1, 1910.

Sec. 5. All acts and parts of acts in conflict herewith are hereby repealed. this act shall be in force and effect from and after the date of its passage.

The document made several omissions of points that probably required little clarification in 1909, but cause some puzzlement today. One is that there is no mention that the student body would consist of local students, but it would include a similar number of boarding students, as did other institutions of higher education at the time. How to finance construction and maintenance of living facilities, along with instructional facilities, was not explained. Nor was there mention of the extent of the curriculum—how many grades and general program of instruction. The more glaring omission was a failure to mention any provision for Anglo and native American students. It seems that very little thought was given to education of all citizens of the Territory. Emphasis on educating Spanish-speaking people is understandable, given place, time and circumstances, but exclusivity, as implied in the Act, would not be justifiable today.

I shall make special mention of Le Baron Bradford Prince, sponsor of the legislative bill to establish the Normal School at El Rito, although he has been written about amply in the history of New Mexico. This is to emphasize his interest and support of education, his seriousness of purpose, and his scholarship. He was born in Flushing, New York on July 3, 1840. It is worth mentioning, because in New Mexico hispanic people point with pride to their early ancestry in New Mexico and the USA, that Bradford Prince was reputed to have had ancestors who arrived in America on the Mayflower. He was a lawyer, graduate of Columbia University (1866). He had served in the legislature of the state of New York as a Republican, when in 1878 he was appointed Chief Justice of the New Mexico court. In April, 1889 he was appointed Governor of the Territory by President Benjamin Harrison and served until April, 1893, when he was replaced by President Grover Cleveland, a Democrat. As territorial governor, he convinced a hesitant legislature to establish public education in New Mexico. It was under his administration, in 1891, that the first Superintendent of Public Instruction was named. The Governor supported public and higher education in the territory. Personally interested in scholarship and in history, he published "A Concise History of New Mexico" in 1912, and other books and sketches about his acquired home state. Although he points with pride to the state's educational system, he does not brag in his writing about the part he played in its creation. With regard to the Normal School at El Rito he states only that, "In 1909 the Spanish-American Normal School was established at El Rito for the important purpose of preparing native New Mexican teachers for the great number of rural schools in the state." Governor Prince makes no mention of his volunteer work on behalf of the Spanish American Normal School or of his membership on its first Board of Regents. He expresses a concern for and chronicles the start of schools by the federal government in Albuquerque and Santa Fe for Indian people. His writing shows strong character and a progressive nature. No doubt some would criticize his association with the "Santa Fe Gang,", I presume one of the risks of the time for any prominent Republican politician.

Venceslao Jaramillo, L. Bradford Prince, and their colleagues had set the stage for higher education to begin in Rio Arriba and its environs. The Spanish American Normal School would have an austere beginning, witness an appropriation of $4,500 to cover all expenditures necessary during its first year. But it was an opportunity for the region, where previously there had been none.

2
THE EARLIEST DAYS

They came from communities in Rio Arriba and Taos counties, but a few students were from as far as Estancia (2), Golden (1), Mountainair (1), and Roswell (1). Two students were from out of the Territory: one from Pagosa in Colorado, a second student from Frankfort, Kentucky. Students from the two adjoining counties were from Abiquiu (1), Alcalde (1), Chamita (1), Coyote (1), El Rito (16), Gallina (1), Monero (1), Ojo Caliente (2), Ranchos de Taos (1), Taos (2), Vallecitos (3), Velarde (1), and Venus (1). Early in the first term, there were 46 enrolled, and later in the year the oldest student joined the class. They came to the Normal School by wagon, on horseback, and on foot.

In the first ten years of the Spanish American Normal School, the student body would be remarkably similar from year to year. The communities from which they came were within traveling distance of the school; most students came from Rio Arriba and adjoining counties. Travel was seldom easy. The younger students—there were twelve students between the ages of 13 and 16—must have been accompanied by parents, because they had a long way to travel. The one thirteen-year-old was from El Rito; he had a sister at the Normal, age 14. Seventeen students were ages 17 to 19; fourteen were 20 to 29 years of age. Two students were in their early 30s. The oldest was 59 in 1909.

Forty-six students determined the curriculum, not by design, of course, but by their lack of previous schooling. Because there were so few rural schools in these communities, most instruction in the first year of the Normal School, and subsequently, had to be conducted at a very elementary level. School began with the teaching of English, sounds and letters. Ciphering was still a word in use, and it constituted the curriculum in math. We have to imagine these circumstances to understand how difficult it was for those in charge of the Normal School in its earliest days. I have mentioned the absence of rural schools in the region. This dictated that many students came not solely for teacher training, but for their general education. A second difficulty was how to begin to hire teachers given the special nature of the Normal School and its students. Elementary school teachers were in short supply and in high demand throughout the Territory. Similar circumstances would prevail for at least the first ten years of the Normal School, and, in one way or another, for close to fifty years. We will revisit similar problems, although seldom as acute, during the remaining history of the Spanish American Normal School.

The rural nature of Rio Arriba, and especially a community in the middle of the county like El Rito, made the situation only worse. In its initial year, the Spanish American Normal School could not attract sufficient favorable attention from potential governing board members. There were two mainstays, loyal to the task to be done. L. Bradford Prince and Venceslao Jaramillo were appointed to the Board of Regents immediately and became chairman and secretary-treasurer, respectively. First, there was the matter of starting a brand-new school far from any center of learning! Luckily for the two principal supporters of the school, Malaquias Martinez from Taos and John Henry Sloan from Santa Fe subsequently to serve on the first Board. Mr. Sloan was the lone Democrat on the Board for a brief while. Both Martinez and Sloan were prominent in their home towns and in New Mexico politics.

Travel was difficult for Board members, as it was for all New Mexicans, but it was especially difficult for Venceslao Jaramillo who became Rio Arriba County treasurer while serving on the Normal School Board. During the planning period, and for much of the Normal School's initial year, Venceslao Jaramillo ran the business of the school. His consultative nature required that he engage Governor Prince in determining whom to hire for educational jobs.

Some of the students, about half of them, would need a boarding facility. The building that had become available, as a result of the old project to establish a reformatory school, permitted classrooms for instruction and living quarters for students. The building lacked central heating and running water. Wood stoves and plenty of wood for the cold months would have to be brought in. Outhouses had to be constructed. Water had to be hauled from a third of a mile down the road in El Rito.

Water, or most often a lack of water, is a subject of much interest, debate, conflict, and so on in New Mexico. During its early period, although the Normal School was free to take as much water as it needed, in fact, on campus there was no water to be had. El riíto, the creek, runs half a mile to a mile from the campus, and there was no ground water available in 1909. In time, wells would be dug, but there was still insufficient water for a population as large as the one on campus. Flow rates of five gallons per minute are common throughout El Rito, more so at the campus. In later years, although the Normal School owned plentiful water rights, in fact there was no water to be had. No one knew this then, but it was a problem that would hinder the campus's growth and require that the school look for other sources for water.

Staff during the first year were few in number. The Board of Regents hired a dormitory matron, Mrs. George Dixon, who also served in the capacity of Assistant Principal of the school. One additional teacher assisted her. Readers will find it curious that Mrs. Dixon was not known, apparently, by her first name. Equally puzzling is the fact that, although she served in the absence of a Principal, she was an Assistant Principal.

Sixteen of the students from the first-year class returned for a second year, 34%. The class the following year was a bit larger, and in communities in which a student did not return, records show that more new students came from the same communities for the second year.

Despite the good intentions of the Board of Regents and the staff of the school, entering students were not performing above fourth grade, as stipulated in the requirements of the Normal School's founding Act. For at least another decade, the Normal School would offer an elementary school curriculum, limited at most to grades one to eight. I point out these matters, not because the leadership of the Normal School was at fault in the least, but because the dismal state of public education in north central New Mexico forced the Normal School to adapt to meet needs of its inhabitants. This tendency of the Spanish American Normal School, to meet the needs of the region, would continue—in its various conceptions and regardless of its name—on up to the present time.

A few students felt sufficiently prepared to take on jobs teaching in neighboring schools. In the absence of more stringent requirements for educational achievement as many as ten of the Normal School's students taught in the public schools of the North. Students would often teach a year or two, and then return to the Normal for further schooling.

3
UNCERTAINTY IN THE FIRST DECADE

The number of students attending the Normal School grew slightly in the second year, 1910-11, and the school hired a new principal. In addition to sixteen returning students the oldest, age 56, did not return. There were 37 new students, making a total of 53. The age range among them was similar to the previous year; there was one older student, from Springer, she was 47 years old.

The Board of Regents, led still by former Governor Prince, continued to govern and to operate a Normal School, in spite of the lack of preparedness of their students. There was a man from New York, who had been in Santa Fe as a patient at the St. Vincent's Hospital in about 1908—then referred to as a sanatorium for convalescence. He thought, erroneously, that he had tuberculosis, which in the early 1900s was probably the dreaded disease of the time. John Martin, who was a son of George J. Martin and lived in Santa Fe at the time, told me this story. George Martin did not have tuberculosis and he recovered quickly. It was his good luck to meet Margaret Allen, a nurse at the hospital. Margaret had come to Santa Fe, and to this country, from Ireland. All of this made it possible for Governor Prince and the Board of Regents to gain the acquaintance of George J. Martin and to convince him to come to El Rito as the principal of the Spanish American Normal School in 1910. A few years later, in 1913, they would change the title of their school leader to President.

George Martin was an interesting individual of his time; today we would view him as a Renaissance man. He had been born in Paterson, New Jersey in October, 1888. In his early life, he resided with his parents in Yonkers, NY. He showed an interest in languages and humanities, and in spring, 1909, he graduated from Manhattan College with a degree in

Modern Languages. I learned from Manhattan College that at the time of Mr. Martin's graduation, the College still resided in Manhattan and the degree in Modern Languages was one of only five degrees offered. From his son John, I learned that George Martin was fluent in English, Spanish, French and German. In addition to his command of languages, he had an ability to manage an organization, such as a Normal School. Several years later when he became discouraged and left the Normal School, he would make his living in business, right in El Rito.

For many years, schools and colleges were affected by the state's political climate, even to the extent of personnel appointments. During the last days of the Territory and early days of the state of New Mexico, Boards of Regents, which consisted of five members appointed by the Governor, included no more than three members from the Governor's political party, but a majority nonetheless. In 1910, the incumbent and succeeding Territorial Governors, George Curry and William J. Mills, happened to be Republican. You can bet that the Board of Regents of the Normal School would appoint a Republican to head the school; George J. Martin was Republican. Consideration of party for selection of the president, whether politically important or not, continued for a long time. This criterion for selection also affected other staff, who had to be—often, not always—from the party in power. The practice slowly died in the 1960s, after adoption of a personnel act by the State of New Mexico prohibiting such practices, with exceptions with which we, today, are familiar. I don't believe that teachers in the schools were affected very frequently by this practice, because there was always a shortage of teachers in our state. I advise that we not judge our forebears too harshly, and that we thank heaven that change has occurred. The law still requires that no more than three of the Board's five members be of the Governor's political party.

George Martin and a small staff had a difficult job and many disappointments. There were other problems, in addition to academic considerations, which had to weigh heavily on individuals committed to creating a real teachers' college at the Spanish American Normal School. The work of the Board of Regents and its new staff was of heroic proportion. Even when statehood was attained in 1912, the state still had insufficient funds to support its educational system, and the Normal School suffered as one of the institutions receiving the least consideration for scarce dollars. Urban areas in the state, and a more or less cohesive east side, made certain that money for the support of educational institutions went to the better known, and larger, colleges, universities and schools. During its first years, the Normal School saw almost no growth in its budget, none. A lot is said annually, still today, about why the state has small resources for education. Still, if the state has been able to address its priorities in a fair manner, the Normal School for most of its history has had difficulty achieving a place on that list.

Despite its poor annual budgets, the Normal School managed to offer an education to its pupils free of charge. The practice had to cease, unfortunately, after a few years because of the obvious need for even the trifle fees that were eventually assessed to students. To this day, people familiar with the old Normal School like to talk about the means by which boarding students paid for room and board. They brought farm goods, vegetables, and fruits; and cattle, pigs, goats and chickens in exchange for boarding fees.

George Martin's personal fortunes took a good turn; his coming to New Mexico and El Rito paid off well. On September 30, 1912 he married Margaret Allen at St. Francis Cathedral in Santa Fe. George and Margaret were to have five children, Tom, Roberta, George, John and Pat.

As if establishing a young school were insufficiently difficult for Martin and a small staff, an accidental fire destroyed a good part of the Normal School's only building in November, 1912. The story of the fire, and the ensuing period before repairs could be made, illustrate the great commitment of George Martin and his wife to the students. They and neighbors in El Rito boarded those students who were displaced by the fire. The care and attention required to boarding and instruction, under the circumstances, must have required an immense amount of work. Yet nothing was said in minutes or in the president's reports about the inconveniences caused by this incident.

When I was president, I discovered a brief paper written by my friend Dr. Robert McGeagh that tells the story of this original building on campus. Dr. McGeagh wrote this as a prelude to its becoming Delgado Hall in 1994, and its subsequent inclusion as a State Historical Building.

There is no record of which I am aware that the Board of Regents was unhappy at any time with the job that George J. Martin had been doing at the Normal. Nor was there any indication of his disenchantment with the Board. But the school was not yet a normal school. It continued to be an elementary school on up to the time that George Martin left the school after four years. Even a high school was not in sight before about 1915. Here was George Martin, exceptionally well-grounded in the liberal arts, having to teach a full day of classes (6) in first, second and third grades. George Martin left the Normal School sometime in 1914. From among their options, George Martin and his family chose to move to Pueblo, Colorado where Margaret Martin's relatives worked in the steel mills. The Martins had apparently liked El Rito, and chose to return, in 1923. George established businesses with John Sargent, buying and selling sheep and wool, and formed partnership in a grocery and dry goods store. The Martin family remained in El Rito and members have contributed to the growth and development of the college since. They are discussed later in this book.

In 2005, the Normal School, by then known as Northern New Mexico Community College, commissioned the manufacture of a bronze bust of George J. Martin. It was done by Allison Aragon, an Albuquerque artist. The Martin family attended a brief ceremony with us in Cutting Hall where this sculpture is located.

Every school, college and university has its halcyon days and its "rough times." The remoteness of the Spanish American Normal School, coupled by a small number of teachers and professional administrators in our young state, contributed to a difficult situation at the Normal School. It was difficult to hire people, and once they came it became difficult to retain them. After George Martin's departure, there were five presidents in succession on up to the early 1920s. Mr. O. C. Zingg served the first year, Ms. O. C. Zingg followed for one year in an acting capacity, until Fremont Osborn came, again for one year. Three years, three presidents. Rosco Hill established what seems to be a good record in a brief two years, 1917 to 1919. Then followed Filadelfio Baca, who came to El Rito in 1919, and whose life ended, truly unfortunately for the Normal School as well as for him, in 1923. There were very important events during these years which we will recount. I list the names of the Normal's presidents of the time to illustrate that instability in the office of the president creates a similar condition throughout the institution. In some respects, this is a cycle that can be interrupted only with new, courageous leadership, as eventually occurred at the Normal School.

During the time of the purely elementary school in this first decade, useful and permanent change was occurring. A group of students was emerging, both at El Rito and in other schools in the north, who were beginning to be ready for more advanced study, although not quite yet for high school. We would view this today as a light in the horizon, where there had been darkness.

However, reports of the president and the Board of Regents of the period are filled with stories of how difficult it was to teach students who were poorly prepared, did not attend regularly, and who faced sometimes insurmountable circumstances that prevented them from attending for long periods of time. It was also difficult for teachers and staff. There was probably some scoffing by people:"Well, this isn't a real normal school. It's nothing more than a glorified grade school," or something like that. It's important that we condense this story ninety-plus years later, and that we not dwell on it too long. Fortunately, some people showed patience and good judgement concerning conditions in this rural, remote and agrarian region; some did not.

One report of the Board of Regents urged that the Spanish American Normal School be closed! The Board issued this recommendation in the winter of 1919, but fortunately Governor Washington Lindsey, a Republican, demurred. We have this information from Dr. Guillermo Lux's book of 1984, which you will find listed in the bibliography. I say this because I have no other evidence. It happened to be a time when the Governor's office changed hands, and the incoming governor was Octaviano Larrazolo, also Republican. Dr. Lux tells this story well, if you are interested in greater detail.

I am baffled about why a president, any president, would not object to the nature of such a communication. The only explanation seems to be that the number of students who could be counted on for the next step in the development of the Spanish American Normal School, a high school, was very small. Also, yet another president was about to depart in 1919. This decade of the founding of the Normal School was indeed a period of some unstable years. Instability gave rise to uncertainty among those who cared about the school, whom you would presume would have included its Board of Regents.

Before this decade ended, however, fortune smiled on the Normal School, with the arrival of a new president, Filadelfio Baca from Santa Fe. Baca was the fifth president, having followed two formally appointed presidents and two people in an interim capacity in the previous ten years of the school. Before he arrived, a high school at the Normal had been discussed; some planning had been done during the administration of Roscoe Hill. The new president made certain that there would be no delays, regardless of the low number of students. We may view 1919 as the start of the high school—an institution that would be important to hundreds of students during the next sixty years of the Spanish American Normal School.

4
THE HIGH SCHOOL IN THE 1920S

Among students who have attended the Normal School in El Rito during the past 100 years, its most faithful and active alumni are students who attended the high school. The first classes were offered in fall, 1919 to a very few students. We have examined reasons why, although founded as a teachers' college, there had been no students ready for a curriculum in teacher training in the first decade of the school. Readers may remember that the purpose of the Spanish American Normal School was ostensibly to train teachers for the education of New Mexicans in the English language. Statehood had been achieved in early 1912. New Mexico became bound to norms and standards of the United States of America for its schools It was barely becoming accustomed to new ideas of the era. We begin the story of the Normal's high school by reviewing public schools in the US in the following decade, the 1920s. (It must be said that the Normal School followed state law.)

Education of the populace alone does not guarantee the perpetuation of liberal democracy. What remains certain, however, is that without education a society is unable to make proper choices concerning policy, or to provide qualified individuals to guide it. After Independence, the United States became embarked in shaping its democracy. It wasn't until approximately 1820 that the US began to support public education, i.e., schools for more than just the wealthy. Change of this nature is always slow. According to "Daily Life in the United States, 1920-1940," by David E. Kyvig (2002), the number of students attending high school tripled during the period 1914 to 1929 a period in which the Normal School was taking steps toward establishing its high school. What was required of teachers? He states that to teach elementary school, a teacher should have a two year certificate from a normal school that read "teachers' college." In order to teach high school it was desirable for the teacher to have a four year, or baccalaureate, degree. Mind you, these were evolving standards across the United States. New Mexico and several of our western states did not meet this norm for several more years.

In 1919, New Mexico didn't have a system of public education, in the same manner that it does not have a system of higher education yet today. This lack of system per se is a remnant of its territorial days. What we mean by a system is a series of schools governed by one set of statutes and regulations that outline the mission, role and function of institutions within the system. It defines a locus of control. The system provides for stability and has moderate, safe guarantees of financial support, and includes a means of change to meet the needs of a society. Evidence is provided by Dr. Tom Wiley "Public School Education in New Mexico" that the 1923 School Code is the result of comprehensive legislation passed for the first time by the legislature and the governor. For our discussion, three matters with which the new laws deal are interesting: first, counties were empowered to initiate high schools by order of their county commissions. The State Board of Education prescribed the curriculum for the public schools. Of special interest to us is the mandate that certification of teachers "be established either by the process of examination or by credentials in the form of institutional credits." (See Wiley p.42.) This gave rise to a means by which the State Department, in consultation with normal schools and universities that offered teacher education programs, would begin to certify teachers, more in line with the second part of the statement in quotations than with the former. For New Mexico, this was a quantum jump a finite improvement in establishing a means by which there would be rigorous requirements for teachers.

The Spanish American Normal School wasn't ready to start training teachers in the manner described above. In 1919, at the risk of repeating, the school had barely enough students to begin the high school curriculum. The new School Code applied to the Normal School, however, insofar as the elementary and high schools were concerned. The role of the State Department of Education became increasingly important, and the Normal School could count on support in its efforts to educate students in grades one to twelve.

High schools in the US had begun to offer vocational education by the turn of the century, and in the early 1900s vocational agriculture, especially, was being offered in many high schools in a largely rural nation. In 1917, passage of the Smith-Hughes Vocational Education Act ensured that federal funds would be provided to each state in support of all vocational education. At the Normal School, this national trend appealed to its new president; Filadelfio Baca who had long shown an interest in agriculture and livestock. Although there were few high school students, only eighteen in the 1920-21 school year according to Dr. Lux, Baca began courses in agriculture and hired a teacher, Ms. Myrtle Knox, part of whose assignment was teaching these first courses in agriculture. Beginning with modest efforts about 1920, the high school would continue to offer courses in vocational education until 1969 when the school finally evolved into a full-fledged vocational institute. This is an important point: thus, the genesis, the original starting point, of an effort in vocational education would commence that would last on up to the present time.

The job done by Filadelfio Baca and the staff is to be admired. From great uncertainty at the close of the previous decade, they had advanced the mission of the Normal School. With absence of competing high schools in the area, the Spanish American Normal School gradually became a school consisting of almost equal numbers of students from El Rito and the immediate area, and boarding students from out of town. The elementary school, the larger of the two, continued to operate. Many of the students became enrolled in the Normal School's new vocational curriculum.

The high school grew slowly, and it had its first graduate in spring, 1922. She was Laura Redman, about whom I have more to say later in this book.

The Spanish American Normal School remained small throughout its history as elementary and high school. Two reasons one having to do with scarcity of water have limited growth of the campus. In the early 1920s, absence of dormitories hindered growth in population. With very limited funds, Filadelfio Baca maintained a small structure in which to board students, in addition to the one central building in which instruction and living quarters were combined. Growth in the early 1920s was steady, but slow. None of the small buildings of that period exist any longer.

Filadelfio Baca provided an important contribution by firmly establishing the high school which would dominate the character of this school for the longest time. A lot has been made of the fact that he was the first Hispanic president of the Normal School, and justifiably. Chief administrators, native to New Mexico, were few. In looking around, Amado Chavez, State School Superintendent would have been equivalent in stature in New Mexico educational circles.

Filadelfio was a well educated individual, having received a Bachelor of Arts degree at Regis College in Las Vegas and a Bachelor of Science from Notre Dame. He had been born in Las Vegas in 1865 to Jose Albino Baca and Dolores G. Baca, according to family, Joe and Sue Baca of Manhattan Beach, California. He was interested in politics and served as Chief Clerk in the Territorial House of Representatives. He spent five years as Secretary of the American Embassy in Mexico beginning in 1894. Upon returning to New Mexico, he turned to a career in education and served as Assistant State School Superintendent, prior to coming to the Normal School.

There is a sidelight here worth mentioning. Filadelfio Baca was a Democrat, appointed by a Board of Regents during the tenure of a Republican Governor, Octaviano Larrazolo. The Governor had to have known Filadelfio Baca; they were both from Las Vegas. I know about Filadelfio's party affiliation from Joe and Sue Baca, who also told me that Filadelfio had been an unsuccessful candidate for public offices in San Miguel County, then largely Republican. If Governor Larrazolo influenced the appointment of Filadelfio Baca, it was to his credit.

Filadelfio Baca was known for his ability in finance and diplomacy. I have mentioned that his interest in agriculture and livestock coincided with the State Department of Education's foray into vocational education as part of the high school curriculum. He brought these strengths to his new job in El Rito in 1919. Unfortunately for everyone concerned, Filadelfio Baca died while in office as President of the Spanish American Normal School on January 16, 1923 at age 57.

With the passing away of Filadelfio Baca, two presidents finished out the decade of the 1920s. José Jordí came in 1923, and there are people in El Rito who remember him. Evidence that the State Department of Education provided support is that John V. Conway, who had also been

Assistant State School Superintendent, provided impetus for Baca's efforts to establish new living quarters erected during Baca's tenure of office. The high school had forty-five students half way through the decade of the 1920s.

Three students graduated high school in 1923; seven in 1924. From the 1923 class, I knew Sixto Valdez, who became Assistant County School Superintendent in Rio Arriba County in his later professional years. His family also attended the Normal School, his son Eli in the 1950s when I was a student, and a daughter, Helen Valdez Bency, whom I met later on.

Lawrence Redman was one of the students who graduated in 1924. Meade Martin gave me a tape recording of a conversation with Lawrence, Laura's twin brother, made in 1977 in which Lawrence describes life in El Rito just prior to 1920. He was interested in construction and was involved in building projects in the community. Lawrence's son, Michael, a retired dentist in Española, has provided leads for me in writing the story of this period of the Normal School.

A second person who has provided me information on this period, Larry Purcell, is the son of Laura Redman Daugherty; he resides in Arizona and Cape Cod. He related to me that, after graduation from the Spanish American Normal School, she returned to the school to teach elementary school and to coach girls basketball. This has to be an innovation in 1990 New Mexico, a girls' basketball team! Boys' basketball had been initiated about the same time at the Normal. These sports were supported very modestly with small budgets for coaches and students to purchase a few supplies. We are pleased to know that it didn't require federal legislation for school officials to support girls' team sports, they just did it. The school didn't have a gymnasium until the end of the decade.

A small book, Children of the Normal School, describes, probably in too much detail, the Normal School's emphasis in sports and it led one reader to comment to Amazon, where many books are sold these days, that the person objected to the description of games, just too many sports. It prompted one member of our Board of Regents, Dennis Salazar, who had attended the high school in El Rito, to state that he had no undying love for sports but that he tried sports to deal with boredom. This much is true for the Normal School and many our small towns across New Mexico, and probably small towns everywhere. The reader had a point: I emphasized much too much how the Normal School emphasized sports, in its early years, for young men and women. As time passed, young women lost interest in sports.

Improvements to the plant followed in the mid-1920s: a water system, sewer line, wood and coal fired heating plant, and electrical generator were still in the distant future. Motor vehicles were coming into use. The school had an all-purpose truck, after José Jordí came, in which it carried administrators, students to ball games in Española, and freight.

Residents in El Rito still remember both José Jordí and John Conway, but maintain a better memory of John Conway who came later, of course. I spoke with Jane Goddard Garcia and John Martin, who were both residents in El Rito and students of the Normal School. Jane and John started school in 1929. They have a faint memory of Jordí, and remember Conway as a good administrator and strict disciplinarian. Conway was president when Jane and John attended first grade with Laura Redman Dougherty, their teacher.

By the end of the decade the high school had grown to about sixty students, the grade school was twice the size. The vocational curriculum had advanced considerably, including emphasis in colonial arts. One regrets that the school's reputation had not advanced as it should, and many people in the state viewed the new vocational programs as a means of exploitation of the school for political purposes. It was a curious way of viewing an effort by the school to help its students earn some money by marketing their products. There was renewed interest in colonial arts, as there is today, and the school helped in selling wood furniture, woven rugs and tapestries that the students manufactured. A sense of this problem can be gained from *The Spanish Redemption: Heritage, Power and Loss on New Mexico's Upper Rio Grande* (2002), written by Charles Montgomery.

John V. Conway, who had reputation as a good advocate for education of Hispanics, in particular, became president to hail in the decade of the 1930s. He had become interested in education while living in Santa Fe and serving on an elected school board. From this experience, he became totally committed to public education, and eventually became Assistant State School Superintendent. He was well-connected politically, and is mentioned by Governor Miguel Otero, Territorial Governor, in his memoirs.

5
1933–1935, YEARS OF DECISION

The 1930s were years of the Great Depression, of course, but also the years of greatest change on the campus of the Spanish American Normal School. What the Normal School came to be, the campus itself, and remembrance of the high school, in particular, remain indelible in the minds of every student who attended and with whom I have spoken.

The first half of this decade was led by John V. Conway; in 1935, Joseph B. Grant became president.

President Conway is reputed to have been insistent on maintaining the highest standard possible during his years at the Normal School. The instructional program became diversified in two ways: vocational education and the teaching staff were expanded, and a few "junior college" courses were made available to those students interested in teaching careers. The addition of courses in the junior college in professional education must have had an immediate impact on regional schools. The courses were well planned, as illustrated below, but evidence of students graduating and taking teaching positions in northern New Mexico is missing, for the most part.

We have a photograph of the graduating class of 1929 There were seven students: Raymond Romero from Vadito, Pauline Goddard from El Rito, Richard Ortega from Chimayó, Olive Parker from El Rito, José M. Valdez from McPhee, Simmie Atencio from Santa Cruz, and Cruz Trujillo from Chimayó. The class sponsor, pictured, is Isabel Ward. The photograph may be found on p. 42 of *Children of the Normal School*, by Sigfredo Maestas, published by Sunstone Press.

One of the students about whom we do know a considerable amount is Olive Parker, who remained at the Normal School after high school graduation and completed the required courses in education. In the 1931-32 school year, she took a job teaching in an elementary school in Truchas. She taught at El Rito in 1932-33.[1] Pauline Goddard and José M. Valdez also became teachers for a few years following their graduation.[2]

Funds that were made available in 1928, almost twenty years after the Normal School opened its doors, were used to construct a small gymnasium, classrooms and student dormitories. As a result, the boarding student population grew, modestly. The project was completed in stages, and final construction was in 1934. This building was called the Junior Building in the 1950s, and has been known as the North Dormitory in later years. The building, which underwent complete renovation during my years as president, is dealt with again later in this book.

Except for suffering from gibes thrown from members of opposing parties, Republican and Democrat, when one or the other was not in power at the Normal School, its reputation did not suffer to any harmful extent. One reason, which I detect from press reports during these times, is that both presidents maintained good relations with the public and press. In spite of the Governor of the state's ability to dominate a Board of Regents, one witnessed, surprisingly, very little of what can be termed as abuse of power, although some preferential hiring continued. The Spanish American Normal School continued to fulfill its mission; partisan politics was not as large an influence as many would like to make it. I refer here to the way in which students' education could have been affected, in particular.

The first twenty years, or so, of the Spanish American Normal School are easily summarized. During the earliest five years, George J. Martin and a very small staff started the school, working against many odds including a fire in the single building that constituted the School. He left in all likelihood because he was well educated and trained for a job of somewhat greater complexity. A humanist, with excellent language skills in at least four languages, could not have enjoyed teaching elementary school. Instability in leadership followed after Martin left, but, at the end of the first decade, a president came who established the high school curriculum. When this president, Filadelfio Baca died, new leaders came who continued the good work, including José Jordí and John Conway. In the next decade the school grew, ever so slowly but perceptibly, and it added vocational courses. Strong leadership produces results, and the arrival of John Conway as president signaled added stability and growth, and beginning of what was called the junior college, for training of teachers. However, a factor that continued to hinder the Normal School's growth was its very poor funding. The problem of inadequate financial support is one that would continue; modest improvement in the school's fiscal condition would not begin until many years later, after the high school had been terminated.

The General Catalog for the Spanish American Normal School published July 1933 is instructive. It describes not only the school's educational offerings, but also a glimpse of the life of a student. The General Information section, in particular, provides a modern reader an idea of conditions in the early 1930s:

> El Rito, the home of the Spanish-American Normal School, is located in Rio Arriba County, on State Road No. 96, fifty-eight miles northwest of the City of Santa Fe, and thirty-two miles northwest of Espanola, the nearest railroad point on the Denver and Rio Grande Railway. The State Highway Department maintains this road. Substantial new bridges and culverts have improved the highway so that students may take the trip to and from the school in one-third less time. Other new state highways now under construction in Rio Arriba and adjoining counties will, when completed and connected, make this institution as accessible to its patrons as any other school in the State. The El Rito Valley, surrounded by scenic mountains, remains in its natural state, as only a minor portion of the available land is devoted to agriculture. The Valley has a population of about one thousand inhabitants. The school is located at an altitude of about seven thousand feet above sea level; the location is favorable to good health, as the winters are mild and the summers cool with freedom from dust, sand and high winds. Since the school is in the center of the community, the students perform their work unimpaired by outside social functions. All social activities at the school are under the direct supervision of the management.

This introduction to the campus betrays the writer's unfounded optimism with regard to the road. People around El Rito tell me it was a very rough road for yet another 12-13 years, when it was paved. I am uncertain what the last two statements mean. The campus is not in the center of the village, nor was it well-integrated with the community. Extra-curricular and school activities were on campus, and were always well supervised.

Separate dormitories for boy and girls were maintained. The General Catalog describes living and dining spaces in separate buildings. It refers to six buildings, some were not very permanent; of the group of buildings, only two are in use today. Supervision of girls was always extraordinarily careful; the practice continued throughout the years of the boarding school. The following statement of policy in the Catalog is not too surprising:

> Girls are required to wear uniform costumes. These costumes are to consist of a navy blue dress and white collar and cuffs. The dress to be made of some serviceable material (such as serge, jersey or wool crepe), which may be readily cleaned and pressed. The garments must be made in a plain one-piece style. The collar and cuffs may be made of any white washable materials such as linen, lawn or crash.
>
> The object of choosing this uniform is two-fold; namely, that the expenses of buying clothes throughout the year may be cut to the lowest possible figure. With care and proper management two dresses and three collar and cuff sets may last the entire year. In addition to the above mentioned articles, it is necessary that each girl provides herself with at least 3 sets of underwear, 3 pairs cotton stockings, 2 heavy nightgowns, and a pair of sensible, low heeled shoes to be worn in the school room and on the campus. Those wishing to play basketball must bring a pair of tennis shoes to be worn on the court.
>
> Students will be permitted to wear silk dresses or other dress-up garments during social functions only and while attending church.

This communication to prospective students *is* quaint. It also illustrates rigor in deportment required of students.

The practice of requiring students to attend church continued, depending on who was in charge of dormitories, on up to the 1950s.

Everyone attended the Catholic Church in the village, the Church of St. John Nepomucene. This was all before the famous case, *Zellers vs. Huff*. This court case-known commonly as the Dixon case for the village in which protest occurred—has given rise to greater separation of public school and church in New Mexico. The specific prohibition that resulted was against the use of school, i.e. state, funds for the support of religion. People in New Mexico, even to this day, do not seem to become too perturbed by practices similar to the one noted above at the Normal School.

Because the school did not have a yearbook, the Catalog contains pictures of the Senior Class, the school band, Future Farmers of America Club, vocational and the home economics classes. There are a couple of surprises: the Senior Class has 20 members; the home economics class has 51, all girls. FFA Club has nine members; the school band has seven members. Also shown are the boys' and girls' basketball teams. Teachers are included in some photos, but are not identified. None of the persons' names are listed, unfortunately.

General entrance requirements for students in any grade include the requirement of a document, usually a report card, indicating that he or she has been promoted to the grade for which application is made. Otherwise a student may "take an examination covering the previous year's work." Entrance requirements for those students applying to the high school for the first time are listed, also. Possession of "an eighth grade diploma" is necessary for admission. A communication from the Principal of the school previously attended will also suffice in the absence of a diploma.

Requirements for graduation with a high school diploma are listed; the list has approval of the State Department of Education: English (4 units), mathematics (2 units), laboratory science (1 unit), social science (2 units), United States history and civics (1/2 unit), New Mexico History (1/2 unit), physiology and hygiene (1/2 unit), and Spanish (2 units). Students may apparently choose from biology or physics as the lab science. In addition the student is to select a major of at least three units.

Cost of attendance was kept as low as possible. There was *no charge* for tuition. A general matriculation fee of $10.00 was for the entire school year. Cost of room and board was $14.00 per month.

In addition to the low cost quoted, students were informed that jobs were available for students who would work nine hours per week, in which case cost of room and board was reduced to $8.00 per month.

The practice of reducing costs for students who worked continued on up to the 1960s.

Prior to times in which cash for enrollment was required, the Normal School had been willing to take farm produce in lieu of these fees. In summary, the considerate and humane treatment of students accorded by the school is one that is appreciated by everyone concerned to this day.

The General Catalog lists the names of members of the Board of Regents and the president:

> His Excellency, Governor Arthur Seligman, *Ex-Officio,* Santa Fe, New Mexico
> Joseph B. Grant, President, Santa Fe, New Mexico
> Tobias Gonzales, Vice-President, El Rito, New Mexico
> Mrs. Margaret M. Lane, Secretary-Treasurer, Albuquerque, New Mexico
> John D. De Huff, Member, Santa Fe, New Mexico
> Ross Olivas, Member, Parkview, New Mexico
> John V. Conway, President Spanish-American Norma School, El Rito, New Mexico

A Calendar For The School Year 1933-34 informs us that student registration occurred on Monday, September 4, 1933 for Boarding Students and on September 5 for Day and College Students on Tuesday, September 5. Note that there were college students in what was viewed as a junior college at the time. The matter of college courses offered by the Normal School in the early '30s became a matter of intense discussion among members of the Board of Regents and President Conway.

With inclusion of the college courses for preparation of teachers in the curriculum–there were three: Psychology, Pedagogy, and History of Education–the Spanish American Normal School was beginning to take serious steps to comply with its legislative mandate of 1909 to engage in the training of teachers. Furthermore, the State Department of Education required, during precisely this time, that an elementary school teacher have completed high school and the three courses listed in order to begin teaching elementary school. This requirement is one that students graduating at El Rito could meet; John Conway saw to that. The Normal School began to serve northern New Mexico in the manner that had been intended.

Faculty who are listed in the program for graduation exercises that year include D.W. Rockey, as Principal; Isabel Ward, Iverne C. Hickey, Roman Jaramillo, Mabel Burleson, George Segura, Caroline Schoolcraft, Earl Newcomer, Mary Gillespie, Helen Kay, Barbara Sena, Mattie Daggett, Celia Redman and Benito Medrano. Eloy Abeyta was Registrar; Ethel Miller and Celestino Martinez were listed as girl's and boy's Advisors, respectively. Twenty-eight students graduated from the high school.

John V. Conway was a native New Mexican born on January 11, 1872 in Cimarron to John W. Conway and María Paz Valdez Conway. He had attended St. Michael's College and the University of New Mexico. Early in his career he engaged in business in Santa Fé, and became interested in education during civic work that he did on behalf of the Santa Fé County Board of Education. He subsequently ran in an election for the position of County School Superintendent and won. He was Republican, a close acquaintance of Territorial Governor Miguel Otero. He knew Venceslao Jaramillo, although there is nothing to indicate that they were friends. He and Venceslao were close in age, John Conway being the slightly older of the two. After acquiring familiarity with the Santa Fé schools, he became Assistant Superintendent of Public Instruction. He came to the Normal School as a mature man, at age about 56. In spite of a stern demeanor that was often talked about in El Rito, John Conway seems to have been well liked. Former students, John Martin among them, tell me that he had very good teachers and that the Normal School was operated well. The school was viewed as a great asset by the community.

What ensued at the Normal School in those early years of the 1930s would affect the future of the Spanish American Normal School for many years on up to the 1970s. Two competing interests developed: advocates for vocational education came into disagreement with those willing to develop the college curriculum further. There were stronger advocates for vocational education, for good reason. This period of the Great Depression made it difficult for the State of New Mexico to support public and higher education in any desirable fashion. As has happened often to the Normal School and its successors, competition from Albuquerque and other urban centers, coupled with indifference in further reaches of the state, has meant that the Normal School has had very little political and financial support. This was the prevailing situation in 1933.

Elsewhere in the United States, the American high school had become the "darling" of the Nation, in particular the comprehensive high school, strong in vocational education. The Smith-Hughes Act of 1917 was extended further and federal money flowed to the states for support of vocational education; some of that money reached the Normal School. Programs were expanded. The General Catalog listed programs in Home Economics, Art (Spanish Colonial Art), Commercial (read Business Education), Agriculture, Beauty Culture, Cabinet Making, Weaving, and a course in wrought iron work. The corps of teachers was expanded to about twelve.

It's apparent that a dilemma emerged that the Board of Regents faced. It is described by Guillermo Lux in his book about the Spanish American Normal School on the subject of vocational education and the junior college. He quotes from a communication of the Board to Governor Seligman stating the Board's intention to emphasize vocational education. Dr. Lux states further that "She and other Regents were opposed to any effort to expand a Junior College program," the communication having been written by Ms. Margaret Lane, Secretary-Treasurer of the Board. I stated earlier that conditions in the state may have dictated that the Board take this position. President Conway would have been aware, however, that Smith-Hughes funds could be applied to vocational education in junior colleges in the US, just as they were being spent in high schools. Here again, competition between public high schools and two-year colleges had to be a concern, thus the Board decided to refrain from building its college program. This was a fateful decision for the Normal School; it would determine that the high school would continue for another 35 years.

There exists a paradox concerning trends involving vocational studies and the choice between the junior college and the vocational high school that was at the crux of the argument at the Spanish American Normal School. The choice that could have been made is easier seen in hindsight today. The extension of federal vocational funds in the 1930s, known as the George-Elzy Act, allowed for support of vocational education in junior colleges–community colleges is what they are called today. An argument has been made among American educators that federal vocational education acts have tended to create vocational education as distinct and separate from academic education. This is a view that may have prevailed within the Board of Regents of the Spanish American Normal School, although it seems that a person of the stature and experience of John Conway would have seen that a choice between the two did not have to be made. Simply put, academic and vocational education were two sides of the same coin.

The remainder of this discussion requires a bit of speculation. I believe that John Conway was determined to make the Spanish American Normal School a real normal college or university, as was happening elsewhere in New Mexico with the normal schools that started in late 1880s. It was a natural course for the Normal School to follow. It makes sense that the school would proceed from offering training in elementary education to begin (1909 to 1919), expanding to include the education of high school students in a subsequent stage (1919 to 1930s), and, in its final stage, to offer a curriculum in teacher education. I did not know John Conway, but I am certain that he knew what I am stating and may have known it better.

It has always been in fashion in New Mexico to blame partisan politics in government for actions that occur that run counter to our preferences. In fact, Republicans and Democrats have coexisted and worked toward common aims quite well. The people have tended to elect Republican and Democratic governors to our highest state office almost in alternating rhythm. Governor Seligman was elected in 1930, preceding by two years Franklin D. Roosevelt's landslide win for the presidency of the United States. The two were Democrats. Governor Seligman's party dominated the Normal School's Board of Regents, but President John Conway, a Republican, seems to have thrived in those early 1930s and to have performed outstanding service as a progressive, hard-working president for the Normal School.

John V. Conway's tenure as president ended unhappily, however. In March 1935 there was a new Board of Regents that included Joseph B. Grant as outgoing Board President, Mrs. Emma T. Oakley, Ismael Ulibarrí, Elias T. Lucero, Octaviano Manzanares, and Mrs. Margaret Allen Martin. Only Grant was Seligman's appointee; the new Governor of New Mexico was Clyde Tingley, a Democrat.[3] Other members of the Board were newer appointees. John Conway was apparently not in harmony with the new Board.

On March 25, according to the Board's minutes, President Conway was asked for his resignation by the Board of Regents. No reason for the action was given. I continue to believe that John V. Conway could not have been entirely pleased with a Board that was opposed to expansion of the teacher education program. From the description that people who knew John Conway give me, he was a person who would have let the Board know that he felt an obligation to build on the teacher education curriculum. The courses shown in the General Catalog in 1933 show a well thought out beginning. The introductory courses in education taught at El Rito still constitute today some of the foundations on which teacher education curricula are built. He would have defended his position as being in concert with the Spanish American Normal School's legislative and constitutional mandate to train teachers for the public schools, or so it would seem.

Instead, the minutes reflect only John Conway's displeasure, probably with spurious comments made by others about his performance as president. He demanded that the Board of Regents order a thorough audit of the school's financial condition, to which the Board agreed. Of course, as time went by, the audit showed that Conway had done an exemplary job, as you would expect from a man of his stature.

In a subsequent action during the same meeting of March 25, 1935, the Board of Regents received the resignation of Joseph B. Grant as president and member of the Board of Regents, and named him President of the Spanish American Normal School.

The departure of John V. Conway left the new president of the Normal School with a good foundation upon which to build. This is precisely what Joseph B. Grant proceeded to do; to expand the Spanish American Normal School's physical plant, and to build upon the curriculum of the vocational high school—in modern jargon, this was the comprehensive high school, even if it was small.

We, readers and writers of these times, would wish to make certain that the needs of the region are viewed in the following way, which is justifiable and causes us an amount of sadness. Needs are simply too many. The argument of John Conway, with Regents and other members of the community, was that Mr. Conway saw that the Normal School should evolve in its natural way that would produce a college, or junior college, as he saw it. On the other hand, many members of the community, former students, and, yes, Regents, were viewing the need for furtherance of vocational education.

Notes:

1. Facts concerning Olive Parker were provided to me by her daughter Katie Bateman Allison. Katie telephoned me at home one day to tell me that she had a picture of the Spanish American Normal School in its very early years. She had read in the *Rio Grande Sun* that I was writing this book, and would I like to have the picture. She and her husband Dana Allison, both former students of the Normal School, visited with me. She mentioned to me that her mother was Olive Parker, who had also studied at the Normal School. It took me a couple of days to realize that I knew one small fact about Olive Parker with which Katie was apparently unfamiliar. I had a 1929 photograph of her mother Olive with her graduating class. "Here is your mother," I said. Had Katie and Dana not visited with me, I would not have known who Olive Parker was, nor Ms. Parker's interesting history as student and teacher. As you may possibly guess, there is more to Olive Parker. You may see Chapter Eight.

2. Information about students whom I have known, or known about, is included in Chapter Eight. Entire lists of graduating classes are included at the end of this book. Except for lists of students that I obtained from minutes of the Board of Regents, these lists are unofficial. Official record of these students having attended the high school does not exist anywhere, to my knowledge.

3. With the election of Arthur Seligman as Governor in 1930, Democrats began a string of years in which they held the Office of the Governor uninterruptedly for twenty years, until 1951. Andrew W. Hockenhull served two years, following Governor Seligman and preceding Governor Tingley.

6
A SCHOOL TO BUILD A DREAM ON

This chapter could just as well be called *The Joe Grant Years*. No one as president[1] has left a thumb print as large or as evident on any campus as Joseph B. Grant did at El Rito in the Spanish American Normal School. The "campus", such as it was in 1934, included a small cluster of buildings on a desolate plain just outside of the village. Joe Grant, as he was known popularly, transformed this place, and the campus changed him. In a period of about ten years, he managed, by being resourceful and prudent, to exceed instructions from Governor Tingley to do something "up there" in Rio Arriba County.[2] Joe Grant surprised everyone, no less himself, by designing and building a campus unequaled anywhere in our state at the time for its beauty and serenity. For several generations, students were to enjoy this setting and grow to love their school for its ambient.

Joseph Grant proved to be resourceful in using local materials, namely stone, gravel, and sand to affect changes in the physical setting. Local masons and laborers constructed rock walls and foundations for new buildings. He had trees, bushes, and flowering plants brought in from neighboring communities to establish, around himself, staff and students, a veritable little paradise. If Governor Tingley wanted something spectacular, that is certainly what he got.

But there is more to this story, a lot more. By obtaining funds for the school, primarily from the federal government, Joe Grant was also able to help the community of El Rito to begin to mend and heal some of the ravages of the Great Depression. Beginning in 1929 with the great stock market crash, the Nation spun into a dismal state of financial and material suffering, but especially in places like northern New Mexico people faced a situation that was bleak. Simply put, *there was no money. Nada*. None.

Into this milieu stepped Joe Grant, who was familiar with the region. He was from down the road in Abiquiú where he had been born on September 1, 1898. His family, after moving here from eastern United States, owned a mercantile store in Abiquiú, one in El Rito, and a trading post in Tres Piedras. Although Joseph Grant's father, Henry, stayed in Abiquiú during most of his life, Joe's mother returned to New York and provided a home there for her children. Joe Grant received schooling at home and in Abiquiu, he left home to attend high school in New York. Upon graduating, he enrolled at City College of New York on scholarship. However, Joe Grant had been a very good athlete while in high school and he decided to pursue baseball while at CCNY. He left college to play semiprofessional baseball in California, and later returned to business school.

In the early 1930s, Joseph Grant was director of the Albuquerque office for the Internal Revenue Service and made acquaintance with Clyde Tingley, who became Governor of the State in January, 1935. Governor Tingley requested that Joseph Grant, a Regent at the time, accept an offer of president of the Spanish American Normal School. According to his son David the request was that he fill the position "for just a few months," and he arrived on the campus without his family. The Governor knew that other Regents would like to replace the incumbent president. This is what has given rise to my view of what happened that caused a change in the presidency at the conclusion of the previous chapter. The Board of Regents that hired Joseph Grant had as members Emma T. Oakley, President; Ismael Ulibarri, Vice-President; E. T. Lucero, Secretary-Treasurer; Octaviano Manzanares; and Margaret Allen Martin to replace Tobias Gonzales after the March 25 meeting.

Joe Grant accepted the presidency in March, 1935 with a reputation as being somewhat of a financial wizard. He was not an educator when he came to the Normal School, nor was he a politician. He had some knowledge of the operation of the Spanish American Normal School from his tenure on the Board. The evidence is, however, that just as he wrought profound change on the campus of the Normal School, so also would he change in ways that would affect him and those around him for the remainder of his life. This shy, seldom-spoken man made lasting friendships and became an effective politician.

The President, at the time, lived in the main building on campus which served also as administrative center. This original old building is said to have included dormitories on the top floor, classrooms on the second and main floor, and a library in the basement, or first, floor. In time, high school instruction would take place in the northernmost Junior Building.

Joe Grant was married to the former Anita Segura, who joined him at El Rito in 1936. Son David was five years old. Mrs. Grant was a nurse whom Joe Grant had met at St. Vincent's Hospital in Santa Fe. According to David, she was the first graduate of the Nursing Program sponsored by St. Vincent's. She apparently continued a remembered practice—remembered by residents of El Rito—of ministering to students and members of the community when there were medical emergencies, as there usually are in rural and frontier communities. Margaret Allen Martin, wife of the first president twenty-five years earlier, had similarly helped local people in need of medical care.[3]

Joseph Grant was hired as president for his technical ability, as I have pointed out. He may have discovered in himself an ability that he did not know he had, however, and Governor Tingley may have discerned it. Joe Grant was to become, along with Carlos Manzanares and E.B. Trujillo in Rio Arriba County, one of the well known political bosses of the era. Reasons for this were more fortuitous than intended. The onset of the Great Depression brought about new political leadership in the United States. New Mexico placed in office a new governor, Arthur Seligman in 1931, and the United States elected Franklin D. Roosevelt as President the following year. In New Mexico, what had seemed like a trickle of Democrats occupying high positions statewide, became a flood of new people after 1933. The new bunch were progressive, as had been Senator Bronson Cutting,[4] Republican of New Mexico, and Presidents Abraham Lincoln and James A. Garfield, both Republican.

New President Franklin D. Roosevelt, recognizing the need for change in the Nation, wrapped his program in phrases by which *The New Deal* is still recognized in the political lexicon. Politics being a game of competition, Democrats intended to solidify a heretofore skimpy base in Rio Arriba and adjacent counties by doing a good job in relieving some of the poverty and misery that existed. Sure, hispanic and Indian people in these parts had their small farms, *huertas* to grow vegetables, a few fruit trees, and small flocks of farm animals, but they had no money, little health care, and only occasional educational opportunity. They needed jobs above all else. We have been close to a financial depression now again in 2008 and '09, and some of our countrymen feel hopelessness that owes to unemployment. Well, the Great Depression lasted 10 years and only the Second World War ensured that the USA and the world would get out of it. Severe economic crises require strong governmental intervention in order to diminish suffering, and avoid war, this much is certain.

It should have astounded anyone witnessing what occurred on campus after the arrival of Joe Grant as president. The beautification and construction boom that ensued on campus owed to two circumstances, fortunately complementary: the campus needed beautification and additional buildings, and people in the immediate area needed jobs. The New Deal was beginning to be felt in America. In 1935 the Works Progress Administration was inaugurated by the Roosevelt Administration with an appropriation of five billion dollars—read that again, $5,000,000,000.[5] Today this seems a modest amount of money to cure the ills of an economy, but all of this amount went for public works, and the Spanish American School received its fair share of these funds.

Joe Grant's staff built roadways, erected stone walls, brought in and planted elm trees and silver cottonwoods, lilac bushes, rose bushes, and an assortment of annual flowers. The administration inaugurated construction of a women's dormitory, a large cafeteria and a beautiful, small auditorium. Almost simultaneously, they built the president's residence, a small home that still stands, and living quarters for teachers. They built a new laundry and storage spaces. As they built new spaces, other rooms were freed in the Junior Building, the older of the dormitories, for student recreation.

Change in the immediately visible parts of the campus included a new gate and stone wall entrance to the campus, eliminating the old pastoral look of the place. Stone walls, on which people walking the campus sat, divided small, attractive parks from the highway and from campus roadways. Stone grottos and fountains were erected; the fountains seldom contained water, too precious a commodity. Joe Grant loved roses and a large rose garden occupied the central park area across from the president's residence. There were so many lilac bushes that in the spring the smell of their flowers permeated the entire east end of the campus.

Other public works in El Rito and Rio Arriba County were part of part of an effort by government to put people to work. Down the road from the campus, there are bare remnants of a park constructed by the CCC, Civilian Conservation Corps. Project such as this one, and many more projects sponsored by the WPA, dotted the county and neighboring counties as well. One consequence was the switch in political allegiance by a vast number of people; they became Democrats, where they had previously been Republican. Joe Grant was one of the individuals responsible for this new phenomenon.

Although there is a great deal more to the administration of Joe Grant than bricks and mortar, examining how he acquired funds, *matériel* and people to build the campus reveals, also, a vision and organizational ability that the man possessed. In time, accolades came his way that were deserved, and some of the stories told about him, although apocryphal, perhaps, are revealing of the high esteem in which he was held by members of the community and political friends.

Construction of the women's residence hall, cafeteria and auditorium is a story often repeated by people in the thirties, and it is about Joe Grant. He and his associates school had envisioned a "signature" building on campus for many years. After work on the building began, completion was slow, and in order for this story to fit chronologically, we should begin with the unexpected death of Senator Bronson Cutting.

The small auditorium in this building is Cutting Hall, named after the man whose portrait has resided in it since late 1930s. The hall includes a bronze bust, also of Senator Bronson Cutting, who came to New Mexico in June 1910. He had been born to a patrician family on Long Island in New York in June 1888. He was educated at Groton and Harvard, as was President Franklin D. Roosevelt and other sons of wealthy families in that part of the US. He came to Santa Fé, as did several people from "back east," to convalesce and to seek cure from tuberculosis. Still a young man, he intended that his stay would be brief, but Santa Fé would be his permanent, and last, residence.

He became a man of many accomplishments, but we'll discuss only those that seem to have advanced him politically. At about the time that New Mexico became a state, 1912, Bronson Cutting decided to become a newspaper publisher and acquired the *Santa Fe New Mexican* and *El Nuevo Mexicano*. He invested time and effort in printing and publishing, opportunities that existed for a man of his background and education. World War I interrupted his life in Santa Fe—he was commissioned a captain in the U.S. Army—which helped him gain appreciation for veterans and their plight, once he, and they, came home. He worked to establish the American Legion in New Mexico, and he especially focused on the need for recognition and participation of hispanic veterans as a means of having their issues heard. Northern New Mexicans would not forget Bronson Cutting's efforts when he became active in electoral politics.

In late 1927 he was appointed United States Senator by Governor Richard C. Dillon to fill a vacancy left by the death of Senator Andreus A. Jones. After one year he stepped aside in order for a newly elected successor, Senator Octaviano Larrazolo, to take office. Cutting did run for the U.S. Senate in the election of November 1928 against Jethro S. Vaught, a Democrat, and won by a large majority, as did most Republicans in their 1928 races. The election of 1928 established Bronson M. Cutting as the dominant figure in Republican party politics. The American Legion, veterans and hispanic vets, in particular, went solidly for Senator Cutting. A note that is attributed to the popular chronicler Edmund Wilson in the 1930s is said to have stated that Cutting became senator from New Mexico "where the 'Mexicans' had rewarded his interest in them by sending him to the Senate."

Cutting earned the esteem of his colleagues in the Senate for supporting liberal and progressive causes. President Roosevelt was not impressed, in spite of the fact—perhaps because of the fact—that Senator Cutting supported issues of concern to Eleanor Roosevelt, the President's wife. It was known that the President would support U.S. Representative Dennis Chavez in the 1934 election against Cutting. This resulted in powerful opposition to Senator Cutting, who managed to defeat Dennis Chavez by only 1,300 votes out of about 150,000 total votes cast. This was an immense triumph for Cutting, when you consider that after the 1934 elections the Democrats held 69 seats in the U.S. Senate to 25 for Republicans. Dennis Chavez contested the election in which Cutting was certified the winner in January 1935. Unfortunately for Senator Cutting and for New Mexico, he died in an airplane that crashed over Iowa on his way home to New Mexico from Washington, DC on May 6, 1935.

During a meeting of the Board of Regents at El Rito in January 1937, President Joseph Grant announced that on May1, 1936 "... a bequest of the late Senator Bronson Cutting in the amount of $150,000 had been delivered to the Treasurer, properly receipted for..." This brought the amount of money in the school's permanent fund to $154,500, which means that the Spanish American Normal School's share of the state's land and permanent fund was $4,500.00 for the year 1936-37. Funds received by the school from the permanent fund were the only really "discretionary" funds that colleges and universities were allowed. Funds could be used for building projects, maintenance, or repairs, at the discretion of the school. One may assume that a good fraction of these funds were applied to the construction of the women's residence hall, dining room, and auditorium-Cutting Hall.

This is a handsome building that required a combination of funds. The school issued bonds in the amount of $60,000 early in Joe Grant's tenure as president, funds from the permanent fund serving as the guarantee of payment. In addition, funds from the Works Project Administration (WPA) started trickling in, and construction on the building began. Progress was slow; federal funds were slow in coming. Joe Grant's political connections and his reputation for attention to the job helped in this instance.

In a meeting of the Board of Regents on August 4, 1937, President Emma T. Oakley asked the school's president to please bring the Board up to date on the progress toward completion of this building. The target date for completion had been September 1937, in time for the new school year. President Joe Grant and his staff faced two problems: one was government "red tape" which limited the number of skilled workers on the project. Second, and worse still, materials that had been purchased by the WPA were late in arriving. Joe Grant had notified Governor Tingley of the delays and urgent need to complete the building. The Governor, traveling to the Nation's capital, tried to acquire necessary funds by visiting with President Roosevelt. Grant informed the Board that Governor Tingley had spoken with President Roosevelt personally and that Mr. Grant "...was assured of cooperation." Only two months later, during the October meeting of the Board, President Grant reported that the women's dormitory was ninety percent completed. On May 22, 1938, Joseph Grant informed the Board that construction of the auditorium was complete.

This hall, which served as the center of students' social life on campus, was dedicated to the memory of Bronson M. Cutting in late summer 1940.

All hiring, including the employment of faculty, was left to the president. In accordance with state law, the president presented to the Board of Regents a list of teachers whom he was recommending for the 1935-36 school year. Mr. Grant pointed out that each of the people whom he was recommending met requirements that were set forth by the accrediting body of the school, the North Central Association of Colleges and Schools. The Board approved the list without dissent. The list of teaching staff includes their place of origin.

    Herbert W. Prather, Principal and Instructor, Duran, New Mexico
    Albertano C. DeBaca, Instructor, Santa Fe, New Mexico
    Josue Trujillo, Instructor, Taos, New Mexico
    Clarissa Bezemek Howard, Instructor, Albuquerque, New Mexico
    Lelia C. Greenwald, Instructor, Socorro, New Mexico
    George A. Segura, Instructor, El Rito, New Mexico
    Caroline Sanchez, Schoolcraft Instructor, Albuquerque, New Mexico
    Barbara Sena, Teacher, Albuquerque, New Mexico
    Celia DeBaca Redman, Teacher, Las Vegas, New Mexico
    Theodorita Manzanares, Teacher, La Puente, New Mexico
    Thelma Ruth Welty, Teacher, Albuquerque, New Mexico
    Ethel S. Miller, Teacher, Dexter, New Mexico
    Blanche Dunn, Instructor, Hurley, New Mexico
    Eloy M. Abeyta, Registrar, Park View, New Mexico
    Charles Brown, Boys Advisor and Coach, Albuquerque, New Mexico

A teaching staff of thirteen, including Mr. Prather, who was principal, seems small, if you consider that the school was grades one through twelve.

President Joseph Grant reported to the Board of Regents concerning other important projects that would get underway in late 1936 and early 1937. One was to re-plaster each of the existing buildings in order that the colors and texture be unified among all visible structures. The second involved improvements to the infrastructure for water and sewage. The matter of securing potable water was to be a problem throughout this administration, when real effort was made to improve on a difficult situation.

Insufficient water from well(s) on campus was then and has continued to be a cause for concern. Four years into his presidency, in March 1939, Joe Grant reported to the Board of Regents that in order for water to be obtained from a site adjacent to the El Rito Creek, a six inch line had to be constructed from the creek a few miles up the canyon. WPA funds were available, but for development of infrastructure the State Board of Finance's approval would have to be sought for a substantial expenditure in constructing the water line. In those days, water arriving at the creek below ground was classified as groundwater, for which the Normal School had a permit from the State Engineer for 58,580 gallons daily. Mr. Grant stated that a great deal less, 14,000 gallons, was being utilized, but the school needed assurance that it could have its full allotment of water, if needed.

Several more years into his administration, in May 1942, Joseph Grant obtained a gift of a tract of land about four miles up the canyon from the center of the village. The land, located on the edge of the El Rito Creek, has a shallow spring that empties into the creek. The spring is, in fact, classified as surface water by the State Engineer and the state's Environmental Department. The donors of this source of water were Arthur N. Pack and Phoebe F. Pack, who deeded the quantity of 10.69 acres to the Spanish American Normal School. The Normal School installed about four miles of concrete pipe and water flowed onto the campus, much as it did in ancient Rome, by gravity flow. This water has been sufficient for all irrigation since that time, but it has had to chlorinated and monitored carefully for drinking and cooking. This source of water has been less than ideal for domestic purposes, as will be discussed later in this work.

A president of an institution learns early that his or her effectiveness as leader and chief executive depends heavily on the individual's relationship with the members of the Board of Regents. Joe Grant brought with him experience as member and president of the Board, but he soon learned that suitable, forward-looking Regents would comprise a Board that not only related well to him, but who got along with each other and viewed themselves as equal and took interest in each member's views and contributions in discussion. Son David told me that his dad strived to maintain continuity on a Board, when its members were working harmoniously. This depended on cooperation from governors of the state, and as time went by he was able to gain their confidence. Between 1935 and 1951 the Office of the Governor was occupied by a Democrat, a help to Joseph Grant.

Since 1937, Joe Grant had been working with a new Board of Regents whom he trusted and liked. Members included: Emma T. Oakley, President of the Board; Roman Baca, Vice-President; E.T. Lucero, Secretary-Treasurer; Roman Atencio and Octaviano Manzanares. They were of the same mind as the school's President, and tended to keep the same officers during this Board's period of service; they reelected the same officers again in 1939. This made it easier for the President to recommend measures in favor emphasizing the vocational high school, given that the Board of Regents of 1934 had eschewed the college program in favor of vocational education.

Instruction continued in the manner set in the early 1930s. Later in the same years, however, Joe Grant was urged by none other than his brother David to strengthen the college program. In order to do this, he needed a good principal, as they referred to the chief academic officer, and a good leader for the college division. He hired some very capable people, but keeping them was another matter. Between 1935 and 1942, when the college division was being developed, he had three principals: Herbert W. Prather, James A. McNeil, and W.D. Caster. The college division was headed first by C.H. Robinson, then by Howard Sylvester.

The team of Caster and Robinson seems to have been particularly effective during the planning and developmental period for the college division. The Catalog of the Spanish American Normal School for 1940-41 states about the College Division:

Purposes
The college division endeavors to carry out the aims that were basic in the establishment of the school: To prepare students for the teaching profession. Progress,
however, has somewhat alleviated the intensity of this need and

other objectives now appear. This department now finds itself in the need of offering opportunities for other types of education as well. The demand is increasingly changing from professional to general education: a broadening, informational, social and spiritual uplift in preparation for the business of living as well as teaching.

By offering in the college division the same or similar courses offered by other institutions of higher learning in New Mexico, the Spanish American Normal School makes it possible for students to begin their college work here and continue it elsewhere without a break. Similar work elsewhere would involve considerably more expense. Because the classes are smaller than in the average college, the student receives more individual attention and comes into closer contact with the faculty.

All work of the college division of the Spanish American Normal School is accepted unconditionally by the State Department of Education toward certification requirements.

For students who are not interested in taking a teacher training course a two year undergraduate curriculum will be offered leading toward the bachelor of arts or science degree.

The Catalog for the school lists the names of members of the Board of Regents and administrators of the Normal School.

Board of Regents[6]

John E. Miles, Governor of New Mexico, Member, Ex-Officio
Mrs. Emma T. Oakley, President, Santa Fe
Roman Baca, Vice-President, El Rito
E.T. Lucero, Secretary-Treasurer, Española
Octaviano Manzanares, Member, Park View
Roman Atencio, Member, Dixon

Officers of Administration

Joseph B. Grant, President
C.H. Robinson, Dean of the College
John H. Black, Director of Teacher Education
W.D. Caster, Director of Academic Work
George A. Segura, Director of Vocational Education
Eloy M. Abeyta, Bursar and Registrar

Note that this is the same Board of Regents with which we have become familiar.

Among administrators, Mr. Caster seemed to have stayed longest, having started with the Normal School as a classroom teacher. Mr. Robinson served the school in later years, in addition to his days at the Normal with Joe Grant. George Segura was the president's brother-in-law. Eloy Abeyta was one of the loyalists on campus, and probably proud of it. He returned to the Normal School during my time when I was a student in mid-1950s. Joe Grant returned to the school as Regent.

Entrance requirements for students are the usual ones today in a modern school and college. What is very interesting is the cost of attendance.

At the beginning of school, college students needed to have thirty dollars. The amount included $5.00 for admission and registration paid only once during the life of the student, $10.00 in fees (included tuition), and $15.00 for the first month's room and board. High school students paid five dollars less, $25.00 on opening day. Boarding students could reduce their monthly cost to $10.00 per month by working at the usual student jobs, in the kitchen, on the grounds, or in the buildings as janitors. The Normal School at El Rito always sought to keep students' costs as low as possible.

The divisions of high school, vocational and college instruction are described:

> Units required for high school graduation are mathematics (2), Spanish (2), social science (2), natural science (2), English (4) and four units of electives. Students may graduate in general education or with a trades proficiency, or both.
>
> The college division had a prescribed curriculum, not unusual for a small school. It is unclear precisely how many credits were required for graduation, but a diligent student could take as many as 78 credits, in particular if the student was preparing to transfer to a university program in teacher education. The Catalog states that students could pursue a program in general education; this may have meant about fifteen fewer credits required for students not seeking to become teachers.

The college division offered a transfer curriculum, important for students interested in the teaching profession. During the late 1930s and throughout the 1940s, academic and professional requirements for teachers were increasing. This meant that new teachers were required to have at least the bachelor of arts degree, which the Spanish American Normal School did not offer. The Normal School made an earnest effort to coordinate with the universities in ensuring that the teacher education courses were equivalent to introductory courses in this field offered at the universities. Joe Grant and the director of the college division kept the Board of Regents apprised of these efforts, and the matter is reflected in minutes of meetings of the Board.

The Normal School did not publish a student yearbook for a long time, and so we do not have a good record of students attending, graduating, etc. In this instance, however, Manuel Eustacio Medina gave us his high school diploma, awarded in 1938. The diploma is signed by Joseph B. Grant and H.W. Prather, the Principal. For the Regents Emma T. Oakley signed as President and E.T. Lucero as Secretary also signed the diploma. On the diploma are listed members of the Class of 1938; the full list is included at the end of this book.

Diplomas awarded are for completion of high school. There is no indication that there were any college graduates. Interestingly, there was a "College Club" in existence in 1938. Pat Vigil, a graduate of the high school whose biographical sketch I have included in Chapter Eight, is a brother to Alonzo Vigil, now deceased. Pat tells me that in Alonzo's possession was a school bulletin that mentioned the college club. This is important to any chronicler of events at the Normal School because its original charter from the state had not changed. Everyone was aware of this, and the Catalog from which I have quoted to you gives evidence of this.

People of that era are still our best source of information.[7] John Martin (Class of '39) tells me that courses in the college division were offered which were automatically transferable to a state university, New Mexico Highlands University being the usual receiving institution. John took some college courses at El Rito after high school, prior to enrolling at the University of New Mexico.

In summary, this is what one can deduce. The Spanish American

Normal School offered a program similar to one offered by junior colleges throughout the Nation, but graduated few, if any, students. Some students took college level courses, much as they do today in what is called Advanced Placement, concurrent or dual credit enrollment. With the onset of World War II, enrollments diminished and the college division ceased to function.

The importance of tracing the history of the Normal School as a teacher training institution is important in that it provides some inkling of the social condition of Rio Arriba County and its neighbors just prior to and during World War II.

The Class of '42 is listed in the May minutes of the Board.[8] Names of students may be found in the list at the end of this book.

Names of teachers are not listed in the Catalog, unfortunately. From personnel actions taken by the Boards of Regents, we know who taught during the period 1935 to 1951, the Joe Grant years. I have mentioned that during earlier years it was difficult to keep teachers and other professional people at the Normal School in El Rito. The same was true during these years. Salaries for teachers were lower than they were in comparable, urban schools. Living conditions on campus were barely adequate. Teachers who stayed did so for their love of El Rito, the campus, its students, and another reason: the school had its loyalists, devoted to Joe Grant and to what the Normal School *was*, what Joe Grant had made it.

Some of the loyalists on the staff had been students at the Normal, other staff simply came and stayed. Some became close friends with each other, and occasionally some married a co-worker. It would be tedious to examine who worked each year during Joe Grant's time, but names are important. These include, in addition to those mentioned earlier:

Eloy M. Abeyta
Ascesion Alarid
Fannie Marie Allen
Helen Anderson
Gilbert Archuleta
Lena Lovato Archuleta
Mary S. Baker

Lucille Borrego	Alice D. Rathbunn
Charles B. Brown	Alice D. Reed
Norma Brown	C.H. Robinson
S. Boyd Calkins	Mary Sanchez
W.D. Caster	Ezequiel Sandoval
D.M. Chavez, Jr.	John F. Schiro
Teresa Chavez	George A. Segura
Carson Creecy	Ralph E. Seitsinger
Waldimir Doering	Barbara C. Sena
Robert Dugan	Teodorita Stewner
Delfina Gonzales	Annette Sudderth
Elacio L. Jaramillo	Howard E. Sylvester
Roman Jaramillo	Josue Trujillo
Florence Kellogg	Sabine Ulibarri
Charles Lopez	Twila Tucker
Pete Maestas	Cleo Trujillo
Ernestine Manzanares	Luis R. Trujillo
Theorodita Manzanares	Alonzo Vigil
Pablo Mares	Opal West Wingfield
James F. Ortiz	

Just as you could see the imprint of Joe Grant on the campus at El Rito, could you also witness the results of efforts of teachers who stayed around at least four to five, or more, years. A strong music program developed after 1940, when Pablo Mares arrived at the Normal. He taught music, voice, and strings. He created an orchestra, *una orquesta típica*, that became well known throughout northern New Mexico. In fact, Pablo Mares and his students would go on tour, bringing to communities the Orquesta Típica of the Spanish American Normal School. The Orquesta Típica played many of the old Mexican and Spanish popular numbers, and a few of his and other New Mexico composers. Many of these songs may be found in the public domain.

I knew from discussion with students who had attended the Normal in the early forties that Pablo Mares and the Orquesta were a great source of pride for everyone. During a large alumni reunion on the campus in El Rito, we invited Pablo Mares, his wife Lucille and daughter Patricia. He gave us some of his memorabilia, including copies of programs presented by the Orquesta Típica at various venues. The earliest record that we have of the Orquesta Típica is a presentation billed as the First Annual Music Festival of the Spanish American Normal School held in Cutting Hall on May 8, 1940. Orchestra members included Mary Gonzáles, Rose Harris, Kayo McDermitt, Mary Sánchez, George Segura, Pat Martin, Alice Greathouse, Mrs. Baker, Ferrell Caster, Eloy Abeyta, Conrad Rivera, Joe W. Trujillo, Liberato Quintana, Fred Catanach, Robert Catanach, Joel Lacey and Sabino García. A larger group of band members included, in addition to some already mentioned, Lucille Velarde, Billy O'Brien, Harold Johnson, Teddy Kuntz, Leroy Gooch, Rodolfo Jaramillo, Juan Manzanares, Aurelio Trujillo, Emilio Felix, Max Gonzáles, Frank Vigil, and Fabiola Lucero.

By 1941, the Orquesta Típica was playing for the Governor's Banquet honoring the 15th New Mexico Legislature at La Fonda in Santa Fe. Numbers included "La Ladera," "La Raspa," "Mexicali Rose," "La Varsoviana," "Panchíta," "La Vaquera," "Amor Chiquíto," "Adios Mariquíta Linda," "Cielito Lindo," and "Jesusíta." Many of the same orchestra members continued, but in addition there were Freda Johnson, Richard Olguin, Ida Johnson, Fabiola Lucero, Della Mente, Cecilia Sena, Guzman Martínez, Antonio Herrera, Rita L. García and Joe M. Trujillo. Other venues included the old Santa Cruz gymnasium ('43), Bruns Army Hospital ('44) in Albuquerque, service clubs and radio stations in the northern part of the state.

Pablo Mares was honored as a distinguished alumnus at New Mexico Highlands University in 1969, long after he had left the Normal School. In 1995, the State of New Mexico adopted his song, "New Mexico/Mi Lindo Nuevo México," as the official state song in Spanish and English. [9]

The sports program at El Rito was always an important part of student life. Interscholastic competition in baseball, basketball, football, boxing and track tended to include a good majority of students. Basketball loomed larger, by far, than other sports, and girls played inter-high school basket, also. Two individuals stand out as coaches during the late thirties and throughout the forties: Charlie Brown and Alonzo Vigil. Gilbert Archuleta was one of the mainstays of Joe Grant's early period at the Normal. The President was a great sports enthusiast and it was probably the reason for the coaches' willingness to stay around. I met Charlie Brown and I knew Al Vigil; they told me how much they admired Joe Grant, enough to spend a good part of a lifetime with him.

Charlie Brown passed away not long after I had met him in about 1979. John Aragon, who was president at Highlands University and my good friend, and his great friend Pat Vigil attended funeral services for Charlie Brown in California. These men were all members in good standing of an informal fraternity—they would say family—some of which continues to exist today.

Students seemed to engage in more than their share of co-curricular and extra-curricular activities, all of which were well organized. The list of organizations resembled that of a small college campus. I refer here to home economics club, glee club, letter "N" club, powder puff, future farmers, press club, orchestra, folk dancing, and homecoming royalty and all of the usual cliques that students dream up for a campus. Staff were always there to help with sponsorship.

One of the vocational teachers' names comes up in discussion continually among the men. Ezequiel Sandoval was synonymous with the institution in Spanish colonial furniture making. His very able assistant was a man, Roman Baca, from El Rito for whom former students and residents express their esteem today. I have seen in former students' homes dining room furniture, tables and chairs of that era. They have seemed to me as timely and well preserved as they were when they were made in late '30s and '40s.

Japan attacked the United States by air at Pearl Harbor on Sunday, December 7, 1941, killing 2,403 servicemen and wounding another 1,200. President Roosevelt requested from the Congress and obtained, immediately the next day, a declaration of war against Japan. Four days later, Adolf Hitler declared Germany at war with the United States; World War II was upon us.

The Board of Regents was meeting quarterly that winter of '41-42, but not much is said about the effects of war until the Board minutes for February, 1942. Owing to the National Emergency, rationing had been implemented. It was becoming increasingly difficult at the Normal to acquire foodstuffs, materials and supplies. The president recommended to the Board that the school should purchase for "spot delivery" whenever and wherever there was opportunity and funds were available. He suggested that a "surplus of commodities" be stored, if possible, while goods were obtainable because it was impossible to foresee which items would be rationed henceforth. Authorization was quickly granted by the Board.

One, among many sad considerations of the war, is that the Spanish American Normal School did not maintain records of the young men who, after life at the Normal School, entered the brutal hardship of war. I happened to know one veteran, because he had married a relative of mine. Among students to whom I dedicated this volume is one Paul Romero. I am justifiably proud because he attended the Normal School, he was featured in *Children of the Normal School*, published by Sunstone Press in 2011, and he was from Velarde. He presently resides in Albuquerque; he is 96 years of age.

In the same meeting, discussion switched to a lighter, more enjoyable subject in short order. Commendations received by the Orquesta Típica from the Albuquerque broadcasting station KOB "poured in", the Board minutes state. Information about an invitation by the orchestra to present a concert at Carlsbad Caverns provided the Board sweet consolation away from talk about the war. Other invitations came in from Colorado, Texas and closer to home.

Joe Grant's pride in the Orquesta Típica was evident in a January 1942 picture that appeared in the Albuquerque Journal. He is there with Pablo Mares and the musicians: Polly C. García, Alcalde; Fabiola Lucero, Anton Chico; Mary Sanchez, Trementina; Eloy Abeyta, Park View; Dondald Evans, Española; Freda Johnson, Albuquerque; Ernestine Salazar, Cuba; Esther Baca, Ratón; Della Mente, Pecos; Cecilia Sena, Trementina; Guzman Martínez, El Rito; La Rue Bostick, Gallina; and Ida Johnson, Santa Fé.

There is a hint in an editorial that appeared in the Santa Fe New Mexican in April 1942 about the direction that the Spanish American Normal School would take for the remainder of the war years under Joe Grant. The article begins, "The recent reelection of Joseph Grant as president of the Spanish American Normal School at El Rito assures continuance of the progress made by the school under his direction." It continues "...the subjects taught are calculated, not only to make the student a better citizen, but to prepare him or her to better fill a position in the economic and business life of the nation."

The school's Catalog for 1943-44 expresses this idea in Joseph Grant's own words.

PRESIDENT'S MESSAGE

It is the aim of the Board of Regents, the Administrative Officials, and the faculty of the Spanish American Normal School to prepare New Mexico Youth to take their proper place in the future of our State. We have emphasized a program of patriotism and shall make all efforts that upon completion of their studies, our students will go out into the world properly equipped to meet competition, and more important, they will appreciate the privileges and the honor of being true American Citizens.

The opening General Information is also written by Joe Grant and seems to be an *apología* for deemphasizing the college division. Take a look at this.

Purpose

The Spanish American Normal School was created early in the twentieth century to provide a source of training for Spanish speaking teachers for positions in rural communities. New Mexico, at the time, was a state of great distances, of villages isolated by long miles of prairie and mountains. To bring education into the communities of the northern part of the state was a problem of magnitude.

The Spanish American Normal School was a courageous and intelligent effort to solve this problem and much progress was made toward its objective. With time and the constantly changing conditions in New Mexico, the automobile and construction of highways did much to end the original isolation of communities and bring our people closer together.

The improved conditions and closer communications naturally were reflected in the policy of our Institution, and we met the new problem by including two years of college work and various vocational subjects which we felt would enable our youth to find work and better meet competition in various industrial lines. We have emphasized vocational subjects for our students which we feel will be needed in the future growth of New Mexico. We have found an interesting response from students who desire to perfect themselves in some trade, with the reasonable assurance of employment. We have found that a great many were quickly absorbed in the business world because of their training in our institution. We feel that progress has been made in our efforts to prepare graduates who will reflect credit upon their state and themselves.

The declaration of the school's intention in the third paragraph and the preamble that precedes it seem like an abrogation of the Spanish American Normal School's constitutional responsibility, it being to train teachers for the public schools. Nowhere is a plausible reason given for this, but one can surmise. There may not have been a sufficient number of students interested in college courses, although the Catalog describes, once again, a college division and its purpose, consonant with teacher training. The curriculum in the college division seems larger, expanded from earlier years, in number and variety of courses. There seems to be an inconsistency present in this document that is not easily explained. It may also have been that state support for the college division was difficult to obtain, in particular financial support. The Catalog repeats statements made in earlier years that the State Department of Education accepted unconditionally all work taken by students in the college division, but we do not find evidence of students having completed a program of study in the college division.

In November 1942, a handful of men, J. Robert Oppenheimer, Edwin McMillan, General Leslie R. Groves, and Major John H. Dudley, decided to locate a physics laboratory—more precisely said, a planned weapons laboratory known as the Manhattan Project—from scattered locations around the United States to a site, the Los Alamos Ranch School, with which Oppenheimer had become acquainted in his youth. Oppenheimer and McMillan were physicists, Groves and McMillan were US Army. Only about a month before that, Groves had decided that Oppenheimer would head a project to develop the atomic bomb, Oppenheimer having been among a group of scientists who had ascertained that this kind of bomb could be developed and manufactured.

Their decision to locate what came to be known as the Los Alamos Scientific Laboratory for many years, then the Los Alamos National Laboratory, as it is today, would change the upper Rio Grande Valley and north central New Mexico in ways, at the time, unimaginable.

The Laboratory changed how people in our communities would earn their livelihood. The creation of thousands of new and unfamiliar jobs at Los Alamos brought to this region unheard of amounts of money. The effect of this new wealth on Santa Fe, Española and surrounding towns and villages was huge, indescribable in a couple of paragraphs of this narrative. An idyllic and pastoral life that local people, mostly Indian and hispanic, had known for several hundred years would be traded for a cash economy...forever after.

The effect on the rest of the world, however, would be much more profound. The Laboratory initiated the age of super bombs—weapons of mass destruction, people talk about these days. The first of these, the atomic bomb, would be tested at Trinity Site, north of Alamogordo, and used in the war against Japan. Two such bombs, dropped on Hiroshima and Nagasaki, destroyed the will of the Japanese government to continue the war, as was intended by the United States. The bomb, and its new, more powerful successors, has never been used again.

In the early years, the Los Alamos Scientific Laboratory hired a few skilled people and mostly unskilled labor from the valley. In time, the educational level of our people in this region would increase as more employment opportunities arose. Locally trained technicians, office and clerical people, engineers and scientists would eventually find their way into good jobs at the Laboratory. It was this phenomenon, principally, that helped to pave the future direction that the Spanish American Normal School would take for many years.

The first half of the decade of the '40s were the war years, and the likelihood of there being many students at the Normal was smaller than usual. Very noticeable about the high school curriculum of the period 1941 to 1946 is the emphasis given to what was called a commercial program, business education or office occupations. There was a "commercial department" described in the Catalog, and courses in bookkeeping, shorthand and typewriting were offered by the department. There existed a home economics department with a wide variety of topics covered in the field, many very apt and useful still today.

The mathematics department listed courses in general math, algebra (2 years), plane geometry, and trigonometry. A music department, which had started in 1940, described its program aimed at preparing musicians for the Orquesta Típica. There was a vocational department described; it presumably included commercial and home economics, and in addition, weaving and woodworking, which were not described at any length.

A junior high school, consisting of seventh and eighth grades was described briefly. Subjects taught were in mathematics, English grammar and literature, spelling, social science, arts and dramatics.

The Catalog for that year described buildings and beautiful grounds, which one can imagine in reading. Three buildings should have been of particular interest to students. The southernmost of three large buildings consisted of a girls' dormitory, dining room, a "large recreation room," and Cutting Memorial Auditorium. The middle building was the high school building, whereas boys were boarded on the second floor. The northernmost building contained the same small gymnasium present, since about 1930, and presumably classrooms for junior high and elementary school students.

Minutes of the Board of Regents in April 1943 listed the graduating Class of 1943, which readers may find listed at the end of this book.

Names of students on the graduating list had been recommended by a committee on graduation credentials: they were teachers John P. Schiro, L.R. Trujillo, Jr., A. Louise Roybal, Pablo Mares, and E.L. Jaramillo.

The administration made it a point to address the matter of drinking water for the campus: "The school supplies its own water through a pipeline leading from the El Rito Canyon, bringing to the school its water in clear and healthful form. The water is tested at all times during the school term by the State Department of Health."

We may be certain that the foregoing statements about water were accurate. The problem with the water source, from which a danger persisted, was that it was immediately adjacent to the bank of the El Rito Creek from which flooding could occur during any runoff. This is indeed what eventually occurred.

In October 1943, a report of the president to the Board of Regents included that a case of typhoid fever on campus led to a flurry of activity owing to concern that the water system could have caused the illness. However, doctors who examined the boy concluded that he had contracted the disease prior to enrolling in school that fall. The state Department of Health was contacted nevertheless and the water system and the school were given a "clean bill." It turns out further in discussion that this very same October day the water system had been cleaned and repaired because it had been overrun by flood waters from excessive rain.

Further precautions against a typhoid epidemic were taken, according to President Grant, and a program of immunization was conducted on campus to include all students, teachers, and staff employees. No more cases of typhoid fever were reported that fall term.

Discussions led by the president concerning the problem of the water system, namely concerns about its purity, continued in early 1944. He reported that every effort was being made to ensure proper chlorination of water, but that inadequate equipment required manual chlorination. Scarcity of the needed equipment was blamed on war regulations. What one may conclude from what was said is that the school was doing its best under trying conditions during that winter of 1943 and 1944.

The war years presented other difficulties for the Normal School, some of which were unforeseen. Not only did rationing of food occur, but rising costs for some items tripled in price. Shortages created by the war required that some students volunteer to do farm work at the expense of their schooling. The Normal School cooperated, of course.

The Class of 1944 was reduced from the previous year by about one third. Thirty-one students graduated that year; the list of students is also available at the end of this book.

Isabel Jaramillo Trujillo was valedictorian; E. Jeanne Belknap was salutatorian. Faculty who certified the graduating class were Pablo Mares, E.L. Jaramillo, Delfina Gonzales, Rose Jordi, Lena L. Archuleta and W.D. Caster, Principal.

A surprisingly large number of faculty were to return to the Normal School for the 1944-45 school year. W.D. Caster and Pablo Mares were not among those returning. L.R. Trujillo succeeded Mr. Caster as principal.

Sadly again, no mention was made of young men who were drafted, or otherwise enrolled, in the armed services.

One result of changes in the curriculum of the Spanish American Normal School in the 1940s was that it produced neither a college nor a full-fledged vocational school, but it did produce a high school that was extraordinarily vibrant. The school that came to be known throughout northern New Mexico, first from its sports programs, especially basketball, enjoyed accolades beginning as early as the 1930s. In spite of its small size, seldom more that 150 students, the high school competed well. Add to this the Orquesta Típica of 1940 to 1944 and you may imagine a happy group of students, all of them busy at one or another of their activities. This atmosphere persisted for a good length of time, on into the end of the 1960s.

After the war years, many of the young men returned to the campus. In 1946 and '47, there were enough veterans on the campus for the young men to form their own basketball team. Many of them were over the age limit to compete interscholastically, but they played challenge games against varsity teams and other league basketball.

Sadly for students and colleagues alike, Pablo Mares had left, but the administration provided other outlets for students talents to be displayed. The age of the Orquesta Típica was followed by the Follies, which were musical, song and dance, groups sponsored by a new teacher, Lena Lovato[10]. Students who attended the Normal School after the war, on to about 1950, could easier remember the Follies, which also played to large audiences on and off campus. Anna Mae King, class of 1948, told me on the telephone that she could remember the Follies being presented at the Lensic Theater in Santa Fe. Extra-curricular and co-curricular activities, including sports, simply grew stronger every year. Finally, Joe Grant's name was occasionally in the news, and always to the credit of the Normal School.

The graduating Class of 1945 was announced in mid-spring; the list of students is provided at the end of this book..

The class was small, 20 students. The war was still on. Students were shielded, as much as possible, from hardships resulting from shortages of foodstuffs and other materials in the campus's rural environment.

Stories that we heard about Joseph Grant, through the years, are often true; some were beyond belief. His ability to get along with the

Board of Regents was a direct result of his influence with governors of the state who were Democrats. Governors renamed the same members to the Board term after term. It is also quite clear in examining the record that he worked very hard, and the Board appreciated this, often having to urge him to take an occasional vacation. An occurrence in a Board meeting in spring 1945 is telling. The Board ordered Mr. Grant to accept a salary increase, to four hundred and fifty dollars monthly, noting that Joe Grant had not had a salary increase since 1938. He had refused yearly increases to which he was entitled. The precise terms of his contract were not mentioned, except to say that the president was required to live in "the president's cottage" on campus.

Despite the vote of confidence that Joseph Grant received from the Board of Regents that spring of '45, the Normal School was having an unusually difficult time financially. Meetings of the Board in May and June suggest that budgets continued to be sparse—state appropriation for the following school year was $78,500—and it was becoming increasingly difficult to hire new teachers. It became impossible to replace a high school teacher who left at mid-year, for example.

On April 12, 1945, the President of the United States Franklin D. Roosevelt died in the Nation's capital. Little in the record of the Spanish American Normal School noted this passing.

The great war ended, first with Germany in May of 1948, then in Japan in early September of the same year. Veterans who had managed to make it through the war started coming home, some of them to El Rito and to the Normal School. Counties like Rio Arriba and Taos lost many of their young men, but luckily some returned, and all of them to be esteemed in the memory of the rest of us.

The number of graduates in 1946 made a small, but abrupt, jump. This was the last year in which the school did not publish a student yearbook. The Class of 1946 may be found in the list at the end of this book.

This group of students was similar to some of the older classes at the Normal School. Vocational education was emphasized. In one respect, this class of students brought the Normal School into the modern age, with its reliance on *El Aguila* the student newspaper, as a means of communicating everything that students felt was important. Some of the biographical information about students that appears in a later chapter in this book I was able to glean from *El Aguila*.

The baseball team in 1946 was the strongest in memory, and took third place in the state tournament. In a less-than-ideal climate for baseball in El Rito—the month of March can be blustery and cold—the boys competed against schools from Albuquerque and powerhouses from farther south, to their credit. Pat Vigil, Class of '47, who was an avid baseball player, explained it to me this way. High school sports were not reported by the newspapers with the wide coverage of today. Nor were athletes groomed for the next step in their careers. This made it possible for a good coach to come along and mold a good team with the talent at hand. Pat credits good coaching for their success at El Rito. During these years, Charlie Brown and Al Vigil, Pat's brother, coached baseball. Pitcher Ruben Archuleta was remarkably talented. Students would remember for a long time that he pitched a no-hitter against Los Alamos High School. The El Rito Eagles beat the 'Toppers 1-0, with Pat Vigil driving in the winning run. So the boys were not without talent, but desire, enthusiasm and pride carried them through several successful seasons.

Chapter Eight in our book contains many more brief stories out of which fond memories were made.

I have had to learn lessons, that as author of two books on the Normal School—the first book, you may remember is *Children of the Normal School*—a book of which I am justifiably proud, although as a first-time author, I made some mistakes of my own making and some not. How life was at El Rito, a very rural community, was an error which I referred to earlier. Emphasizing sports was a matter that I could not avoid, although there were some errors that resulted from poor record-keeping on the part of the Normal School.

After publication of the first book, I have since discovered that many students, whose children and more distant relatives would maintain that their forebears were among those graduates of the Normal School whom I missed. At the time of publication of *Children of the Normal School* I knew that faulty record-keeping would reflect on this book. You may be distressed to know that no fewer than half a dozen people have noted that I am missing names. I truly regret this.

When I was president of the Normal School, in its incarnation as

Northern New Mexico Community College, I learned that, following the closure of the high school in 1969, records of attendance of students was not done. If I am repeating a story that I have related before, I am truly sorry. However, I am sorrier for those students, long after they had left the Normal School, discovered that there was no record associated with them. The method that seemed appropriate, and which had followed in the past, is that the State of New Mexico would notify the new high school, the Mesa Vista Schools, of students having attended the Normal School. I suppose that the uniqueness of the Normal School, in its founding and operation, was the cause of this omission. It is a serious omission.

Please bear some of this in mind, if you read this book. Many of the same sources are used in this book; I regret that the same sources are all that exist.

The new year, 1947, was one of modest growth for the school, the number of returning veterans having gotten larger. The eleventh grade class, in particular, grew to almost forty students. Classes of '47 and '48 were indistinguishable in important ways, important for students, that is. They were all great friends, and would remain in close touch throughout their adult lives. They loved the campus, their teachers and staff, student activities such as basketball, baseball, football, the student newspaper–El Aguila–and their new student yearbook, named, appropriately, *El Chamisal*. Then there were The Follies, it seems that we were to hear about The Follies to the end of time. It seems, also, that if classes of students can possess their own character, the classes of 1947 and '48 had character. One tradition that received renewed vigor was the matter of sticking nicknames on people. This was a bit like the inside joke, only they would know whom they were talking about, and they did, all the time.

This was the last year in which the school would be known as the Spanish American Normal School. The student yearbook, the creation of David Grant, who graduated high school in '47, was a modest beginning, published on inexpensive paper. Binding was with spiral. Students cherished it, those living still do.

Joe Grant got into the news, as was his wont. People of the time say that he wasn't the greatest communicator, but, in fact, what he left in writing and in interviews with newspaper people, was superb. A long article appeared in El Nuevo Mexicano[11], the Spanish language newspaper, in 1947, written by J.E. Medina. This is the same gentleman who was a new appointee to the Board of Regents of the Normal School. He dealt beautifully with matters about the Normal School to the elucidation, one can be certain, of a largely uninformed readership. For example, there was the name change to Northern New Mexico Normal School, undertaken by the state legislature with approval of everyone concerned. Medina explained that it was not meant that the school should be exclusively for Spanish-speaking Americans, but that it had been founded to deal with a population at the turn of the century that did not speak English. Teaching the English language to future teachers had been its intended mission. He recounted that when he first visited the school in 1935 there were fewer than 100 students.[12] He alluded to the stark picture of the campus of two buildings on a lone prairie. Medina remembered the remaking of the campus as I have described it to you, and ended by saying that all of the progress in establishing a school—an oasis in this desert, he called it—was owed to Joseph Grant. He ended a two thousand word essay by lauding the president's efforts, his tenacity, energy and determination in creating a modern and progressive school.

We may regret, as we do the history of these United States, that apparently no thought was given to a Native American community, especially in Rio Arriba, Santa Fe, and Taos counties where many communities and reservations reside. The tendency then, as it often is today, that people saw, in its title, a means of exclusivity of the Normal School, that Mr. Medina described well when the name change of the Normal School was announced.

We are fortunate that a good number of the members of the Class of '47 and Class of '48[13] are living; I interviewed a number of them for this book. Returning veterans who eventually graduated at the high school include the following members of the Class of '47: Ernest Gurulé from Cuba, Atanacio Martínez from Truchas, and Sam Romero from Santa Fe. We lament the scarcity of student records remaining from the days of the Northern New Mexico Normal School, among other reasons because no one makes mention of other deserving veterans of this terrible war. It was a war in which more young men died, by far, as a percent of the population of the world, than in any previous, more recent war.

A piece of evidence of students' pride in their campus was to be found in a graduation issue of *El Aguila* on a Friday, the 23rd of May 1947. It was an exceptionally nicely done edition on good paper, printed by press, not the usual mimeograph sheets of the news bulletin. David Grant, editor, wrote a farewell to his classmates and Concy Romero wrote the piece to which I refer. She called her brief essay "Preserve Nature's Work." The middle paragraph says,

> Like the poet and the artist let us not only glorify nature's work but preserve it. Our own campus is replete with flowers lawns, shrubs and trees. We find, however, that the vandals of Nature are in our very midst. There are those who trample the lawns, those who pick the flowers, those who desecrate shrubs and bushes, and finally those who, not satisfied with Nature on the ground, ape the monkey and climb trees. The result? Dry lawns, broken branches, deserted flowerbeds and distorted shrubbery.

Focus on student life in the late 1940s brings to light the beauty of the campus and its ambient, all of which students, unaccustomed to another similar environment in northern New Mexico, grew to love and filed away in memories that they cherish to this day.

Sports and sports-related activities entertained students, as did dramatic and musical presentations. Although basketball outranked baseball, football, track and boxing in student interest, one of the real prizes eluded the basketball team for a long time. For the 1948 season, Frank Byers joined the Northern New Mexico Normal School as head basketball coach. It would be six years before the Eagles would win their first district title. A note of explanation is necessary: until 1955, high school athletic association did not divide schools by size. This meant that for close to forty years the smallest school in the state, say the Normal School at El Rito, played against the largest schools, say Albuquerque and Santa Fe. It is interesting that so many small schools competed successfully, as was the case across the Nation. This indicates characteristics in the American culture at the time that are beyond description in a book of this scope.

These early years of *El Chamisal* gave rise to student behavior that carried forward for another twenty years. Students designated their favorites from among them: most handsome, most beautiful, best athlete, best student and so on. Surely communication among students state wide, or at the very least among neighboring schools, took place, with students emulating behavior among a wide set of peers. I am lifting this passage in the 1947-48 *El Chamisal* as an example of usual practices that students enjoyed:

Homecoming Day and Football Queen

On November first we celebrated our annual Homecoming Day. The main events were a football game in the afternoon, and a dance that night. At the half of the game, football captain John Aragon crowned Miss Anna Mae King the Football Queen, and she received flowers from the co-captain Buzzy Newbern. Miss Mary Mascareñas and Miss Belen Espinoza were the Queen's attendants.

Although readers may chuckle, this is what youth of our day did, and the young today probably continue to do.

Rural electrification reached El Rito in 1947. Joseph Grant reported to the Board of Regents as late as September of '48 that a transformer was needed by the Kit Carson electrical cooperative before power could reach the campus, on the far side of the community from Taos County where electrical power originated. In the meantime, Prokosch Electrical Company of Santa Fe would provide a route for electrical power to be brought to the school's generating plant in order that power could be assured for the campus even during power outages at Kit Carson.

During the same meeting the Regents were informed of a contract that the school had entered into with R.K.O., a distributor of movies of the time, including those from Walt Disney.

New teachers for the 1948-49 school year included Lou C. Funderburk, Frutoso López, John D. Villa, Nellie Trujillo, Paul Valerio, Cipriano Trujillo and Mary R. Martínez.

Boys' State, a project sponsored by the American Legion, had been held at the Northern New Mexico Normal School that year and was being recommended to the state legislature for continuation by the sponsor.

President Joseph B. Grant had informed the Board of Regents of his intention to resign in September. The Board entered a lengthy letter into the record expressing its deep satisfaction with the performance of Grant as president, urging him to reconsider. Even Governor Mabry interceded on the Board's behalf, and Grant elected to stay until the end of Mabry's term of office.

The first serious, and acknowledged, spread of typhoid fever on the campus and in the community of El Rito occurred that fall of 1948. Apart from records kept by the school, which focused on dealing with the emergency, obtaining help from the state Health Department in analyzing the source of the problem, and preparing to avoid future cases of the disease, human testimony that is still available paints a picture of hardship and despair. The disease seems to have affected the younger children especially, although the record is scant. Richard Garcia and Ted Martinez, two very young boys from Albuquerque at the time, in sixth grade, had to go home. Richard didn't know that it was typhoid fever that he had contracted. He remembers only that it seemed "like a long time" before he was able to return to sixth grade. Ted had come to the Normal School only that fall at the suggestion of his cousin Richard. He left ill in mid-fall and was quarantined at home until April of the following year. He did not return to El Rito until 10th grade. *El Chamisal* published a memorial to two of the boys who died in that epidemic: Nicomedes Sanchez from Park View and Orlando Griego from Albuquerque.

Measures that were undertaken, with the cooperation of the Health Department, were effective once the illness had been diagnosed. Students were inoculated against typhoid fever. Dennis Salazar, a boy also in sixth grade at the time, remembers well *not* becoming ill. The president and the Board held a long discussion of steps to be taken to avoid a repetition of this incident. Chlorination of the water was key. It was felt that the existing anti-bacterial system had been inadequate and that an apparatus that guaranteed timely and strong chlorination was needed. Joseph Grant requested funds for purchase of a new chlorinator from the state's "emergency fund," and was allowed the sum of $2,800 for this purpose. The apparatus was acquired in Denver. This was the last of any similar epidemics to be witnessed again.

In a subsequent meeting that year, minutes stated that President Grant addressed the Board of Regents that, "...this had been one of the most difficult periods that the school had ever undergone, and he complimented everyone for the calm manner and efficient work which had been done so as to cause no undue worry to the parents, as well as to avoid any panic." It was at this meeting, however, that the grave condition of the two boys for whom the disease would ultimately prove fatal was announced to the Board. One matter became amply clear to me as president, years later. The tendency of the El Rito creek to overflow the adjacent springs would continue to be a problem; indeed, *any flooding* of the domestic water system by the creek continued to be dangerous. The watershed, possibly for another forty miles up the canyon, is contaminated by grazing animals and human activity. The contamination of the water system by the creek became evident in the manner in which I have described here, in the 1940s.[14] I regret that we had to discover this much later…

By late May 1949 the Normal School was acquiring a semblance of normalcy following the epidemic of the previous fall. The Board of Regents rehired Joe Grant, extending his employment contract to August 1950. Many of the faculty whose names we have seen earlier in this book would be returning. New teachers included a mathematics instructor, Glenn C. George, who was to become a beloved individual on campus for several years thereafter. Instructors also included Bonnie Kissee, who had newly acquired a masters' degree, Audra Nell Kuhlman, F.B. Lopez, Ramona Chavez and Nellie M. Trujillo. Two very popular teachers, Lena Archuleta and Frank Byers, would be returning for the '49-50 school year.

Residents in El Rito recall that old State Highway 96, that extended from the community to the turnoff to Española and Abiquiu, was paved beginning in 1946. Northern New Mexico Normal School turned in its old bus—no one remembers just how old it was—for a new 48-passenger Ward bus on a Chevrolet chassis purchased for $4,340, less $1,840 for the old one. It was bought from the M&S Garage in Española, the low bidder.

The president informed the Board of his correspondence with Governor Mabry concerning request for a share of a state bond issue. Northern New Mexico Normal School requested funding for improvements of boarding facilities and a new gymnasium. The school was allowed the sum of $75,000, the smallest amount received by any state school, from a total bond distribution of $2,500,000. This continued the usual pattern of treatment of the Normal School at El Rito by state officials.

Many of the same teachers indicated that they would return for the 1950-51 school year. New teachers included Mary Ellen Montoya, Clare W. McFall, Julia J. Martínez, and Marilyn Barrett.

The president of the school and the Board took a great deal of interest in student life and their activities. At the end of the '49-'50 school year, probably to compensate for gloom that had beset them in fall of this school year, there was great celebrating and self-congratulating for public praise that the Northern New Mexico Normal School had received for its athletic teams and the "Follies of 1950." The Follies had been presented on campus and in Española, Las Vegas and twice in Santa Fé.

One of the consequences of a prolonged war, World War II being the example, is that a large national debt was incurred. This led to an increase in the cost of acquiring money and, ultimately, in the fear of inflation. The president advised the Board of the need to acquire provisions, specifically canned foods, for the ensuing year while prices were still sufficiently low.

It was in the late forties that new living quarters, small apartments, were built on campus for teachers. This kind of construction was the type that members of the maintenance staff and student workers knew well. Dennis Salazar remembers remaining on campus during summers, making adobes, erecting walls, and roofing El Pueblito, which became a landmark on campus. This is a good example of self-sufficiency enjoyed at the Normal School. Although state government did not provide much financial support for these needs, neither did it interfere with bureaucratic "red tape" that would impede small projects. Building codes were known and followed in these instances, and safety of the buildings was seldom questioned.

Need for new large-scale construction was discussed among the staff, the president and the Board of Regents. President Grant presented the case that enrollment of boarding students had to be limited by the school because of insufficient dormitory space. Request for state assistance in expanding dormitory capacity at the school was almost a yearly occurrence. Two additional projects, a new gymnasium[15] and a student union building, were items that received next priority. The Normal School was unsuccessful, as it had been throughout most of its history, in obtaining help from the state for building projects.

The gubernatorial election of November 1950 resulted in the choice of Edwin L. Mechem, a Republican, to occupy the Statehouse for the first time in twenty years for the minority. Other state offices would remain in the hands of Democrats, but the election of this governor portended vast changes at the Northern New Mexico Normal School.

With the exception of statements that would reenforce his legacy at the Normal School, you would not have guessed that Joe Grant was planning his exit. One matter that Grant wanted noted, and it was in the New Mexico Tax Bulletin, was his fiscal management of the institution. The Bulletin noted that, although the approved institutional budget for the present year was in the amount of $239,990, expenditures of the Northern New Mexico Normal School were $183,813, leaving an unspent balance of $56,177. Cash balances at the institution were in the amount of $70,963. He felt justified in being proud of this achievement, although today we would find this odd. A surplus in excess of twenty-three percent for the year simply seems high, although fiscal responsibility as defined at the time may have required it.

In March 1951, Joseph B. Grant presented a letter of resignation to the new Board of Regents of the institution. In a very gracious statement, he expressed his wish to leave the Normal School at the end of May, but pledged to assist the Board in anything that was within his ability. Joe Grant would probably enjoy seeing this sentence reproduced from his letter: "I shall always have a place for El Rito in my heart as it constitutes a great part of my life." He had been president sixteen years, and he had been a Regent for four years earlier.

Fortunate we would be if we knew exactly what effect our actions have on others throughout life. In the instance of Joe Grant and the Normal School, his legacy is a far more important one than management of the institution's finances, important though this was. He built a campus and directed its operation so as to serve its students in ways in which they were unaccustomed. Most youngsters were made to feel that they were important, and thereby secure. Perhaps this made it easier to be accepting of one another. They were happy to please, because students were already pleased, just being there. I have tried to describe the beauty of the campus, but its ambient was even more pleasing, in ways that are difficult to put into words. Since in our youth we tend to romanticize a lot, even our meager existence, this tendency among students led us to ascribe to the campus an ethereal quality. I am phrasing in summary fashion what I heard dozens and dozens of students of the time, and those of a time after, recall of their days at El Rito.

In his own way, Joe Grant was dead on target in knowing what young people needed. Part of his quietly generous personality also made him naive. He felt that, since on his campus no one knew prejudice, ideal citizens would be formed of the students there for the "melting pot" of America, owing to the opportunities and privileges that the Normal School accorded its Spanish American students. He was partly right.

The school that Joe Grant was leaving bears more, let's say less teary-eyed, analysis. Northern New Mexico Normal School was not Groton, or Andover Academy, or like any college prep school in eastern United States. It was not very strong academically, but neither were other schools in northern New Mexico. The establishment of the Los Alamos Scientific Laboratory, about fifty miles away, probably did more to wake up the population about the need for better schools in a modern era than any single event prior to or since then.

Emphasis came to be placed on the high school, with less attention to the grade school. This was because it was expected that Rio Arriba County would begin to take greater responsibility for the grade school, and it did, by sharing in the financial burden. With greater emphasis on the high school came greater attention to the boarding population of students. Local students, day students, from as far back as the thirties, have complained that they did not receive the attention accorded to boarding students, nor equal privileges. I am not quoting malcontents. Long after these halcyon days of the Normal School, students from El Rito would speak to the news press about their displeasure with their treatment by the school.

Some of the neglect of day students was plainly visible. Day students tended to be excluded from evening and weekend activities on campus. Several factors contributed to the injustice, one being a lack of transportation for students from El Rito or nearby communities. Another cause may be attributed to parents of students from the community who did not rise to defend their children's rights. This hesitancy on the part of parents stemmed from other concerns, like the need for jobs. The Normal School was one of the few places of employment in the community, the other major employer being the U.S. Forest Service. Hindsight, as they say, is always better than foresight. Every boarding campus in America has or has had a "town-gown" problem. This one is lamentable, because it affected children.

Boarding students tended not to voice complaints about common practices that still tend to take place on campuses around the nation. One of these was student hazing. Seniors, 12th graders of the high school, would unload punishing tasks on freshmen, on penalty of paddling. Similarly, members of the lettermen's club would haze new initiates, occasionally in degrading fashion. The attitude about activities like these are viewed often as "well, boys will be boys." We will discuss hazing some more in the next chapter, and why we put a stop to it.

On the other hand, if you are a reader of Britishers, like George Orwell, who attended English prep schools, you know about the near-atrocities perpetrated on, not only children from modest homes, but youngsters from the upper classes of that society. Northern New Mexico Normal School was nothing like that.

The school to build a dream on is the high school that Joe Grant built. After he left in 1951, it was to last another eighteen years, and a lot of what he left behind persisted. It may seem odd that the campus achieved its zenith during war years and immediately after. The older students whom I knew from the Joe Grant years wished that their high school would have continued forever.

Notes:

1. Although I refer to the chief administrative officer as president throughout this book, in some cases the individual was known as superintendent. Joseph B. Grant, as an example, was known as superintendent during his early years. In their wisdom, Boards started referring to him as president in late 1930s.

2. Most of this information concerning Joseph B. Grant I obtained from his son David during a three-hour interview at his home in Albuquerque on September 18, 1997. The purpose of my visit was in preparation for a high school alumni reunion which we held at El Rito in summer 1999. We honored Joe Grant during this event to which his sons David and James were invited. David was the older of the brothers. I learned this past year, regretfully, of the passing away of David Grant.

3. We northern New Mexicans tend to undo and redo our acquaintances

and associations quite frequently. Margaret Allen Martin returned to the Spanish American Normal School as Regent and she was, in fact, on the Board of Regents that hired Joseph Grant as president.

4. Senator Bronson M. Cutting was one of American history's most progressive individuals, a liberal man. In this same chapter there is further discussion of Senator Cutting and his association with northern New Mexico and the Spanish American Normal School. He may have been a friend or close acquaintance of Joseph Grant. It is likely that they knew each other before Grant came to the Normal School. Grant owned a home in Santa Fe, where Bronson Cutting resided when he wasn't in the Nation's capital.

5. How much was five billion dollars in 1935 worth in today's currency? If we assume a modest inflationary growth of three percent annually, the amount would be worth something in excess of eighty billion dollars. Although estimates of this kind are difficult, clearly this is an amount similar to what would be required today for government intervention in a very weak job market. Q.E.D.

6. I point this out more in admiration of Joseph Grant than for any other reason. In April 1943, Governor John J. Dempsey reappointed the exact same Regents to the Board.

7. Members of the Class of 1939 may be found in the list at the end of this book, also.

8. During Joseph Grant's tenure as President, he acted as clerk of the Board of Regents and produced minutes of meetings. Each set of minutes was signed and dated by Joe Grant.

9. Readers may find "New Mexico/Mi Lindo Nuevo México" on page 53 of the state's "1997-98 Blue Book."

10. Lena Lovato married Juan (Wallace) Archuleta who was utility manager and coached the grade team. Students of that era remember Lena Archuleta, who was very popular with them, as was her husband Wallace.

11. *El Nuevo Mexicano* ceased publication in 1958. Supplements by this title continued in The New Mexican and The Española Valley News. Readers may still see this publication now and then.

12. The author must have been referring to the number of students in the high school. The number of students in elementary grades added up to more than this number.

13. *El Chamisal*, the student yearbook, contains graduating classes from 1947 to 1969. Readers of this book may find lists of graduates for these years at the end of this book.

14. In later chapters in this book, I describe for readers a better and more lasting solution to the problem of providing pure drinking water for the campus. This was finally achieved in 2010, almost six years after we began to address the problem as described in Chapter Ten.

15. The small gymnasium to which I refer was not your typical "cracker box gym" usually referred to by spectators in Smalltown, USA. It was smaller. First, it was not built with any spectators in mind, and their feet along the sidelines got in the way of the game. The length of the gym did not accommodate a regulation court. The ten-second time line had to alternate to the opponents' backcourt when the team in possession brought the ball down. But in winter in El Rito, the gym beat playing outdoors, no doubt.

7
FINAL YEARS OF THE SPANISH AMERICAN NORMAL SCHOOL

The decade following the Joe Grant years started with little change in daily lives of students. Enthusiasm, always the hallmark on campus, still centered around the same student activities that they had enjoyed, and the campus was almost as beautiful. The fifties were a good time for students to be on campus. There was a reason to resist change; many students had been at the Normal School while Joseph B. Grant was president.

The spirit of the Normal School, and students' dreams to build their futures upon, were bolstered by friendships among them that were to last a lifetime.

Most of the cultural history of this region has been told through newspapers, which perforce fail to provide continuity in the story of its development. For example, how people adapted to a world around them that was changing, and in which the only choice they had was to acquire new skills in order to survive and prosper, has seldom been told. This book has illustrated the absence of, and dire need for, schools in the early part of the century. To our good luck, advocates of statehood had been anxious to educate hispanics in the use of the English language. By the 1930s, education in English was viewed as imperative in order for children of the old Spanish and Mexican families to earn a living in the coming new society. This had been the genesis of the Normal School. Thus it was that the language of the home and playground was Spanish for all these children, but the language of school was English. John Conway, the old president of the early thirties, recounted that he himself had grown with Spanish as his first language, but he emphasized the need for English if Hispanics were to thrive in the United States, as he had done, for example.

Students at the Normal School, mostly Hispanic—there were a

few Anglos, as there always had been—were an interesting mix of rural and urban. Kids from Albuquerque, Santa Fe, and Roswell, and other small cities, spoke fluent English when they arrived on campus at the Normal and English had become their language of choice. We rural youngsters[1] spoke English considerably less among ourselves, although we were perfectly capable in the classroom. Even this slight cultural distinction dictated that rural kids, from El Rito, Española, Velarde, Coyote, Tierra Amarilla, and so on, were my first friends on campus. In short order, I became acculturated to the mix of students on campus and everyone became my friend. Unlike the experience of American Indian children in their schools, run by either the Bureau of Indian Affairs or the church, we were not prohibited from use of the Spanish language. We felt very comfortable being, as we were, almost perfectly bilingual. One interesting peculiarity is attributed to Hispanics in the US and Canada, and that is the use of Spanglish, the hybrid language. We tended to anglicize a few words, not many, usually indicative of emerging technologies such as the automobile, radio, telephone and television.

Students who attended school during the fifties have pointed out to me how little we were affected by the outside world, secure in our own environment. But there were external influences, and for music lovers it was wonderful. When I arrived on the campus in 1953, there were crooners, older boys and girls, who sang perfectly the songs of Johnny Ray, Frank Sinatra, the Andrews Sisters, and many other American artists. One of them was a young man, now deceased, Sammy Esquibel from Tierra Amarilla. Two young women, Elva Jaramillo from Vallecitos and Gloria Ortiz from Santa Fé, harmonized beautifully. But the late forties and the decade of fifties brought an explosion in music that bore names like rhythm and blues, rock and roll (then rock 'n' roll) and its many hybrids. We didn't know this, but kids like us, half way around the world in the British Isles, were listening to African-American blues straight out of the South in the US. We rural kids knew nothing about this music, but we learned from the boys from the city. When the great explosion occurred with Bill Haley, Elvis Presley, and other southern boys in that music scene, we already knew about Joe Turner, Chuck Berry, Fats Domino, Little Richard and other rock artists and about blues singers like Jimmy Reed, B.B. King, the Howling Wolf and many others. It was through the wonders of late-night radio that we knew about this music, because television did not feature black people very much in those days. Our classmates on campus grew beyond the music programs offered in classes and started their own rock bands. They performed for our dances, on occasion, and if they weren't the most polished rock groups in America, we appreciated them just the same.

Team sports were to loom larger and larger in the life of the Normal School, but there were other forms of entertainment that were almost as interesting.

We came away from this experience knowing that it was not proper to discriminate against anyone for any reason, although there were subtleties. Girls spoke more English, urban or not, than the boys. When we spoke in confidence, for example, the language of use was Spanish, even with the girls. Only a few students spoke English exclusively and students accommodated to each other when they spoke, without a thought. In an earlier period, Anglo students spoke Spanish fluently, but by the 1950s this was not usually the case. All of this is to demonstrate that, slowly but gradually, English was becoming the language of use.

The new Board of Regents reorganized and set about selecting a new president of the school. Members on the Board the spring of 1951 were:

Filiberto Maestas, Chairman
Elizabeth L. Eckles, Vice Chairman
Tom A. Martin, Secretary-Treasurer
John V. Conway, Member
Elias T. Lucero, Member

You will recall the name of John Conway. This is the same gentleman, indeed, who was president of the Normal School back in the early thirties.

The Board of Regents selected Edward Medina as President of the Northern New Mexico Normal School on May 11, 1951. A well-known educator in Rio Arriba County and a man known in Republican party circles, Edward Medina was offered and he accepted a one-year contract with a salary of $7,200 during a meeting on May 23.

The Board immediately went about accepting Medina's hiring

recommendations of new teachers and staff for the new year, 1951-52, but only in part. According to minutes of the Board for May 23, only a handful of teachers were rehired: Frank Byers, Glenn C. George, Theodore J. Henry, Bonnie Kissee, Florence Kellogg, Ezequiel Sandoval and Audra Nell Kuhlman. Two teachers simply elected to resign. Message was clear; there were several more changes in personnel coming.

The first year of the Medina administration was difficult insofar as hiring of faculty and staff. One was the Board's expectation of change, but a more serious problem was the school's inability to attract new teachers. This owed to the fact that the Northern New Mexico Normal School was not a member of the State Retirement System for schools. Once the administration was apprised of guidelines required for a new applicant school, the matter was resolved by early in the following year. In 1952 and 1953 the school's ability to hire seemed improved, if one can judge from the lists of applicants that President Medina presented to the Board for its approval. For the 1952-53 school year, Medina presented and the Board approved the following teachers: Frank Byers, Physical Education and Biology; Fay F. Garcia, Cosmetology; R. A. Crider, Principal; Glenn C. George, Mathematics; T.J. Henry, Laboratory Sciences, John Romero, Band Director; Ezequiel Sandoval, Industrial Arts; Joseph Serna, Business Education; Ray Leger, Librarian and Commercial teacher; Sam Ortega, English and Guidance Director; and, Tom Ortiz, Social Science. In the elementary grades, one through eight, teachers were Effie Baca, Julia J. Martinez, Tom D. Roybal, Raymond Gabaldón and Carlos Castillo. There continued to be a shake-up in faculty and staff ranks. Even students could discern a lack of harmony among administration and other employees

Beginning in fall 1951, the president and the Board began to make inquiries with the Governor and the State Board of Finance about means to acquire funds to build classrooms for the high school, and a gymnasium. They were told of several possibilities, the more expedient route being the issuance of bonds and retirement of mortgage on buildings by pledging income from the permanent fund. A large sum of money from the Cutting trust fund still resided in the school permanent fund. In August 1952, the Board authorized the administration to request bids for construction of a high school building based on building plans that had been prepared by the architectural firm of Herkenhoff and Turney. Bids for construction of a new high school building were received. The amounts bid by six building contractors were high by a factor of about two. The architects redrew plans, and bids received the second time produced a price for the building that was more affordable: $135,900 approximately[2]. The financial condition of the Northern New Mexico Normal School had not changed very much. Funds for new construction remained scarce, but the school did a very good job, in this instance. The new high school building was first occupied in September 1953. The staff worked long and hard to make certain that sidewalks were installed and the building furnished for the new school year. Dedication of the building had to be postponed until spring 1954. We, students, were particularly pleased to meet Governor Edwin L. Mechem, who came for the dedication of Venceslao Jaramillo Hall.

In March of 1953, prior to the President presenting his recommendations to the Board of Regents for the '53-'54 school year, the El Rito Teachers Association met with the Board to express their concerns. Their first request was that notification of reemployment (for the following year) be provided at least 30 days prior to the end of the current school year. A second request was that a policy concerning tenure for teachers be adopted, similar to policies being adopted elsewhere in the public schools. The Board heard positive comments about the Teachers Association from Regents and stated that tenure would be placed on the agenda for discussion during a future meeting. Teachers were perturbed, it seemed, about rumblings concerning anticipated dismissal of some teachers, which the president denied. A month later the president recommended that four teachers not be reemployed for the '53-'54 year, but the Board of Regents determined that it was better to review the cases carefully prior to any action being taken. They were, in all likelihood, anxious to stabilize the cadre of teachers and other staff after the initial change brought about two years earlier.

For the '52-'53 school year, the Board approved the employment of Glenn Teske, Frank Byers, Faye García, Glenn C. George, Mela Leger, John Romero, Reuben Rose, Tom Roybal, Ezequiel Sandoval, Arla Scarborough, Ray Leger, Noé Lucero, Julia Martinez, Charles Solomon, Laura Solomon, Frank White and Vincent Martínez. Later in the year they were joined by Edward Grant, Corine Myers, Viola Ulibarrí, Faye García, Caroline Velásquez and Sam Ortega in the high school. Helen Gonzáles was the head librarian. Eloida Herrera, N.B. Lucero and Lola Valdez taught the elementary grades.

In the summer of 1953, Edward Medina faced a new Board of Regents. Filiberto Maestas, the chairman, and Tom Martin, secretary-treasurer, were holdovers, but there were new members including Isabel L. Eckles, vice-chair, Celia Redman and Rudy Velarde. In June, the Board held discussions behind closed doors with Edward Medina that led to his resignation at the end of his employment contract. Without delay, the Board of Regents obtained applications to fill the vacancy of President of Northern New Mexico Normal School and offered the job to Clory B. Tafoya.

I was a boy up in Velarde that spring of 1953 when County School Superintendent Plácido García had given me a letter of introduction for Edward Medina stating that I should be provided a scholarship and a job at the Northern New Mexico Normal School where I wished to attend. The departure of Edward Medina caused me some anxiety, since he had offered me the terms requested by Superintendent García after examining my school record. In mid-summer I went to El Rito to visit the new president who assured me that a place had been reserved for me for fall term under the conditions agreed upon by his predecessor. In early September 1953, I joined that trickle of students that had been making its way to the Normal School at El Rito for forty-four years.

What I witnessed was unique in the annals of twentieth century United States: the social and cultural development of children in attendance at the Northern New Mexico Normal School. I experienced personally what other students have verified for me from their observations: the Normal School was sometimes refuge from an undesired[3] home life, or it provided access to a high school for children in very rural areas where no high school was available, not for miles around. Some students, and their parents, felt that it was simply a good place to stay out of trouble.

That September, as I walked up the narrow road into the campus—I was coming from the little store across the highway owned by Fred and Lola Valdez—I marveled at how happy these newly arrived kids seemed to be. Naive though I may have been, this was a new experience for me. This is the most vivid memory I have of four years of high school at El Rito.

The '53-'54 year was, socially, the most educational for me and, as a result, the happiest. Although later during my stay at the Normal

I would be recognized for academic achievements, in this first year I learned to live in close contact with other students, and in this regard, the Normal School fulfilled the first requirement of a public school: to help the child to become socialized. I have stated elsewhere that the Normal School was not the most academically rigid environment nor the most intellectually stimulating, but it was as good as we had in northern New Mexico of that day. Our school was not very different from the few public high schools in the larger towns and cities of northern New Mexico. When we competed interscholastically, in debate, science fairs, written exams of one kind or another, we did well. Interestingly, in the years 1953 to 1957 I was to witness the most remarkable achievements of our school in team sports. I would also get to know some of the finest high school athletes of the time. Before the end of the decade of the fifties, the El Rito Eagles—not the Northern New Mexico Normal School Eagles, this was too much for one mouthful—won two state high school basketball championships. It seems that the Eagles were strong every year. I've covered these and other feats in more detail later in this book.

I thought the campus was still beautiful even in 1953 when I arrived there. Other people who had been observing the grounds in the previous few years, after Joe Grant left the Normal School, maintain that even as early as '53 the campus was not in the same condition that it had been during the late 1940s. Some of the flower gardens were gone, there were fewer lawns, and so on.

Living conditions for a boy of thirteen, which I was, were spartan, but okay. In the Junior Building, there were four large dormitory rooms, almost identical. Each room had a closet and every boy had his bed and a foot locker, which he brought. That, and the space immediately around you, is all that you had. You could reach over and almost touch the next guy's bed.

We were up before seven each morning, including Saturday and Sunday, stayed gone from the dorm most of the day, and returned after dinner. There was a brief study hall from seven to eight each evening, Monday through Thursday, for about an hour. I tended to do homework during the day in one of the classrooms at the high school building, so that study hall tended to be a bore.

At this age, I was pleased to make adult friends. The first of the staff whom I remember fondly for the attention that they gave me were Cloide Trujillo and Willie Jaramillo. Cloide ran the laundry; Willie was the bursar. Cloide, her husband Abel and her children have remained friends during most of my adult life. Willie Jaramillo and his family would invite several of the students to view major league baseball on television. Unfortunately for us, Willie left the Normal School during my third year for a long while. I didn't see him again, although I know that he returned to the school a few years later. I make mention of both of these fine people in our later chapters.

During warm weather it was a lot of fun walking around campus, meeting new friends, especially girls, and hearing about what the Normal School had been and what life would be like during the year. There was a canteen, some music, occasional dancing, and ping-pong tables. I took a great liking to table tennis, but it was difficult to get the older boys to play—I was just too small a kid. I remember two outstanding players, although the best one by far was Reuben Rose, the art teacher. I would enjoy seeing him play Sammy Esquibel, a fourth year student. It turned out Rose, as the students called him—"mister" was not in students' lexicon—was one of the school's most popular, and truly loved, instructors. I didn't know him at the Normal School, since I didn't take any art classes. He was the best ping-pong player around during my year in ninth grade, so I never did play him, and he left at the end of the school year. Everything I knew about Reuben at the Normal I learned from other students. Many years later I got to know Reuben and his family. They lived in Santa Fe, where he worked at the State Department of Education for a while. I knew him for several years beginning then, until his death in the nineties. He was a great guy, cosmopolitan, educated, and interested in you as his friend: little wonder the students at the Normal School loved him.

Stories about the days at El Rito are something everyone who was there wants to tell, and why not? For many, this was the happiest time in their lives. I have to tell you a bit about Sammy Esquibel, who has passed on and who seemed very happy being there, although he often seemed to brood. He seemed to me like the artist caressing his soul. He was a quiet guy, pleasant, and a terrifically talented art student. He sang at our talent shows. "Cry" was his favorite song; it had been popularized by Johnny Ray. He was not only a great ping-pong player, he was a tailback on the football team and played basketball. The Eagles were pretty good that year. I heard Frank Byers tell an assembly of students that the '54 Eagles had won the district basketball championship for the first time in the history of the school.

The 1954 basketball Eagles had a guy named Joe Martínez playing forward, not very tall, five/ten maybe. I'll tell some more about him in the next chapter. Suffice it for now to let you know that he was the finest basketball player I saw in a lifetime, until about forty to fifty years later along came two guys named Michael Jordan and Kobe Bryant, whom I've only seen on television. Yes, that good. It's worth speculating why Joe Martinez didn't go on to college, or make his name and fortune in the world of professional basketball.

Three twelfth graders that year were to have a significant say in the future of the Normal School. They were all quiet kids, as I remember. Dennis Salazar from El Guache was our dorm proctor and played football. Priscilla Trujillo from El Rito was a studious girl and very attractive. Michael Branch from Dilia was also a good student, played football, and like me, was a fatherless boy. Dennis has spent many years in helping to shape the future direction of our school. His story is in chapters nine and ten. Priscilla and Michael have been on Boards of Regents of the new Normal School, and Michael still is. Dennis has been a Regent three times, on three separate boards.

I know now that I arrived at El Rito just a bit late to witness the campus in its zenith, and to meet teachers like Reuben and others whom I mention in this and next chapter. Another teacher whom I missed knowing was Charles Solomon, but about whom I heard from other students. He had been rehired as an English teacher the spring of '53, but Chuck was too liberal and worldly to stay around. He left the Normal and became a lawyer. I met him years later, in 1985, when I needed a lawyer, preferably a person of great moral conscience, and I was lucky that someone mentioned him. He was another fellow like Reuben Rose, who had come to attend college in New Mexico from "back east." He fell in love with our state and became a great addition to the intellectual community of Santa Fé, in time. Chuck Solomon has passed on, also.

Teachers seem more important to a ninth grader than for an older kid, for some reason. In younger years, you sort out whom you will like, and not, and thereafter you nurture friendships as they should be attended to and cared for. Two teachers whom I particularly liked were quite popular with serious students: they were Ed Grant, the science teacher, and Glenn C. George, who taught math. Ed Grant was very young, a graduate of Yale University, and Joseph Grant's nephew. Glenn George was in his late sixties when I knew him, a very sound math teacher and excellent advisor. Mr. George[4] gave me confidence in my academic ability; Ed Grant gave me reasons why I should push myself to do better.

Corine Myers taught Spanish during my first year at the Normal School. I considered her an outstanding language instructor. She taught me to love the Spanish language, and to look fondly at Mexico and Spain as the land of some of our forefathers. She taught Spanish as it should be, a living language related to a culture and a geography belonging to the people of those countries. Because of Corine Myers I would develop fluency in reading and writing, so much the case that I won a Fulbright Scholarship in later life to teach at the National University of Honduras. Corine Myers was a graduate of New Mexico Highlands University, which had a good program in the teaching of Spanish.

The old saying, "Time flies when you're having fun," is unfortunately so true. After ninth grade, it seemed like just overnight it was 1957, and we would be graduating and leaving the Normal School. In any case, I can capture events during those years, but time becomes condensed, making it difficult to recall important features of the times, and not to report the purely mundane or banal occurrences of life on campus.

For about forty years, the Normal School had been refuge, or a cocoon almost, for rural kids from northern New Mexico and a few youngsters from cities. The Normal School provided security for us, no doubt about that. A few teachers—four or five of whom I spoken in this chapter—knew that the school had to be a window to the world, in addition to being our own little wonderland. There were important events in our nation that would affect us eventually, and it was important that we know about them. Ed Grant introduced us to an environmental scientist, Peter Van Dresser, who had to have been among the first of these forward-looking people. He also had us visit Georgia O'Keefe, who in addition to being a well known artist, was among the more influential feminists[5] of the period. About six months later, we also learned about the confirmation by two British scientists that deoxyribonucleic acid (DNA) held some of the secrets of life. Biochemists, James Watson and

Frances Crick would henceforth become familiar names in the world of modern science, if not in a majority of households in the more affluent parts of the Nation. Now, not everyone cared about these things, but some of us did, about these and a number of other things which occurred in the "outside world."

The McCarthy witch hunts were real, make no mistake about that. They scared the daylights out of liberals like Ed Grant, Reuben Rose, Ray Ledger and others. Me? I didn't know very much about the meaning of words tossed about during the so-called Red Scare, and I didn't know what a communist was, never having seen one. Many years later I learned that J. Robert Oppenheimer had been treated by one of our governmental agencies, the Atomic Energy Commission, as though he were a communist, which wasn't true, and by then I knew enough to be properly indignant about the matter as were other clear-thinking Americans. This discussion is only to show that, in spite of our insularity, we were preparing for life on the outside.

In 1954, just more than half of American homes had television. We did too, in Cutting Hall. We didn't watch much TV in the mid-fifties, except for rock 'n' roll shows. "Rock Around the Clock" hit the music charts in 1955, and although we were past the "kid stuff" in our musical sophistication, it was nevertheless a sign of the times, and, like Elvis, not to be ignored.

Clory Tafoya was fortunate to work with the same Board of Regents for a number of years after he was first hired. He managed to maintain a fairly stable teaching staff. Some of his upper-level administrative staff remained. Facundo Rodriguez was principal of the high school. He was a good disciplinarian, although he had a kind heart and took interest in every one of the students in his charge. He married Eloisa Gallegos, a member of his staff, who was also a graduate of the Normal School, Class of 1950. Years after we had all left the Normal School, Facundo and Eloisa remained friends with many of the former students, and they were active with the high school alumni association.

The only two sources of information from that time are the student yearbook and the minutes of meetings of the Board of Regents. The minutes were well kept and are instructive, containing data and information about the social and cultural history of El Rito and the Normal School.[6] For example, in fall of '53 the Bond-Willard Company of Española offered a bid price of 23.8 cents per gallon of regular gasoline and 25.8 cents for premium. The Board held discussions with the president on the matter of uniforms for the girls, on several occasions. Clory Tafoya had to do some fast talking in order to dissuade some Board members from this idea. As students, I don't remember hearing much about this, thanks to our school president.

Another example of the state's inability to support the mission of the Northern New Mexico Normal School surfaced during the 1953-54 school year. The Board of Educational Finance[7] informed Clory Tafoya in November that it would hold one of its regular meetings at El Rito the following April 1954, a seemingly harmless request and within the BEF's normal method of operation. It turned out, however, that on April 12 there was a surprise in store for the President Clory Tafoya and the Board of Regents. Governor Mechem was in possession of a confidential report that had been submitted to him by the Executive Secretary of the BEF, John Dale Russell, and the State Superintendent of Public Instruction, Tom Wiley. The exact contents of the report were not revealed, i.e. do not appear in the Board minutes, but it is certain that the Board of Regents had concerns about the tenor and some of the language in the report. The Board of Regents would have preferred that the report provide a more positive view of the school's mission and educational activities. Quite coincidentally, two weeks later The New Mexican carried an article in which a recommendation was made that the campus of the Normal School be converted to a vocational school for "problem youngsters." The article went on to say that the vocational school would help the state to cope with juvenile delinquency. The Board expressed its support of "improving the vocational structure of the school, " but opposed "having to take in the problem youngsters of the State." We note again for readers of this book the state's inability to recognize the original intent expressed by the legislature in establishing the school, and its hesitancy to continue support of grades one through twelve.

In a separate action, the Board of Regents instructed President Tafoya to begin the process of transferring responsibility for the grade school to the County of Rio Arriba, at the insistence of the Board of Educational Finance.[8] The Board of Regents had entertained this idea earlier, and was not opposed to the change.

The improved ability of the school, during Clory Tafoya's tenure as President, to maintain stability in its administrative and teaching staff did help. A little later, in 1954, the Normal School received moral support from an unanticipated source, the North Central Association of Colleges and Schools. In late '54, the Board of Regents extended the president's contract for an additional year and rehired Facundo Rodríguez and Willie Jaramillo. It extended reemployment for the following school years to teachers: Frank Byers, Faye García, Glenn C. George, Edward H. Grant, Vincent Martínez, Corinne L. Myers, John Romero, Reuben Rose, Ezequiel Sandoval, Carolyn Velásquez, Frank White, and Tom Roybal. During the same meeting, the president announced the resignations of Sam Ortega, Viola Ulibarrí and Eloida Herrera.

The Normal School needed the state's financial support for a decaying physical plant and it was not receiving it. The condition of one of the dormitories, in particular, was becoming intolerable for students. There was flooding in the basement of the middle building where the bathrooms for senior boys were located. It took some resourcefulness on the part of the administration to "hold things together." The Normal School acquired a surplus boys dormitory that was located in White Rock belonging to the Atomic Energy Commission. It was a long wooden structure that was moved to a site on campus for $1,998 by J&B Construction of Española. Some of the boys were moved to this barrack building during the 1954-55 school year. I can remember that, during winter, the furnace operated day and night to heat this flimsy building. It seemed to me that the administration tried very hard to make improvements on campus, but the odds it faced in acquiring the state's assistance seemed insurmountable.

The visit by the North Central (NCA) accrediting agency conducted during the 1954-55 school year was helpful in two ways: it did much to improve morale of teachers, administrative staff and the Board of Regents. The visiting team also emphasized the need for administrative stability and recommended that the president be awarded a contract for three years. NCA recommended improvements to the campus, for instruction, but, in particular, it stressed the need for a new gymnasium. The Board took the recommendations to heart, and it extended a contract to Clory B. Tafoya for three additional years beginning in summer 1955. It also sought funds successfully for a new gym to replace the one in use since about 1930.

Grant Gym, as it became known, was not ready for use until 1957, but indeed it was a great time on the campus. This is a good place in this narrative in which to summarize high school athletics at El Rito in the 1950s.

I have mentioned to you Joe Martínez, who played for the district-champion 1954 Eagles and is probably the outstanding basketball player to have been seen in our state until very modern times. There were some splendid athletes who played with Joe on teams as early as 1951, '52 and '53. Among them was Arthur "Casey" Martínez, whose older brothers played at the Normal School also and were known, yes, all of them, as Casey. Arthur was a great athlete and played professional baseball in the San Francisco Giants organization. He, along with Gilbert Archuleta in the 1940s, are the only two fellows who played in professional leagues, to my knowledge.

The only genuine "All American" at El Rito was Lupe Juárez from Albuquerque, and it was in football. Lupe was a marvelous all-around athlete who played baseball, basketball and football. During the 1953-54 school year, Lupe played end on a good football team, but he attracted personal attention for his pass-catching ability. You know that a guy from a small school of 160 students has to be good to make first-team All-American.

Frank Byers left El Rito after the 1955 season, much to everyone's dismay. He had done a very good job with El Rito athletics; everyone remembered him and liked him.

Vincent Martínez, who had coached football, was given the job as the new basketball coach. Everyone had a wait and see attitude. Vince Martinez was a quiet man who had brought enthusiasm to the football team. He was well known for having played football at Highlands University. No one knew about his credentials in basketball. He surprised all but those who knew him for his good organizational skills and his seriousness of purpose. He took a very young group of boys who were headed by one senior, Estolano Márquez, a fine, all-around athlete from San Isidro, and won district and regional tournaments and took third place at state.[9] The other boys on this team returned, some as many as three more years, and established a basketball dynasty that lasted from 1956 to 1959. In '56 the team included, in addition to Estolano, Dennis Branch (Coyote), Porfirio Sánchez (Dixon), Ralph Martínez (El Guique), David Valdez (Dixon), Mel Archuleta (El Rito), Sam Martínez

(Vallecitos), Johnny Jaramillo (Vallecitos), Chris Quintana (Garita) and Leo García (Española).

In the 1957 season, Dennis, Porfirio, David, Ralph, Sam, Johnny, Chris and Randy Velarde (a ninth grader) made up a team—together with some new, younger boys like Albert Sánchez (Porfirio's brother), and Joe Valdez (David's brother)—that was strong, fast, quick and unstoppable. They established an all-time record of success with 31 wins and only two losses. Dennis Branch set a new standard for scoring in New Mexico high school basketball, 904 points. This unusually talented center and post man was not much taller than about five/ten or five/eleven, but he had quickness and a head fake that enabled him to run circles around two, or as many as three, opposing players. Throughout the season he averaged about thirty points per game. The Eagles were a high-scoring team, much more so than any northern teams of the past, and scored more than 80 points per game five times and exceeded ninety twice. Towards the end of that 1957 season, the Eagles were so dominant that they not only beat all opposing teams, they virtually destroyed the opposition. In the state championship game, they beat a good Ruidoso team by more than forty points. This was basketball at a higher level, not seen heretofore.[10]

I asked Estolano Márquez to help me analyze what produced these amazingly successful teams. He pointed to coaching, including stern discipline. In '57, the front line of Dennis, Ralph and Randy was big, strong and quick. These weren't the tallest boys in New Mexico, but they dominated space around them. David Valdez and Porfirio Sánchez were excellent shooters from the periphery, and again, exceptionally strong and quick.

During the 1958 season, Vince Martínez and the basketball Eagles took time to regroup. The loss of Dennis Branch would have spelled the end of dominance for most teams. The Eagles had also lost, through early graduation, a very fine player in Porfirio Sánchez. In 1958, the Eagles lost only five games and won their district again. A team down the road in Pojoaque was exceptionally strong that year, and the Elks managed to beat the Eagles during the regular season and in the Northern Rio Grande Conference semi-final game. El Rito managed to beat the Elks for the district championship, but a visit to the state tournament had to wait another year.

During the 1959 season, I was away at college and didn't follow the Eagles very closely. Ralph Martínez, Randy Velarde, David Valdez and Sam Martínez were a good nucleus that any coach would have been very pleased to have back for a new season. I learned later that the 1959 Eagles had won 26 games and lost three on their way to the state tournament. I drove up to Albuquerque from Socorro for the tournament and witnessed that, again, there was little doubt that the Eagles were the best team in New Mexico. They defeated good teams from Estancia and Lordsburg in early rounds with little difficulty. In the final game, for their second state championship in three years, they defeated San Jon by a score of 55 to 45.

The El Rito basketball Eagles were never to be as successful again. One reason, at least, was that, after the decade of the fifties, sports programs at other schools in New Mexico were getting stronger.

Northern New Mexico Normal School was often a splendid place for students, but its worth to the state of New Mexico was seldom recognized and its original mission was most often lost and forgotten. It seemed that after Venceslao Jaramillo and L. Bradford Prince, in and around 1909, and after John Conway and Joe Grant in the thirties and forties, the school simply lacked a good, effective advocate. Even Conway and Grant encountered their difficulties and frustrations in trying to develop a good school in remote northern New Mexico, as I have indicated.

Once in a while there was cause for hope. In January 1955, the president and the Board of Regents met with members of the state senate in Santa Fe to discuss the institution's financial needs. President Tafoya was present, together with Board Chair Phil Maestas, and Regents Isabel L. Eckles, Tom A. Martin, Celia deBaca Redman and Rudolph Velarde. Senators Horacio DeVargas, Murray E. Morgan and W.P. Cater were also present; Senator DeVargas chaired the Senate Education Committee. This proved to be an important meeting in a manner that was unexpected. Senators tried to be helpful, although they explained that it was becoming increasingly difficult for the state to provide funds for the school because it did not offer any work beyond the high school. They suggested to the president and the Board that they should be planning to establish a junior college on campus within five years. We should note that Senator DeVargas represented Rio Arriba County and had familiarity with the Normal School and its history. This kind of gentle nudge, and promised support, was exactly what the Northern New Mexico Normal School needed, in view of the fact that there was decreasing interest on the part of the state to support a high school, and there was the constant urging, at various times in the history of the school, to convert to a purely vocational school. In fact, the course that the Normal School would follow would be circuitous, including, in future years, components of both a vocational school and a junior college. A fuller story unfolded, fifteen to twenty years later.

Only one matter was fully settled with regard to the school's mission and responsibilities: the elementary school, while remaining on campus, would come within the charge of Rio Arriba County and its School Superintendent, J. Plácido García.

Nineteen fifty-four was an election year, and John F. Simms was elected Governor of the state. [11] By March of '55 the Governor had appointed four new members to the Board of Regents; only Filiberto Maestas remained as incumbent. When the new Board organized in March, Joseph Grant was elected Chairman, Juan E. Medina became Vice-Chairman and Mrs. E.C. Cabot was elected Secretary-Treasurer. A fourth new member was Gilbert Archuleta,[12] a former student and staff member of the Normal School and one of its better-known athletes.

This board immediately went to work with the president on bringing about much needed improvements to the campus. Clory Tafoya and the previous board had convinced the state Governor and legislature of the need for the new gymnasium. The new board focused on the Middle Building, a senior boys' dormitory, which needed renovation. The dormitory building was renovated for occupation in fall 1956, and by summer of that year bids for construction of the new gymnasium had been obtained. The architect of record was Lawrence Garcia, an alumnus of the school, and the contractor was Ismael Trujillo from Chimayó. The bid price for construction was $136,180.

The new gym, dedicated as Grant Gymnasium, became ready for the 1957 basketball season, one of the big years for this sport at the Normal.

The presence of Joe Grant on the Board of Regents was especially valuable in seeking campus improvements. Opportunity arose to expand the campus and the Normal School acquired an additional twenty-five acres from the Burea of Land Management. The additional land was helpful in that the school had to have its own sewage plant (to the south and west), away from ball fields.

Discussion of baseball and football fields has always been accompanied by jokes that in El Rito rocks grew out of the ground. Students could remember that these two sports were always played on dirt fields, and a yearly ritual involved picking out rocks from the playing fields. Before the end of each season, those rocks were there again.

Students had reason to be happy with their school for considerations that they were granted. President Tafoya and the Board devised a payment schedule for students, $150 for a full semester of room and board, in which every student was required to work twenty hours per week. Tuition and fees amounted to $17.00 *per year.*

On the other hand, students lamented that some teachers were leaving; Frank Byers and Humberto Gurule left the Normal School at the end of the '54-'55 school year.

Many of the teachers in '55-'56 were present also during the following year: Facundo Rodríguez, as Principal; Ada Archuleta, Benito Chávez, Phillip Felix, Fay García, Glenn C. George, Francis Gonzáles, Aurora W. Lea, Neffie Quintana, John Romero, Tom Roybal, Dan Trujillo, Vince Martínez and Brenice Valdez. In addition there were Elvira Jaramillo, the Librarian, and Joan Odom Roybal, the School Nurse.

For the school year 1956-57, the president recommended and the Board approved the employment of additional teachers: Bertha Estrada, Edward Grant, Consuelo Torres, Ben Martínez and Charles Maes.

In March 1957, the new gymnasium had been in use by the state high school basketball champion Eagles. The Board took two actions, neither unexpected. It authorized a letter of commendation to Coach Vincent Martínez, congratulating him and 1957 Eagles, and it resolved to dedicate the gym as Grant Gymnasium. It was noted in the minutes of this meeting that Joe Grant was a former president of the institution who had served two tours of duty on the Board of Regents. Tributes were well deserved by Vince Martínez and Joe Grant, who had each served their school during very different times.

President Clory Tafoya, with concurrence of the 1955 Board of Regents, had taken the initiative of beginning to plan for establishment of a junior college, as had been suggested by members of the state senate. He apprised the Board of Educational Finance of the school's plan, and requested the BEF's assistance. In response, Tafoya received a reply from John Dale Russell, who signed his name as Chancellor and Executive Secretary, stating a response to Tafoya's letter: "The Board of Educational Finance, at its meeting of April 4, 1957, gave consideration to your letter of February 15, 1957, in which you request the Board to encourage your proposal for development of a junior college in connection with Northern New Mexico State School. After a thorough discussion of the situation, the Board of Educational Finance voted not to approve your request, on the basis that the time is not opportune for the development of a junior college under the supervision of Northern New Mexico State School." The Board of Regents did not challenge this latter assertion made by Russell on behalf of the BEF.[13]

In April 1957, Frances R. Shipman was installed as a member of the Board of Regents and elected Vice Chairman. She replaced Juan E. Medina, who died in December of the previous year. This same spring the Board of Regents gave Clory Tafoya a list of fifteen items in the general area of facilities maintenance that required attention. First among the concerns expressed by the Board were items pertaining to plumbing in dormitory buildings and maintenance of the water and sewage systems. The Board was concerned with the gradual degradation of facilities that had been occurring over several years. It was a period in which the school's requests for financial support by the state were ignored, or else the amounts granted to the school were substantially less than the amounts needed.

Members of the class of 1957 parted ways in May of that year. *El Chamisal* lists thirty-four members graduating; you may find their names in the list at the end of this book.[14] As one would expect, I grew very fond of some of the members of that class. They were all exceptionally kind and helpful to me. I was class president all but ninth grade and led the student council. I mention this because during our final two years at the school we made some useful changes, which were intended to make life more pleasant for everyone. For example, by consensus of everyone concerned, we eliminated all hazing. This had been a system of particular annoyance to me, having the consequence of demeaning younger students, in most instances, and physically hurting them, also on occasion. My classmates readily understood my interest in abolishing oppressive practices, and engendering means by which we could live together. It was an important lesson in growing up for me, and it would help to shape an underlying social and political philosophy for the rest of my life. I think about this often.

During my last year at the Northern New Mexico Normal School I was unaware of the difficulty that the school was having keeping doors open and continuing to serve students. I should have realized this by examining the slow deterioration of the campus and its buildings. The minutes of the Board of Regents of that time show the concern expressed by its members, but the President could remedy only maintenance items that didn't require much money. In the ensuing year, 1958, the Normal School found itself with diminishing support for its high school program. The Board of Educational Finance, its funding agency, could withhold funding recommendations that were needed because of its dim view of the high school program, but it failed to suggest or entertain ideas that may have constituted a useful alternative.

The presence of Frances Shipman on the Board of Regents produced an interesting and long-needed advocacy on behalf of day students from El Rito. She recommended in June 1957 that the school consider a free lunch program for day students and that the school provide a dining room where students could have their lunch. Mrs. Shipman spoke on behalf of children in both the high school and the elementary school. President Tafoya promised that the dining room would be afforded to students at noon, but he stated that the County of Rio Arriba had discontinued the free lunch program.

During the same meeting in June, the President announced that the Board of Educational Finance had reduced the Operating Budget for 1957-58 by an amount of $29,000, suggesting that the school dip into its fund balances, $100,000. Years later, it seems paradoxical that the school would maintain balances this large in the face of the campus's need of repairs.

During fall 1958, the Board reiterated its interest in commencing the junior college program. Neither the Board nor its president had yet taken occasion to remind everyone, state officials in particular, that the Board had sole prerogative for the offering and management of educational programs on the campus. There were other complications that would impair the ability of the Regents to assert their prerogatives as a Board. This was about the same time in which the school was having difficulty submitting budgets for approval to the BEF, and in which the school was uncertain of its funds on hand. The school took an action that would serve it well for several years: it reemployed Guillermo (Willie) Jaramillo as bursar.

Beginning with the 1957-58 school year the Normal School was once again enshrouded in a period of uncertainty, although students had no way of knowing about three-way discussions among state officials, the Board of Regents and President of the school concerning the future of the Normal School. The state would issue encouraging signals at times, depending on the official who spoke about the school, and at other times it would withhold encouragement of any sort. This state of affairs would, in fact, continue through the remainder of the decade and well into the 1960s.

During March, April and May of '58, individual members of the Board reported that the Executive Secretary of the Board of Educational Finance, Dr. Russell, did not think that a vocational program at El Rito was a good alternative for the school. Another report was that the new Governor, Edwin L. Mechem, who was elected again in November 1956 after an absence of two years from the Capitol, considered that initiation of a junior college was an effort which he would favor. It seems certain that the Governor and the Executive Secretary at the BEF had entertained some discussion about the matter of the mission of the Normal School, and were declaring mutually compatible statements about what should be in store for the school. The Board of Regents instructed President Clory Tafoya to begin to plan for the junior college. At about the same time, the Normal School issued a bond in the amount of $85,000 for building improvements, which presumably would help along the notion of the junior college, providing housing for the college.

A list of teachers for the 1958-59 school year was approved by the Board during a meeting of May 4: Benito I. Chávez, Bertha D. Estrada, Phillip J. Felix, Glenn C. George, Albert Jenschke, Ruben O. Lucero, Charlie S. Maes, Manuel F. Martínez, Vincent J. Martínez, John J. Romero, Brenice I. Valdez, Amado O. Valdez and Carolyn B. Velásquez. Approval of vocational instructors was postponed until the State Vocational Department approved the list and released funds under the Smith-Hughes Act for vocational education.

The three-year appointment of President Clory B. Tafoya came to an end that June 1958. The Board had been quite insistent that the

President pursue the (re)initiation of the junior college, and although we do not know what Clory Tafoya's point of view may have been on the matter, we do know that the Board of Regents decided to bring in a president who would help to establish the junior college as soon as possible. The Board chose not to renew Tafoya's contract, and quickly hired Charles H. Robinson to fill the position as President. Robinson, from Las Vegas, had been Registrar at New Mexico Highlands University. Robinson was issued a two-year contract beginning July 1, 1958 at an annual salary of $9,000. During the same meeting, Willie Jaramillo was reemployed as bursar, also for two years.

Clory B. Tafoya served ably from our point of view, which was that of a student. We know now that there was not very much money, and that the campus was not receiving the attention that it required as it aged. The program seems to have been underfunded, but financial management of the school was not precise, making it impossible for every cent at the school's disposal to be used.

The second matter that weighed heavily upon those in charge of the school was that state support, financial and moral, were no longer forthcoming, because the Board of Educational Finance, and others in state government, did not view the mission of the Normal School in secondary education as being important. The continued existence of the school was tolerated, but with little encouragement for either a new direction or for staying the course.

The success that the school enjoyed in team sports—I have already mentioned two state basketball championships in two years, and strong contention for honors in most years—must have been some consolation to administrators, staff and teachers.

Academically, the school was sound, or another way to view it is that, although very small, its students did not seem to be at serious disadvantage in comparison to the state's northern schools. The Normal School's insufficient funding by the state probably influenced education at the Normal more than any single factor.

During late summer in '58, additional teachers were hired: Melvin Cordova, Principal; Gilbert A. Vigil, social science; Silas López, mathematics; Ruth Willis, physical education and science; Fay García, vocational beauty culture; Rubél Montoya, vocational automobile mechanics. Carmen Segura was hired as school nurse.

By early December, capital outlay funds had been received and renovation of the Middle Building, a boys' dormitory, was begun under the direction of Lawrence García, Architect.[15]

President Robinson was moving as rapidly as possible to try to begin the junior college. The meeting of the Board of Regents of January 27, 1959 was held at La Posada Inn in Santa Fe in order to accommodate State Senator Horace DeVargas and Representatives Arsenio J. Martínez, Delfin Sánchez, and Rafael García. After lengthy discussion concerning the proposal presented by Dr. Robinson, "...it was mutually agreed that a Junior College at the Northern New Mexico Normal was greatly needed to furnish educational facilities beyond the high school for the children of this area of the State." Again in February, the Board and the President of the school met with the legislators named in order to acquaint them further with plans for initiation of the junior college. Melvin Cordova was reemployed as Principal for the 1959-60 school year, the highest ranking member of the Normal School's academic team at the time.

A gubernatorial election had been held in November 1958 and John Burroughs of Portales was elected. He named new Regents, who were installed in office in spring 1959. After reorganization, the Board included Del Miera as Chairman; Filiberto Maestas, Vice Chairman; Frances R. Shipman, Secretary-Treasurer; and members Albert Amador and Carl Turner. During the May 23 meeting of the Board, President Robinson apprised the Board of the direction which he had been following in establishing a junior college. A resolution was approved unanimously by the new Board which read, in part, "RESOLVED: That the plans for the college program of the Northern New Mexico Normal School be wholeheartedly approved."

President Robinson and the new Board persevered in spite of uncertainties that lay ahead with regard to the junior college. Robinson recommended that the name of the school be changed to Northern New Mexico College; the Board concurred. That same June 1959 the school hired John W. "Jack" Flynn as Acting Dean for the college program. Soon thereafter the Board reemployed the President for a period of five years and its bursar, Willie Jaramillo, for three years. The Board, President and administration worked harmoniously and seemed to achieve successes initially. The Board of Educational Finance, responding to the Normal School's request for assurance of approval of the college program, acted in the affirmative, according to minutes of July 31, 1959. We should note that the tenor at the Board of Educational Finance, in its correspondence with the Normal School, had improved significantly during the tenure of Donald C. Moyer as Executive Secretary. This helpful attitude evinced by the BEF would appear again, during Moyer's tenure with the BEF.

The plan was to add the college program to the existing high school on campus. This being the case, more space for instruction would be required. The school decided to renovate the old Middle Building (called now the "Central Building"), to accommodate the college.[16]

In late September 1959, Jack Flynn reported to the Board of Regents that the Board of Educational Finance continued to view positively the effort to start the junior college, and furthermore the BEF had approved the issuance of a bond in the amount of $205,000 to modify the Central Building (old Middle Building) to house the college program. The Board included in the record correspondence, kind in tone though it was, from a member of the BEF which did not reveal knowledge of the constitutional mandate nor mission of the Spanish American Normal School. The message conveyed some cautions, the usual purpose of most communications received by this school from state agencies.

For some unknown reason, Jack Flynn requested an Attorney General's opinion requesting to know whether Northern New Mexico College possessed legal authority "to re-inaugurate a first and second year college program at the school?' Why the school would not first seek its own legal counsel on the matter is not explained in any documents. An Assistant Attorney General, Philip R. Ashby, responded that the school did not have that authority. A second-to-last paragraph in the gentleman's response which he adds "parenthetically" is itself contradictory of his letter's content. He points out that other similar "institutions" founded by the state for the same purpose were "by their very nature" college level institutions. He stated, however, this in itself did not grant the authority required to operate a college. This is the kind of exceptional treatment that hindered progress of the Spanish American Normal School for a long time. The fact is that nothing in the constitutional mandate regarding the state of New Mexico's teachers colleges has changed. In the case of Northern New Mexico College, the Board of Regents is still charged with the control and management of the school, including its educational programs. This fundamental premise has been stated, in modern times, by Sigfredo Maestas in official public forums affecting this institution. In the year under discussion, 1959, the

President of the school and the Board of Regents understood that the opinion of the Attorney General was, in all likelihood, in error. It had, however, a most serious consequence of discouraging the effort that had been started on behalf of Northern New Mexico College.

President Robinson was obviously concerned. In a letter of November 19, 1959, he states to the Chairman and members of the Board of Regents:

> After serious and considered review of the present status of the program of Northern New Mexico College, particularly after the ruling of the Attorney General of New Mexico that the institution did not have sufficient authority to inaugurate a two-year college program, the institution's Administration is submitting herewith a proposal for an Advanced Technical High School Program, a summary of the present situation of the Junior College Program, and certain Recommendations in relation to both programs.
>
> Your attention to and careful consideration of the material submitted herewith is earnestly solicited.

The letter is signed by C.H. Robinson, President, with copies indicated for Governor John Burroughs and Donald C. Moyer, Executive Secretary of the Board of Educational Finance.

Robinson may have been hedging, or he may simply have been trying to prepare for an uncertain future. The proposal described the Advanced Technical High School Program and mentioned the possibility of simultaneous operation of the junior college. Robinson pointed out in his proposal to the Regents that the opinion received from the Attorney General simply may have been in error. With the Board's concurrence, the Administration would prepare to offer the technical program *and* the junior college. Robinson worked diligently to ensure that the college program was sound, and that students would profit by attending.[17] In preparation, he held discussions with officials at the University of New Mexico to ensure transferability of credits earned by students in the college program. Chester Travelstead, a member of the College of Education at UNM and eventually an academic vice-president, assured him that UNM would be pleased to have the Northern New Mexico College's transfer students.

President Robinson stated a strategy that included approaching the

1961 legislative session with this dual proposal.[18] He was doing all that was possible to save his school from further erosion by showing some initiative, which the Board supported initially.

The C.H. Robinson's Administration pushed ahead with renovation of the Central Building. Bond was issued in the amount of $105,000 at a rate of 4.75%. Transactions involving state agencies and sale of the bond went smoothly. The Board of Regents advertised for bids for construction, with the assistance of Lawrence Garcia, Architect. The Board employed the services of E. Montgomery of Taos, a building contractor, to complete the project for the price of $88,598. The project was completed by late August, 1960, just in time for the new school year.

In July, prior to occupation of the newly refurbished building, the Board resolved to name the Central Building, the oldest building on campus, Francisco Delgado Hall.

In late August 1960, Jack Flynn resigned his position as Dean of Northern New Mexico College.

The reader may ask the question, how were students, faculty and others concerned affected by discussions and proposals involving Northern New Mexico College? The evidence is that the high school was the only program of the Northern New Mexico Normal School, and in its other communications, it was still the Normal School. The 1960 *El Chamisal* makes no reference to Northern New Mexico College, and the people whom it includes are high school students, their teachers and staff. A brief message from President Robinson makes no mention of the college, thanks students for their cooperation and commends their achievements. He ends by saying, "May we all look forward to an even brighter future."

Vince Martínez, the head basketball coach, who had stayed on at the Normal for several more years following the Eagles' brilliant showing in late 1950s, was someone that students loved and respected. *El Chamisal*, the 1960 edition, was dedicated to Vince Martínez by the staff. It was a well-deserved reward and recognition for a job well done.

The graduating class of 1960 numbered 34, as the high school entered its final decade. I knew perhaps five or six of these students: Leon Baca, Erlinda Gonzáles, Lorraine Vigil, Dora Martínez, Joseph Valdez, Priscilla Jaramillo and Herman Trujillo. Leon was class president, Erlinda and Lorraine were the top students academically, and Joe Valdez was a fine athlete and student. Herman Trujillo, a quiet boy, became a pharmacist and operated a business in Pojoaque; he was appointed to the Board of Regents in the late seventies. Joe worked at Los Alamos. Erlinda obtained a doctoral degree and taught Spanish at the University of New Mexico until a few years ago. Dora Martinez and her brother Sam have been active with the Normal School Alumni Association.

Name changes of an educational institution very often simply convey a change in mission at the school, and are cause for some satisfaction, at least. This was regretfully not the case for the Normal School at El Rito. The change to Northern New Mexico Normal School during the latter part of Joe Grant's tenure as president was a good idea, and students, in particular, rejoiced in the name and acronym, NNMNS, if the school song and other slogans were a good indication. The change to Northern New Mexico College in 1960 was premature, but it was a good effort by the Board of Regents and the President C.H. Robinson, to point to an important change in mission. The following little story adds emphasis to indicate that the school simply did not receive moral support from the state during times when it was needed.

The school had advertised for bids for engineering services to refurbish its water and sewage system. It must have been institutional practice to refer contracts and similar documents to the office of the Attorney General for review and approval. When the Northern New Mexico College submitted its contract, the reply was that the contract could not be approved until a recommended change to the name Northern New Mexico State School was effected. The latter name had become the institution's official name in 1960 after passage in a general election of an amendment to the constitution by voters. Whether or not the school was consulted about the desirability of the change to Northern New Mexico State School is the question. Likely not.

Beginning in 1961, President Robinson held to the name Northern New Mexico College for the school. The Board of Regents during this time, and northern legislators looked favorably on the effort to create the college and on the name change. *El Chamisal*, which was one of the principal means of communicating among students and a publication that helped them to memorialize their days at the school, indicates wide use of Northern New Mexico College in its publications 1961 to 1964. It was a college in name only, however.

Teachers are listed who taught between 1959 and 1964, during Robinson's presidency:

    Melvin Cordova, Principal
    Silas López, mathematics
    Ruben Lucero, biology and physical education
    Charles Maes, arts, crafts, electricity
    Josue Trujillo, Spanish and mathematics
    John Romero, band and chorus
    Gilbert Vigil, social studies
    Bertha Estrada, home economics
    Caroline Velásquez, Librarian
    Amado Valdez, commercial
    Ben Martínez, woodwork
    Faye García, beauty culture
    Vincent Martínez, physical education and Athletic Director
    Al Jenschke, commercial
    Benny Casados, science
    Philip Felix, English
    Carmen Segura, School Nurse
    Brenice Valdez, English
    James Rosenberry, drafting
    Clyde Mantooth, woodwork
    Jerry Thompson, mathematics
    Mrs. Adkinson, home economics
    Louise Hilswick, Librarian
    Mrs. James, business
    Charles Esquibel, social science
    Rose Marie Espinoza, mathematics
    Esther Gallegos, English and Spanish
    Benjie Espinoza, mathematics
    Linda Sánchez, chemistry and biology
    Ruth Wymer, Librarian
    Seledón Martínez, Dir Guidance
    Margaret Todd, English and Speech
    Leada C. Hutchison, English

Although President Robinson had managed to maintain stability at the school with most of his senior staff and teachers, the Board of Regents became subject to change again after the 1960 general election. Governor Mechem was elected for a third term in November 1960. The new Board reorganized in April 1961, as is customary when membership on the Board changes.

    Reinaldo M. Valdez, Chairman
    Luis M. Salazar, Vice-Chairman
    Frances R. Shipman, Secretary-Treasurer
    Roque M. Abeyta, Member
    Carl Turner, Member

The previous Board seemed to have understood that the future of the Normal School, as constituted now for about fifty years, was in jeopardy. The high school was unlikely to continue much longer; this seemed an appropriate time to offer the junior college program. The new Board was apparently unconvinced.

In a letter of January 1963, the school indicated to the Joint Appropriation and Finance Committee that there were matters of urgency requiring more money than was being recommended by the Board of Educational Finance for the coming school year. The approved budget for 1962-63 was $284,911. The BEF was recommending the amount of $293,000 for the following year, the year in question. The recommended increase was $8,089, or less than three percent.

Communications between President Robinson and legislative committees seem to indicate that there was at least tacit agreement that the Normal School was preparing for its new and expanded mission. In examining background of teachers who were employed after 1960, it is evident that the Advanced Technical High School Program was well underway. Preparation for the junior college continued. But the school lacked money for the usual maintenance of old buildings and equipment, and no money for new typewriters, for example The school was requesting consideration from the Appropriations Committee of an additional $62,327 for the next year. No frills; in fact, the additional amount for any administrative costs was only $2,450.

Minutes of the Board for April 1963 indicate that the school did not receive the additional consideration. It states, "The budget was discussed on how very close and tight it was."

During a meeting of the Board in August 1961, the Board took an action that must have been disheartening for President Robinson. The Board of Regents, fearful of criticism from the State Capitol, or conscious of a difficult financial situation, ordered that junior college courses not be started if there were not an enrollment of 25 students. The issue seemed to be that additional teachers would have to be employed, indicating that the school was not yet fully staffed to offer college-level courses. In fact, the President and Melvin Cordova, the Principal, made very good choices in subsequent hiring in order to staff both senior level high school and junior college courses. The point is that very good management was required in order to "pull off" the programs that were being planned, and the Administration seemed quite capable in this respect.

In late 1962, the President and the Board hired Seledon Martinez as Director of Guidance and Special Services and assigned him the task of helping to develop the technical and vocational curriculum. Funds for this purpose could be sought from the State Vocational Department, the agency that administered federally appropriated funds. The program in business and secretarial education seemed to be thriving. Basic courses for which equipment was needed were in carpentry, radio and electricity. Some of the courses were similar to ones that had been offered in an earlier period in late 1930s and '40s, but they were packaged differently to appeal to an older student, in accord with the Advanced Technical High School Program. Martínez recommended to the President and the Board that students in this advanced curriculum should begin to be separated from high school students, a clear indication that the plan was to begin to offer the program in the way junior and community colleges operated. Enrollments that were reported by Seledón Martínez seemed satisfactory.

C.H. Robinson had been hired to start the junior college and he had given it his best effort. By 1964, it became evident that there was more interest, again, in vocational education for El Rito than there was in an academic institution. Training of teachers for the public schools did not seem to be a concern. Robinson did not indicate in any additional documents what his thoughts were on the matter, but it must have become evident to him that the effort to get the junior college underway had failed.

In January 1963, there was a new Governor, Jack M. Campbell, who was acquainting himself with state government and its institutions. Governor Campbell met with the Board of Regents in El Rito on September 25. The same month, he appointed Joseph B. Grant to the Board of Regents. Grant, who was a replacement for Reinaldo Valdez, immediately became Chairman.

The Campbell administration was interested in economic improvement in our state, and viewed northern New Mexico as the example of needed change to spark its development. He set up *ad hoc* committees to study what he needed, one of them being the Subcommittee on El Rito, chaired by Robert Pringle. William McConnell, Executive Secretary of the Board of Educational Finance and Robert Pringle attended the September meeting in El Rito with Governor Campbell. Joseph Grant took opportunity to explain to guests that the Normal School seldom had support for funding that it needed, and that it was seldom included in bond allocations made by the state for building renewal and construction. Governor Campbell, who incidentally was of Joe Grant's political party, had his own reasons for meeting with the Board, however. His presence, along with McConnell and Pringle signified that change was in the wind for the Normal School. There clearly was not much interest in Northern New Mexico College, although Robinson continued to issue reports to the Board on the subject.

The Board of Regents was advised that Pringle would be issuing reports of his study of the school at El Rito. The general direction that was indicated during meetings that winter of '64 was vocational education. The Board became resigned to the fact that Pringle would be "working out the program for Northern New Mexico College."

President Charles H. Robinson announced his resignation effective June 30, 1964. In one of his final actions on behalf of the college, he announced to the Board that a transfer program for NNMC's graduates had been agreed upon with Adams State College in Colorado. Even as interest in Northern New Mexico College waned, the clear-thinking Robinson continued to persevere on behalf of the junior college.

The Board advertised the vacancy in the presidency and at a meeting during spring 1964 it hired Louis F. "Lito" Martínez as Superintendent. The Board had seen some changes also; in addition to Joseph Grant, members included Mrs. Shipman, Mr. Salazar, Mr. Turner, and Mr. Reinaldo Valdez. The President's annual salary was $12,000.

The Board was being urged in a report entitled "Education for Employment Program" by Robert Pringle, with the tacit approval of Governor Jack Campbell and the Board of Educational Finance, to develop vocational education. Since the school had little expertise in post-secondary vocational education, it resolved to advertise and hire a person in this field. The die was cast. The junior college would henceforth be ignored in favor of a vocational school.

The Administration of Lito Martinez chose to adopt, almost immediately, the name of Northern New Mexico State School, which most people associated with the school had avoided but this Board seemed to accept. In late June, the Superintendent and the Board hired Leon Wagley as Director of Vocational Education. In an organizational chart provided to the Board, there were three divisions: the high school, vocational school, and guidance and special services. The bursar, Guillermo Jaramillo, reported to the Superintendent.

The school proposed an increase in its operating budget of $386,877. It also made a request for assistance to build a new dormitory at a cost of $586,320. It could not obtain the support needed from the Board of Educational Finance. It became obvious, once again, that in spite of Governor Campbell's push for vocational education at the old Normal School, state support for any ambitious program would not be forthcoming.

Charles López was appointed to a Board that included Grant, Salazar, Shipman, and Valdez; Joe Grant continued as Chairman of the Board of Regents in early 1965. In March of that year the Board demonstrated its ambivalence about the loss of control in the matter of the high school. One member advocated limiting entrance to students who were enrolled in the high school only if they were also enrolled in the vocational program. The Board concurred, thereby demonstrating its lack of interest in becoming a purely vocational school.

In a letter of May 10, 1965, the Executive Secretary of the Board of Educational Finance wrote to Superintendent Martínez in a manner more imperative than encouraging, outlining for Martínez his understanding that the school would expedite the start of programs in office occupations and clerk stenography, beauty operators, barbering, auto mechanics and building trades. It emphasized that support for new programs would come partly from state and federal sources, and in part from the operating budget of the institution. The BEF, he stated, was willing to consider costs of additional dormitory space for girls. The letter suggested maintaining a contingencies balance of $25,000. It further requested an indication of agreement with these points. In summary, control for management of the institution was no longer solely a local matter by this stage in the development of the school.

In late May 1965 the school adopted a policy stating that it would, "Admit first all students who indicate on their application that they are interested in taking vocational courses offered in our school at a high school level..." and, "If room is available in the dormitories at the end of the summer, then other non-vocational high school students may be admitted."

The end of the chapter of the Normal School that, to include a high school in its program of offerings, became less important in June 1965. After all, the Governor of the state being behind new changes that would be wrought for the Normal School made it apparent that this was a fact. A committee of citizens in El Rito transmitted a request to the Superintendent and the Board of Regent through its two representatives, Jo Ann Martin and Jane G. Garcia. They requested consideration and approval of a resolution to be presented to the State Board of Education for the creation a new school district with its high school to be located in existing facilities of the Northern New Mexico State School. The new school district would result from combination of districts 24, 9, and 54, and including Taos School District No. 6. The Board of Regents adopted the resolution. The Executive Secretary and staff of the Board of Education al Finance were present during this meeting and voiced no objection to the resolution or the Board's action. The BEF's posture, then, seemed to be that there was little objection to the presence of a high school on the campus, but expressed no interest in its continued support.

The old Normal School no longer faced uncertainty about its direction for the next few years, but there were numerous questions concerning viability of its newly adopted mission.

The Administration headed by Louis F. Martinez persevered one more school year, 1965-66. In addition to the Superintendent, there were the Director of Vocational Education, Leon Wagley; Business Manager, Guillermo Jaramillo; Director of Guidance and Special Services, Seledón C. Martínez; and the School Nurse, Carmen Segura.

The glory days of team sports at the Normal School were clearly over. Especially during the final four years of the high school, 1964-69, when the boarding population of students declined. No longer were these programs top-notch as they had been in an earlier day.

For performance in individual sports, however, no one in New Mexico has matched the prowess of Gerry Garcia, a boy from El Rito, who from a very young age showed strength as a long-distance runner. In cross-country, his achievements were unsurpassed prior to his time or since then. He captured state championships consecutively beginning in 1961 on up to 1965, five years! His story is told more thoroughly in Chapter Eight in our book, and in *Children of the Normal School*, published by Sunstone Press.

After 1965, the Administration and the Board busied themselves with acquisition of new equipment and facilities for the vocational school. Although in Fall 1965 enrollment in the high school was still strong, 187 students, the time would soon come when the Board would have to spell its end. In the vocational school, there were 66 students in attendance, almost equally divided among auto mechanics, building trades, beauty culture and barbering. There were four students in office occupations.

As if to drive the nail home, the school was informed by Callaway Taubee of the state's public school division that Northern New Mexico State School was not eligible for public school funding in its present status.

Morale among staff at the school could not have been very high, given only the certainty that the high school was being phased out, but with uncertainty about possible enrollment in a vocational school. Leon Wagley resigned as Vocational Director, followed shortly thereafter by the resignation of Superintendent Louis Martínez in June 1966.

The alumni of the high school must have been reading the teacup and anticipating the adverse result for their old high school; its abolishment.

A new Director of Vocational Education was hired for June 1966. Shortly thereafter the Board of Regents announced the employment of their new Superintendent, Albert F. Catanach. New teachers were hired for the '66-67 school year, with a large smattering of vocational instructors:

 Henry Allen, Industrial Arts and Government
 Iris Brown, Library and English
 Benjie F. Espinoza, Mathematics
 Bertha Estrada, Home Economics
 Albert F. Jenschke, Business Education
 Amado Valdez, Typing and Shorthand
 Ruben O. Lucero, Biology and Physical Education
 Robert Bal, Auto Mechanics
 Toribio Lovato, Science and Spanish
 Alfred López, Barbering
 Vicente Martínez, Physical Education and Athletic Director
 Carmen Segura, School Nurse
 Seledón Martínez, Guidance and Special Services

School enrollments continued with similar pattern; 184 high school students and 99 students in vocational programs, some of whom were also counted as high school students. This was the situation in 1966, still not a bright outlook for the vocational school.

One indication that the vocational school would be a hard sell was that many students in vocational programs were supported by federal grant funds, principally from Manpower Development and Training (MDTA). The program for clerk stenographers, for example, was itself supported by MDTA. Shortly thereafter, in early 1967, students at the school became eligible for National Vocational Student Loan Act funds.

Governor David Cargo was elected in November 1966 for a four-year term of office. He named one replacement to the Board of Regents in winter 1967, Henry Abeyta. The Board continued with Francis R. Shipman as Chairman.

For the school year '67-'68, the following teachers were either employed or reemployed, in addition to those whom I have listed above: Dean Brewster, Alfred López, Florentino López, John J. Romero, Raymond Torres, Lucas O. Trujillo, Brenice Valdez and Emily Westbrook.

In spite of the fact that the new public school district was having logistical problems in becoming ready for a new student population, the Northern New Mexico State School declared on May 3, 1967 that it would no longer accept boarding students for the high school. The policy pertained to new students; only those students finishing by spring 1969 would be admitted.

At the same time that changes were taking place in El Rito concerning utilization of the campus, another bit of social history of northern New Mexico was unfolding that is worth recalling. After the middle of the 1960s, Rio Arriba County and its governmental seat, Tierra Amarilla, exploded onto the news in ways that reverberated beyond the borders of our state. This is the background: education in these parts has been viewed principally as a means to prepare to earn a livelihood. In the face of insufficient educational opportunity, economic deprivation of the vast majority of people has been a fact of life. In our past history, land and water were exceedingly important, especially during the period in which ours was an agrarian and pastoral society, say pre-1940. By the 1960s, any semblance of a way of life sustained by small farming and ranching in northern New Mexico was only part of a distant past. These factors, among others, contributed to what happened beginning about June 1967.

People who felt grievances about the loss of land, in particular land that was granted by Spain and Mexico to citizens of this region prior to the coming of the Army of the West in 1846, organized around a charismatic individual who came up from south Texas and formed the nucleus of the Alianza Federal de Mercedes. He was none other than Reyes Lopez Tijerina, who was a self-educated scholar on matters involving the land grants. The fundamental notion held by members of the Alianza is that people with money, who knew American law and conspired to use it to acquire lands owned by hispanics, in some cases stole the land from under its rightful owners.

The Alianza started out trying to use government to reverse previous actions, leading to loss of lands, that were viewed to be unjust. The movement evolved and adopted methods involving civil disobedience. Finally, notoriety resulted from criminal charges brought against some of its members for actions such as the Tierra Amarilla Courthouse raid of June 5, 1967. This condenses a very interesting history far too much, and I would refer readers to a summary published in book form by Peter Nabakov, "Tijerina and the Courthouse Raid."

Students of the Normal School have emphasized to me that they felt safe and secure at the school. They tended to be unmolested by outside events, except perhaps by the Great Wars. In this, the case of a social movement in their own region, their own communities, they were similarly unaffected. Although the period of the sixties and early seventies were periods of unrest in American and European universities where forms of civil disobedience figured prominently, at the Normal School none of this occurred. Nor did anyone attempt to link the issues of economy, education, land ownership, water rights, and so on as being part and parcel of people's ability to live and prosper in this environment.

The absence of concern, and the inability to provide the voice of reason, was not the fault of this school. Simply put, its scope did not reach into social and cultural fields, nor did it have very much that it could contribute during this time. Perhaps, in time, it will, but it did not in the 1960s. One reason was that students at the Normal School did not and could not accept the basic premise upon which the Alianza was founded. Students felt, as students will on occasion, that reasons for the decline in prosperity had to do with reasons that were much too complex for ordinary citizens to comprehend, the influence of the Great Depression in the 1930s being one of them.

Northern New Mexico State School undertook some needed changes that would affect the institution during many years into its future. One was to petition the Economic Development Administration for funds to redo its water system. The process was long and involved, but it did come to fruition in March 1969. I should state here that scarcity of water, ground water, was a case that the town of El Rito and the Normal School would face for several more years.

A second initiative was undertaken that included an effort to open off-campus attendance centers for vocational education. The first one was in Española, in which an actual campus would one day be established. State officials were quite enthusiastic about this, as were the Española Public Schools. Leo Murphy, Executive Director of the North Central New Mexico Economic Development District, was four-square in favor of the project. In time, this led to erection of a very large and functional building in Española dedicated to vocational education.

Finally, it was determined to create a snack bar in Cutting Hall, which would change the character of the campus considerably.

In April 1968 staff and teachers were reemployed for the '68-69 school year.

Albert F. Catanach, Superintendent
Carl O. Westbrook, Dir Vocational Ed
Seledón Martínez, Dir Guidance and Counseling
Guillermo Jaramillo, Business Manager
Carmen Segura, School Nurse

Teachers:

Bertha Estrada
Toribio Lovato
Vicente Martínez, Coach
John J. Romero, Band Director
Lucas Trujillo
Amado O. Valdez
Emily Westbrook

Instructors:

Henry Allen, Drafting
Robert Bal, Auto Mechanics
Mary Bard, Nurse Aides
Janice Brown, Nurse Aides
Ralph García, Electricity
Albert Jenschke, Office Occupations
Fred López, Barbering
Perfecto Maestas, Auto Body Repair
Raymond Torres, Auto Mechanics

By 1968, an Española Branch of the vocational school was established, owing primarily to the efforts of Seledon Martinez. Total enrollment of the institution was 350. Slightly more than one hundred students were in high school and the remainder were enrolled in vocational programs. Many of the approximately 250 remaining students attended in Española, although records of enrollment by attendance center were not kept.

In spring of 1969, the association of Joseph B. Grant with the Normal School finally ended. He was replaced on the Board of Regents by Louis Saavedra, from Albuquerque. The Board of Regents held a dinner in honor of Joe Grant, who had served the Normal School as a member of the Board and in his capacity of President since 1934.

The same month, May 1969, the Normal School graduated its last class of high school students.

Notes:

1. I came to the Northern New Mexico Normal School for ninth grade in 1953. As I review the period of the fifties I will tend toward use of the first person and first person plural.

2. Institutions will often include items as part of the project that may be eliminated if deemed unaffordable during the course of construction. The amount quoted above is the most the project would cost, in any case, and did include the desired items.

3. I am stating here "undesired" as opposed to "undesirable," although some of us were from an undesirable home environment, also. A few children had lived in orphanages, not many. These were matters that were seldom discussed. We students had no reason to discuss them, since we had a shared understanding far beyond what words could add.

4. I mentioned earlier our wont to dispense with "mister" in addressing male teachers. Glenn George was an exception, toward whom we were almost reverential, not only because of his age, but because he was such a caring person. And we were respectful in the presence of all our teachers.

5. The use of the term "feminism" first came into use in France as the French equivalent in the latter part of the nineteenth century, and was

first used in America sometime during the early twentieth century. I point this out because we didn't know this. But in about 1953 we met this woman who opened our eyes to how wonderful freedom and independence can be.

6. El Rito Normal School was the more popular name by which the school was known during the high school period.

7. The Board of Educational Finance (BEF) became the Commission on Higher Education (CHE) in 1984 during Governor Toney Anaya's administration. The Commission was abolished by the state legislature and Governor Bill Richardson in 2008 at which time higher education became another of the governor's administrative departments. We heard frequently, during the life of these two organizations, that the reason for their existence was to place a buffer between colleges and universities, on one hand, and the legislature and the governor, where funding requests were concerned. I cannot bear witness that this plan ever worked.

8. The evidence is that during these years, and for several more years, the Board of Regents was willing to cede its constitutional authority for the control and management of the Normal School. In the early years of the school, say prior to 1950, it made sense that the Normal School would operate as it did in preparing a number of students for "college work", who could, if they wished, elect to enroll in a program for potential teachers. As time went on beyond the early fifties, however, it became obvious that the need for a state-operated grade school, junior high and high school was diminishing. The point to make here is that the president and the Board of Regents should have asserted the Board's prerogatives and sought to modify the instructional program to meet the need of students in an emerging modern age. Ceding this responsibility to a funding control agency, which was the BEF's *raison d'etre,* was not in the best interest of people in northern New Mexico.

9. The El Rito Eagles, along with teams from Santa Rosa, Wagon Mound and Maxwell, dominated some of the early years of Class B New Mexico basketball. In the early 1950s, the New Mexico schoolboys' athletic association decided that certain schools in New Mexico were becoming too large, and therefore small schools could no longer compete fairly

for state honors. They created two classes, A and B. This still meant that winners had to be capable of playing very good basketball, and other sports. In many respects, this system in the fifties was superior to the current alphabet soup of divisions in boys and girls athletics. On the other hand, what has been done on behalf of girls' athletics is certainly to be commended.

10. There is an example of another high-powered offense, and a strong defense to go with it, that dates to the 1950s. Clear across New Mexico in Hobbs, another team known also as Eagles achieved even greater dominance over Class A teams. Coaching is very important in basketball. A man named Ralph Tasker became a living legend, coaching the Hobbs Eagles to many state championships. In 1957, in fact, while the El Rito Eagles won the Class B state championship, the Hobbs Eagles won Class A.

11. For readers who follow state politics closely, during this time governors served two-year terms and could run for election twice consecutively. Governor Edwin Mechem, the Republican incumbent, had served two terms, since 1951.

12. I have included a discussion of Gilbert Archuleta as a student of the Normal School in the chapter, *"Children of the Normal School."* Although I didn't know Gilbert, I learned about him from his brother Ruben, who resides in Española and who was also a student athlete at the Normal.

13. Perhaps the Board of Regents and its president saw nothing to be gained in challenging the Board of Educational Finance. The agency's power, to determine the amount of financial support for the Normal School, may have seemed too daunting for officials of a school that lacked the political influence that other, bigger, institutions seemed to wield.

14. Graduating classes 1947 to 1969 are listed at the end of this book. Most of the information is taken from *El Chamisal*, the student yearbook. I am less certain of earlier graduating classes of the high school. Some years names of students graduating were included in minutes of the

Board of Regents, in some years the students' individual diplomas included names of classmates graduating.

15. Lawrence García, whose architectural firm was in Santa Fé, was an alumnus of the Spanish American Normal School.

16. During this meeting in Santa Fe on September 12, 1959, a reporter for the Santa Fe New Mexican attended, Tony Hillerman. Mr. Hillerman, now deceased, was beginning what turned out to be a distinguished career as a mystery-story writer, and it was while in Santa Fe that he wrote *The Fly on the Wall*.

17. Charles H. Robinson showed academic leadership that had not been present at the Normal School for many years. His proposal was innovative and the dual effort that he described was essentially the mission of a community college. Similar programs were in existence in other parts of the United States, and although community colleges were late in arriving in New Mexico, their mission soon proved widely attractive.

18. C.H. Robinson's proposal was innovative, although the dual effort was imbued in the mission of what came to be called the community college. Similar programs were in existence in other parts of the United States, and although community colleges were late in arriving in New Mexico, their mission soon proved widely attractive. More about this later in this book.

8
SONS AND DAUGHTERS OF THE NORMAL SCHOOL

The high school lasted fifty years, 1919 to 1969. Instruction tended to favor vocational education for more than half of this period of time. This chapter deals with students in the high school. I know of no single, consolidated record in existence of students who attended the Normal School during these fifty years. After the high school closed in 1969, records were not transferred to the Mesa Vista Independent Schools nor to the State Department of Education, to my knowledge. In the list at the end of this book, I have listed, therefore, as many of the graduating classes in the high school as I have been able to locate.

Although the vast majority of students who attended the Normal School were from New Mexico and this region, they each had similarities in background. There was as much diversity over the years, and even year to year, as you would have in many American schools. When students left the Normal School, however, they took with them a love of their school and an appreciation for one another that would last a lifetime. The manner in which they said this to me—I was, after all, president of their old school and much interested in what had happened in life to them—in words and in expressions of body and face, led me to believe that the Normal School and their schoolmates would remain in their being forever. Odd, banal or sentimental though this may sound, it is certain that the Normal School affected its students in ways not completely describable, perhaps incomprehensible.

I first started to called them "children of the Normal School" by using the United Nations definition. However, I soon got the idea that an entire book was appropriate for these young people whom I had known. And I knew many of them well, because I had made it an effort to get to know students, both older ones and younger ones. I attended the school when I was thirteen, in ninth grade, and I felt an old fellow compared to some of the younger ones who were sent to the boarding school while yet in elementary grades.

In addition to providing a list of names of many students who completed 12th grade at the Normal School, I have included a few of their personal stories. Every student has a unique story, of course. Would that I had been able to meet and talk with each and every student who attended the old Normal School. For this book, I interviewed those within my immediate acquaintance and others whom I sought out. Their individual stories begin to tell the tale of the Normal School as I knew it.

When students arrived at the Normal, there was enough diversity to provide a mild cultural shock. It was the difference among students of urban and rural—not a difference in names, ethnicity, or language—that was so different. In the old days, say prior to 1940, there was always a preponderance of Hispanics studying at the Normal with a good number of Anglos in the mix of students. The opposite tended to be true about teachers, Anglos were in the majority. I found it fascinating that while hispanic students were studying English, perhaps for the first time, Anglos tended to be quite fluent in Spanish. Students have told me many times and in different ways how different it was, like a new window to the outside world, when they arrived on campus for the first time. This gave rise to an initial hesitancy to say very much, and it heightened listening skill. Inside of a month, however, the best friend of a kid from Cebolla, or another village, might turn out to be from Albuquerque, or Santa Fe, or perhaps El Paso.

I invite you to take a look at the list of students who first came to the Spanish American Normal School in its early days, 1909 to 1912, included in the section at the end of this book, "Students During the Early Years."

Lists are incomplete, I am certain, for reasons that I have mentioned to readers, but apart from this I know of no reason why I should not include them.

The *Rio Grande Sun* in Española and Dr. Guillermo Lux, in his history of the school published in 1984, have names of students whom I have included in this book for the sake of providing one volume where we may find as many new or familiar names as possible.

In this narrative, I have included the stories of students of the Normal School as a college. Although the number of students who attended Northern New Mexico Community College is too huge to include here, the names of these students *are on record* at the present college.

I have included, toward the end of this chapter, accounts given by recent students of Northern New Mexico College who have completed programs in teacher education.[1] This I have done namely to contrast the circumstance of modern-day students training to be teachers with older ones who found admittance to the profession after, often, a long and hard struggle.

Laura Redman has to be recognized as the first high school graduate of the Spanish American Normal School. She was also the school's only graduate, completing a prescribed student completing course of studies, in 1922. Following graduation, she became the first teacher on record who attended the Normal School.

Although any student who had completed sixth grade and three courses in pedagogy could begin a teaching career, Laura persevered throughout life by advancing her education. She taught elementary school in El Rito in the early '20s, was married and left El Rito briefly. Laura continued taking courses at Highlands University and the University of New Mexico, and returned to teach first grade at the Normal School in 1929. A picture of Laura Redman and her first grade class is included here. It is one of the oldest pictures in this collection in which we can identify most students.[2]

Laura and her twin brother Lawrence had been born on April 20, 1903 in Pagosa Springs, Colorado. The Redman family moved to El Rito early in May 1913, and Laura and Lawrence enrolled at the Normal School.[3]

Laura was married twice and had four children, a son Larry Parcell, a second son Hale Dougherty and adopted daughters, Hyda Marie and Geraldine. She had fourteen grandchildren.

Laura moved to Kansas with husband Gerald Dougherty in early 1930s and worked in Atchison and Kansas City in social work. She continued studies at the University of Kansas and took courses at Wellesley College and the National University of Mexico.

In 1953 she sought and obtained the directorship of the Garcia Street Club in Santa Fe. At the Garcia Street school, a kindergarten, Laura earned plaudits for her dedication and innovation in early childhood education. Her reputation spread beyond Santa Fe. Hyda Marie and Colin remember that the University of Michigan would send students to intern with Laura Dougherty at the Garcia Street Club.

This great woman[4] used a second innovation at the Garcia Street Club. It is a technique which is not widely used in teaching, but it should be. She would involve the parents of children in her classes by setting up an educational environment for them. She engaged the parents in art classes, drawing, painting, macrame, and dance. Laura worked with children and parents who were not the more affluent people in Santa Fe, and she created learning communities in which parents and students could learn simultaneously.

In October 2003, the Garcia Street Club honored "Mamacita", as the former director had been known, with a Sunday afternoon of storytelling. This was almost exactly eleven years after Laura Redman Dougherty had passed away, in October 1992.

In 1923, there were three students graduating: Sixto Valdéz, Sarah Vargas and Glenn Redman.[5] I knew Sixto Valdéz and two of his children, Helen and Eli. More precisely, I knew Sixto Valdéz the public servant—he was Assistant Rio Arriba County School Superintendent—and teacher.

Sixto Valdéz went to very rural villages to teach immediately upon graduation, according to his daughter Helen. Sixto had been born in Los Brazos in April 1900. Sixto's father Clemente had worked for the Denver Rio Grande Railroad in the mountains north of Chama, in Cumbres, and so Sixto was no stranger to remotest northern New Mexico. At an early age, he was taken to St. Catherine's School in Santa Fe. He also attended the Menaul School in Albuquerque prior to enrolling at the Spanish American Normal School. Upon graduation at El Rito, Sixto taught school in remotest northern New Mexico in fall 1923. He taught, according to his written account, a total of 19 years in Rio Arriba County Schools.

Early in his career, Sixto attended Highlands University where he met, and married, Mercedes Martínez from La Madera, who was also a graduate of the Spanish American Normal School. Mercedes, who had been born in 2003 in La Madera, the village she considered home most of her life, also prepared to teach school. During her first year of teaching back in her home town, she had 57 students as the only teacher available. She enjoyed a career lasting forty years, all in the northern region of our state.

Sixto served an interesting and varied career. In the late 1930s he served as principal at a school in Ojo Caliente, followed by a stint in Tierra Amarilla in the early '40s. He worked for the state of New Mexico in the Public School Finance division during the 1940s, before returning to Tierra Amarilla to teach during the time that Albert Amador was in charge of the schools.

Sixto Valdéz had an aptitude in finance and worked as business manager on different occasions for the Rio Arriba schools' superintendent's office and for the New Mexico School Tax Division.

Helen remembers that her father was Assistant School Superintendent for Rio Arriba County during her first year at the Normal School, approximately 1949.

After retiring from his work in public education for thirty years, Sixto worked as field man for the New Mexico State Treasurer's Office.

Sixto moved to La Madera to farm, while Mercedes was teaching back in the place she called home.

Sixto and Mercedes, who were married in December, 1930, had three children, Helen, Eli and Ernest. Helen and Eli attended the Northern New Mexico Normal School. (More about this later in this narrative.)

Mercedes Martínez Valdéz passed away in 1965.

Sixto Valdéz moved to Albuquerque and enjoyed the opportunity to be engaged in the arts. He had been a man well-steeped in the folklore of the region and recited *dichos*, adages, proverbs and other sayings in Spanish, with ease. In his later life he joined *La Compañía de Treato de Albuquerque* and took an acting part in a play, *"Sí Hay Posada."*

Sixto Valdéz died in July 2002, at age 102.

Lawrence Redman[6] was a member of the Class of 1924, he together with Anita Arellano, Pablo Flores, Bolivar Martinez, Jose B. Trujillo, Lafayette Varela and Cornelio Vigil. Lawrence was the twin brother of Laura Redman, and of course they had been born in southern Colorado before the family moved to El Rito. You will note that the older brother Glenn graduated the previous year, 1923. The boys had to work and earn some money while Laura was preparing to be a teacher.

Lawrence attended Highlands University in Las Vegas where he met Cecilia C. de Baca. They were married, and although Lawrence did not work in public education during his professional life, Cecilia did. Cecilia Redman joined the faculty of the Spanish American Normal School in late 1920s, during the Conway administration. She taught at El Rito five years during which Lawrence was employed in Española

The Redman couple had several children, including Michael, who was a dentist in Española until fairly recently.[7] Michael's wife, the former Mary Ellen Montoya, was a teacher at the Normal School in 1949-51. The grandson Michael, Jr. has his dental practice in Española.

The graduating class of 1929 is prominent for a handsome photograph that is in this book, and for the record of its graduates. In the picture, they are from left to right Raymond Romero from Vadito; Pauline Goddard, El Rito; Richard Ortega, Chimayó; Olive Parker, El Rito; Jose M. Valdez, McPhee, CO; Simmie Atencio, Santa Cruz; Cruz Trujillo, Chimayó; and Isabel Ward, seated, is the class sponsor.[8]

Raymundo Romero was class valedictorian. He also became a teacher; he lived and taught in Vadito his entire life. He and his wife Orcibiana (Anne) were married 67 years, and had children Louis, Benito, Isaac, Eleanor and Annabelle.

Raymundo Romero is featured as one of state's notable elders in the February 2000 issue of the New Mexico Magazine.[9]

Pauline Goddard was the daughter of John Goddard, who came to El Rito from Kansas, and Augusta Carrillo Goddard from Roswell. The Goddards had nine children, six sons and three daughters. Pauline followed in the footsteps of a sister, Genevieve, also a graduate of the Normal School, as a teacher in the rural schools. Most of what we know about Pauline is from her younger sister Jane. Pauline taught elementary school in Gallina and Ensenada and other villages of northern New Mexico . (There is more concerning the Goddards in a discussion of Jane Garcia later in this narrative.)

Olive Elnora Parker was a member of the class of '29; her story was told to me by her daughter Katie Bateman Allison.[10]

Olive Parker was born in 1910 in Mancos, Colorado and grew up in Albuquerque. In the late 1920s Olive enrolled at the Normal School to prepare for a career in teaching. Olive's younger sister Marguerite was also enrolled.[11] Olive was a very photogenic young woman as evidenced from three photographs that I have seen. Olive and Marguerite were very good students. [12]

After completion of high school at the Normal, Olive attended the University of New Mexico to complete her teaching credential. She then taught at Truchas in Rio Arriba County.

Olive was married in 1933 to Albert Bateman. They had three children: Katie, Dorothy and a younger brother born in 1935. Olive Parker died as a result of childbirth, a day after her baby was born. Olive was 25 years of age.

I knew José M. Valdéz when I was a young boy, but I did not know him well. In our village, Lyden, he was refined in manner, short, but handsome, well dressed and soft spoken. He was someone whom I admired.

José Manuel Valdéz was born in April 1912 in Lyden to Perfecto and Elvira Valdez. Perfecto moved as his job required with the Denver and Rio Grande Railroad Company, and so José lived in several communities in southern Colorado and northern New Mexico prior to residing in Lyden.

José came to the Normal School from McPhee, Colorado and enrolled in the high school. After graduation from the high school, he returned to El Rito in 1934 to take the college courses that had been made available for prospective teachers. He subsequently enrolled at the University of New Mexico to complete his teaching credential. He taught in very rural schools in Monero[13], three years, and in Ancon, very near Lyden, an additional year. After about 1938 he worked for the state's Department of Public Welfare and as County Director for Guadalupe County.

José Valdez married Candelaria Romero in November 1934. They had four children: Joe, Barbara, Consuelo and Donald. Joe, Barbara and Connie attended the Normal School, also, in 1950s.

José was a studious man; his favorite pastime was reading. He had studied music and played the piano by age six. José was athletic, liked sports, and played basketball and baseball at the Normal School and in later life. He was well traveled and worldly. He was national secretary for the League of United Latin American Citizens.

When I knew José Valdez he was employed at the Los Alamos Scientific Laboratory (until 1972.) He retired at the Laboratory and took a job with the Los Alamos Federal Employees Credit Union. He made his residence at Los Alamos for a while.

In his later years, he lived in Albuquerque where he died in May 2005.

Gilbert Archuleta, Class of 1934, is one of the legends of high school athletics at El Rito. He was from Española and went to the Spanish American Normal School as a boarding student in fall 1930 at age 14. If nothing else, he would be known still for his long association with the Normal School and with President Joe Grant.

He was, however, one of those gifted athletes who seems to come along about every ten years or more in northern New Mexico.[14] He was an all-around athlete at the Normal, but since basketball was the favorite sport, Gilbert starred on the hardwood floors in northern New Mexico. He was lucky. Although it was a tiny gymnasium, it was completed around 1930 in time for Gilbert and teammates at the Normal.

It was in baseball, however, that Gilbert really made his mark and for which he is remembered. While in high school, he pitched summers for the Terrero Miners in the Central New Mexico League; he was at age 17 and 18 the outstanding pitcher in the league. He repeated outstanding seasons in a Northern Rio Grande League, semi-pro baseball.

After high school, Gilbert took a job with the Normal School as coach, boys' advisor and dorm proctor. He remained in this capacity until 1939 during which year he informed the Board of Regents that he would likely be leaving to play professional baseball. Joe Grant, the President, beamed as Gilbert made his announcement; Board members wished Gilbert well but failed to grasp the significance of what Gil had just said. Grant knew his baseball and understood that this was a big opportunity for Gilbert, who was 23 years old. Joe Grant knew that this young man had a bright future as a pitcher in organized baseball.

According to Carlos Salazar, sports editor for the old *Albuquerque Tribune*, in '39 Branch Rickey of the St. Louis Cardinals made "a special trip to Albuquerque on the Santa Fe Chief" to sign Gilbert Archuleta to a contract. In summer 1939 he posted a record of 11 wins and two losses for the Albuquerque Cardinals of the Arizona-Texas League. He had moved up in the Cardinal farm system to the Pocatello, Idaho and

Sacramento, CA farm clubs, but he joined the Navy in early 1942 in response to the attack by Japan on Pearl Harbor. That summer of '42 he had been slated to pitch for the parent Cardinals club in St. Louis. He served with the Seabees in Guadalcanal, according to the *Tribune*, where he also played baseball against guys like Dominic Dimaggio and Phil Rizutto, who went on to play for the New York Yankees. As happened in the early 1940s, the Great War took the best years from young men who might have otherwise excelled on the ball field.

Gilbert Archuleta came home at the advanced age of 30 to play for the Albuquerque Dukes in the Class C West Texas-New Mexico League. He posted a record of 11 wins and two losses that year and won 17 games with no losses at Tingley Field in 1947. His pitching career was over for practical purposes. Gilbert had a job with the New Mexico Employment Security Commission and he pitched for the Dukes who paid him for each game, sixty bucks a game. The Dukes would not get many deals like that one.

Gilbert was great influence on Ruben Archuleta, his brother, who came to the Normal School in fall 1942 after Gilbert had left for the Navy.

Gilbert married Norah Sandoval; they had a daughter Juliann. Toward the end of his life, Gilbert lived in the state of Virginia. He died in Martinsburg, VA in December 2003.[15]

Cloide Trujillo is loved by the students who knew her. When I came to the Normal, she was running the laundry and supervised five people, but she held several positions at the school as chef and as girls' dormitory advisor. But before she married her husband Abe in El Rito, she was a student. She is more like the many kids who came to El Rito, and tells about the experience better than most of us. Cloide speaks to the joy of life, even when times were tough.

She was born Cleofas Herrera in Blanco, NM in April 1917; she is 92. She was named after her grandfather, Cleofas Herrera; her dad was Telesfor. She was orphaned at a very young age, but she managed to remain in Blanco and started Catholic school, affiliated with the Santa Rosa de Lima Church and the Ursuline sisters. The grandmother Anastacita Valdéz and aunt Teresita helped her to grow up. Young Cleofas showed an aptitude for math, geometry and languages, was a good speller. Her aunt and uncle Fernando saw her potential and brought her from Blanco to El Rito and the Normal School to board as a student.

Quite naturally, she was homesick but she soon made friends and excelled at basketball. The Normal School had a new gymnasium by late 1920s and she joined the basketball team, then coached by Father Bikhaus. The good father was parish priest down the road at the church of San Juan Nepomuceno and volunteered to help with the girls' team. Cloide likes to recall that toward the end of one game she threw the ball up and back, partly in self defense, and sure enough the ball fell through the hoop, swish!

Cloide grew to be a young lady on the campus, now in eleventh grade, where she met a very young, quiet fellow who was working the beautiful grounds while he prepared to leave town for a better job. Abe worked for the New Mexico Highway Department then decided to take a job in the shipyards in San Francisco, but he and Cloide had the good sense to marry in 1936. Her old coach, Father Bikhaus, married them. Not long after this, Abe was drafted into the US Army and shipped off to Okinawa.

Cloide consoled herself as best she could; she had a cousin in Chili, that helped. She started her own employment career, occasionally at the Normal and at the El Rito Post Office. After the war, she and Abe, who is now deceased, settled in El Rito and raised a family: daughters Olivia, Eva, Paula and Anna Marie, and sons David, Herman, Alfonso, Benjamin and Patrick.

Dana and Jewell Allison, brother and sister, came to the Normal School about 1936 when their parents moved to Canjilón from Oklahoma. Dana remembers that he started school in fourth grade. He didn't complete high school; he left after 11th grade to take a job. Jewell did complete high school at the Normal; she graduated with the Class of '38.

Like many young men at the Normal School, his first love was basketball. He played, and was on the starting five, in 1941, '42 and '43. Charlie Brown was already the basketball coach. The Eagles had several successful seasons. Rivalries were maintained with large and small schools alike: Santa Fe High School, Española, Las Vegas, but also St. Catherine's and other smaller schools. Dana was the Eagles top scorer by the time he was in his final year at the Normal School.

Dana married Katie Bateman, daughter of Olive Parker, all

originally from El Rito and Canjilón. I know Dana and Katie, who reside in Española. I have not met Jewell.

Alonzo Vigil, Class of 1938, is best remembered by students of the '40s and '50s as coach and boys' dorm proctor. Alonzo had two brothers, Paul and Pat, and sister Laura who all attended the Normal; they were Albuquerque kids. A younger brother Billy also attended the Normal School to 11th grade.

Al Vigil was a veteran, and one of Joe Grant's favorite people. Alonzo was one of the staff members who remained at the Normal, largely influenced by Joe Grant. I like to refer to them as the "loyalists." They were among the staff who left in 1951 when Joe Grant resigned (following the election of Republican Governor Edwin Mechem.) Alonzo returned to the Normal School when I was in my final year as a student.

Al enjoyed a career at the Normal School, but he could have made his living in construction, particularly with wood. He was one of the original superb wood furniture carvers. One example of his work is a dining room suit that sits at his brother Pat's home in Albuquerque.

Pat referred to Alonzo as "one of the kindest people" whom he has known. Pat and Al *were brothers*, but this is the sort of memory that students at El Rito retained about someone, or two or more brothers and sisters.

According to John Martin, the Martin family returned to El Rito from Pueblo, CO in 1923 when John was eight months old. John is New Mexican through and through; speaks Spanish and knew some good stories, funny tales, too. One of his first recollections about life back in El Rito is that his family had a 1927 Buick. You can guess that this set them apart from the community more than anything, not many people had cars. John says there wasn't much money, but darned if their parents would let him and his brothers and sister feel poor. John had older brothers named George and Tom, sister Roberta and a younger brother Pat, the boys attending the Normal School. Roberta went to Santa Fé to the Loretto Academy.

John, who is of the graduating Class of 1939, attended first grade at the Normal School in '29 with Laura Dougherty, their teacher. Most people who were born in the past century know that this was the year of the great stock market crash and the beginning of the Great Depression. When you talk with John Martin, you get the feeling that this singular event in his young life left him a humble man, and someone resolved to be a good person. For years when I was president of the college, the new Normal School, John was a member of our Foundation Board, raising money for scholarships for area students. In the early days of the 20th century, the Martin Store had a truck because provisions had to be hauled from Santa Fe, no one else would bring them to El Rito. John also remembers the great number of local men who had to leave town to work, many of them to herd sheep in Colorado and Wyoming.

During the depression years the Civilian Conservation Corps built roads to Canjilón and La Madera. John told me few of the men went to the armed services during World War I. Communities in northern New Mexico were still pretty isolated, still no electricity, phones or good roads. Not much English was spoken in these northern communities, so John learned Spanish.

John V. Conway was president when John started school. John Martin credits Conway with hiring good teachers. In addition to Laura Dougherty, John remembers fondly Barbara Sena (who was the late Senator Dennis Chavez's sister) and Carson Creecy at the high school. John remembers that the predominate number of students attending during the thirties were academic, rather than vocational, students.

The big event that *really* affected his generation of people was the Second World War. John graduated high school in 1939. His family couldn't afford a second child in college, George was at Regis College in Denver. So John remained in El Rito and took courses in the college division. Most of the courses available at the Normal School were in preparation for teaching, but he took courses not in the teaching curriculum, nevertheless. He was drafted into the US Army in October 1942 and joined the many young men from northern New Mexico in the service of their country.

John talked with me about a changed way of life during the war years and shortly before. The economy had changed with rationing of food, meats and gasoline. After the war in January 1946, John enrolled at the University of New Mexico. Many of the young returnees from the war were going to California to work during the same time. A few returned to El Rito, but John did not. John studied business and Spanish while at UNM. Spanish was his first love, so he concentrated his studies in language.

His brothers Tom and Pat stayed in El Rito, Tom ran the store and Pat became a rancher. George and John earned BA degrees and set out for the world.

John was recalled into the Army during the Korean war; he was commissioned a second lieutenant.

John Martin made a career in banking and worked with the US Agency for International Development in El Salvador. He lived in Santa Fe with his wife Barbara; they were married in December 1951. They have two sons, Meade and Christopher.

Jane Goddard García completed high school at the Normal School in 1940; was awarded the diploma in 1941. Jane was the youngest of eight children belonging to Clarence Goddard and Augusta Carrillo. She was younger than her oldest sister Genevieve by about twenty years.

Jane has a most vivid recollection of life in El Rito during her childhood.

Jane's father worked all over the region, drove around in a Model-T truck. As a result, the family did not suffer much during the Great Depression. She remembers how important village life was—*fiestas* on July 25 related to Santiago, patron saint of men on horseback, but most revered in Spain for the reconquest from the Moors—and treats, such as ice cream, available for the children only during feast days.

Jane learned English at home; her father didn't speak Spanish. She remembers that her mother spoke Spanish with a Mexican inflection. So Jane learned local Spanish from neighbors' children, in particular a small girl who befriended her.

She began school in first grade at the Normal School in 1929; she is in the picture with Laura Redman Dougherty's class. Jane also had classes with Cecilia de Baca Redman in elementary grades. Jane has a good recollection of President John Conway and the discipline that was maintained at the school. Jane remembers well Barbara Sena, an elementary school teacher, and Josué Trujillo in high school.

Jane was an avid reader and the library at the Normal had many, many books from which to choose. She enjoyed the education that she received at the Normal and thought it quite good. Regretfully, she complains, as did many of her classmates from El Rito, that there was little consideration shown to day students. There were no activities for them to attend, there was not even a designated place for lunch. She stated to me that school dances were off limits to kids from El Rito, and, as a result, she did not even attend ball games. She felt that day students in general did not have a good feeling about the school, as a result of this negligence on the part of the management of the school.

Jane graduated from high school and soon thereafter married Fabián García in 1941. Fabián and Jane had ten children.

Jane's parents lived in El Rito until Augusta died in 1945; Clarence passed away in 1951. Jane Goddard is the only child of the Clarence Goddard family living. Her husband Fabián died in January 2005.

Jane and Fabián had at least an acquaintance with every one of the presidents of the Normal School from the time of President Conway.

Only a few of the children of the Normal School who attended in the 1930s are living. You have met a few of them in these pages. Many of the students of the early '40s we don't know; they are of the generation of World War II, as were those of the late 1930s. We have maintained contact with many, beginning with the Class of 1943, and students who attended in the 1940s.

The Classes of 1943 and 1944 were particularly hard-hit by a war that had expanded to Europe, via England, Normandy and Belgium on the way to Germany and Berlin. A bitter conflict was underway in the Pacific islands with Japan. World War II depleted the student population. A welcoming message in September 1943 from President Joe Grant published in *El Aguila*, the student newspaper, told part of the story. After his opening remarks, the President said:

> Due to our war effort, we cannot expect the many advantages provided in the past, but I know that each and every one of you is more than anxious to play a part to preserve those ideals of our country which we love so well.
>
> Today, hundreds of our students are scattered all over the globe, boys who a few years ago were in school, and we also have about thirty-five girls who answered the call of our Nation. I feel the utmost pride that when danger came near our standards of liberty, those boys and girls, knowing the value of a free America, responded eagerly to offer their own lives, that the way of life they had so enjoyed would not be denied for you who came after.
>
> Each week, letters come from those loyal boys and girls, and

each expresses the thought that some day they may return to El Rito, perhaps not to continue their schooling, but merely to visit once again the school and the campus that holds so many cherished memories for them, to see old friends, to talk over their school days, and perhaps to shed a tear for those who failed to return to their native land. The patriotic program of your institution for the past eight years for these boys and girls must also come to you, a desire to protect at all costs the privileges and rights which were prescribed for us by men and women, who preferred death than to live under a yoke of slave laws.

I know you all join in a prayer for the return of our former students and all those connected with our cause, and for those who have already made the supreme sacrifices, and now lie sleeping in a foreign land, let us pray that they may have found peace with their God, knowing that they died for us and that we will never betray those ideals for which they gave all.

The President then closed with a blessing and a patriotic statement.

A problem for all of us who came to the Normal School later, is that there was very little way of knowing who went to war, neither men nor women. Joseph Grant is eager to remind us that among all of the young men who went to Germany and the Pacific Islands, as a result of their participation in World War II, included at the very least 35 young women. These young men and women were the Greatest Generation.

Very soon that fall term, the football season at El Rito had to be canceled. There were not sufficient students to constitute a football team. Two statements, published in the November '43 issue of *El Aguila,* summarize the depth of feeling among students concerning the war. Alfonso Lujan, the Assistant Editor stated:

> Few of our parents and grandparents realized when World War I broke out in Europe in 1914 that the United States would eventually become a participant in the great struggle. Thousands of American soldiers gave their lives so that this nation might live. Fortunately the German Empire asked for an armistice and on November 11, 1918 the cruel killing and destruction of property ceased. This day has been declared a holiday.

Today we face the same problem, or even a greater one, but we sincerely hope that again the axis powers will be vanquished. Let us pray for a quick victory."

These word were followed by another statement, this time from the Editor-in-Chief, E. Jeanne Belknap, who expressed from her meditations:

Time has really skipped by this year it seems. Think back and see how near last Thanksgiving seems. How Armistice Day of "42" is yet vivid in the photo album of our minds. Yes, we were in this war last year too, but now it makes a year longer since we've had any peace of mind concerning our loved ones. Let us all hope that we celebrated this Armistice Day by buying more war bonds and stamps and by making new resolutions concerning the conservation of vital war materials.

We must pledge ourselves to a sacrifice that is true. We must remember that what we are doing without is helping to feed our loved ones who in turn are laboring and fighting for the day which will be our next national holiday--Peace Day for World War II.

Gordon Darling came from his home in southern California for our largest reunion, held in 1998 at El Rito. I was very impressed with his love of the old school and his schoolmates, and with the sincere gratitude that he shows for the opportunity that the Normal School at El Rito offered. He particularly enjoyed talking about President Joseph Grant.

Gordon's first experience at the Normal was not a memorable one, however. He had started first grade in Estancia in 1932, but in 1934 he was taken to El Rito. He wasn't happy there and he states in his memoirs that, when an opportunity occurred, he "ran away." He spent the remainder of the mid-thirties in Albuquerque and Stanley, and returned to El Rito in 1938. Gordon wondered why his mother was bringing him back to a school and a place which he had not liked.

His new circumstances at the Normal School turned out to be entirely different from his one earlier experience. For one, Joe Grant paid special attention to him and made certain that he would be comfortable there. Luckily for Gordon, his second stay at the Normal was successful;

his mother died a victim of an automobile the following year, 1939.

Gordon met new people, including Ruben Miera and Pat Martin, who became his best friends. He became involved in school sports, under the tutelage of Charlie Brown.

Gordon has provided me with written observations about the Normal School between 1938 and 1943. He summarized: "Most impressive was El Rito's *esprit de corps*. To be associated with El Rito Normal School mean(t) belonging to a community stressing caring, culture, sharing, pride, and achievements and reaching one's full potential."

Gordon Darling was president of the Class of '43, and in parting thanked the faculty and President Joe Grant "for all they have done for us."

Throughout his adult life, Gordon Darling has engaged in civic activities, striving to improve the life of his community. His leadership in civic organizations has been well-documented in newspapers in our nation. One of the impressive awards that Gordon has received is the Roberto Clemente Humanitarian Award for his twenty-five years of service to Vallejo, his home town in California. Gordon stated that, had he stayed in New Mexico, he probably would have served as senator, or governor, or perhaps as president of the school, because he was well-known here. Such words ring true still today.

Ruben Miera is a well-known political figure in New Mexico, and a friend to many New Mexicans. He also is of the Class of '43.

When Ruben started school in Sandoval County, the public high school in Bernalillo "barely existed" in his memory. The Catholic school, Our Lady of Sorrows, was better known. Ruben was, of course, interested in athletics, and so El Rito seemed the better place to be.

Ruben loved football, played for Charlie Brown. He turned out to be a good running back.

Of his days at the Normal, Ruben remembered sharing his money, since there wasn't much of it, with schoolmates. He told me they were "the happiest four years I ever had. We lived like brothers and sisters." Later, but in his younger days, he visited El Rito quite often. Ruben Miera would probably be surprised to know that he, among many former students of the Normal School, who gave me the idea of expanding this chapter into *Children of the Normal School*. Ruben Miera has passed away since I began work on this book more than 10 years ago.

After graduation at El Rito, Ruben managed to survive World War II, serving as a dental technician while in the US Navy. Upon his return, Ruben ran a store and bar in Algodones, his home. He told me that Senator Joe Montoya had promised to "make a politician out of you." He did, readily. Ruben served as *de facto* chairman of the Democratic Party in Sandoval County for about fifty years, finally becoming the elected Chairman in 1955.

Ruben served in various elected and appointed capacities in state government in New Mexico. He served in both the administrations of Governors Bruce King and Jerry Apodaca as Secretary of Transportation. At various times, he served as Assistant State Auditor and as Assistant Secretary of State.

Ruben was widowed and remarried; he lived in Algodones. He is deceased.

Pat Martin was of the Class of 1943. He was the youngest of the five children of President George J. and Margaret Allen Martin; he was born Patrick O. Martin in July 1923.

Pat attended elementary school in El Rito and enrolled in high school at the Normal School. I saw his picture with the *Orquésta Típica*, and it occurred to me that this kind of participation was one reason to be popular among students; he was. After graduation at the Spanish American Normal School, Pat remained on the ranch and had a deferment because he was the only boy at home to do the work. After 1946, when his brother John came home, Pat was drafted into the US Army.

Pat attended the University of New Mexico one semester. He resumed his life ranching in El Rito and married Joann Severns in August 1957. The Martins had two boys, Mike born in August 1957, and Timothy, born in June 1958. Michael Martin was member, and he is currently the Chairman of the Board of Regents. Thus the Martins have contributed immeasurably to the continuation and good health of the Spanish American Normal School.

Pat was one of the few *real* ranchers, real cowboys, left in New Mexico, and his sons have followed in his steps. Joann Martin is the person about whom I have written in the previous chapter, concerned about the fate of the high school to serve students from El Rito and this region. Pat was a Cattle Inspector for the Livestock Board and a member of the New Mexico Cattle Growers. Pat was also a founding member of the El Rito Fire Department, across the road from the Normal School campus.

Pat's son Mike was on the Board of Regents of Northern New Mexico Community College during my presidency. I have more discussion elsewhere in this narrative about his work on behalf of our school.

Interestingly, this past January, the Governor of the state of New Mexico, Michelle Lujan Grisham, appointed Michael Martin to the Board of Regents. Soon thereafter, the Board of Regents elected Michael Martin as its new chairman. I worked with Michael; there is no better chairman for this Board of Regents, and at this time, than Mike Martin. Michael is an unusual man; he is quiet, pensive, and, moreover, will add to the president's authority at the Northern New Mexico Colllege.

Pat Martin passed away in February 1976. Tim, the Martin's son, died in June 2006. Pat, Mike, and Tim are remembered around El Rito for their very pleasant disposition and their ethic, hard work.

Paul Romero, who is of the Class of 1944, came to the Normal School two years earlier for eleventh grade. Paul was from Velarde; his father Flavio wanted him to have a better education, as did his mother Cirila, who was a school teacher. She taught in tiny schools in villages like Lyden, La Canova and Velarde. She was known as *la maestra.*

Paul's girlfriend Cecilia (and my mother's aunt) was preparing to be a schoolteacher while studying at the Normal School. There were only two students in the college division, as Paul remembers.

Paul graduated in May 1944 and was immediately drafted into the US Army. World War II "disturbed everything" is how Paul describes the period. He and Cecilia, although young, were to be married but decided to postpone the wedding because of the uncertainty of life for a soldier.

As you hear Paul speak about those days, clearly a happy memory of life in El Rito is overshadowed by flashbacks of the war.

Paul Romero was an infantryman. He said to me, "Recall that General McArthur is remembered for saying to the people of the Philippine Islands, 'I shall return.'" Well, he did, on the backs of the US infantrymen who retook Luzon and the capital, Manila, inch by inch, because the Japanese would not surrender. Paul remembers the rejoicing when the war with Japan ended in August 1945; he and his buddies were still on Luzon.

It changed the man's view of the world. Better said, the boy who had known security of home and people at the Normal School whom he liked and enjoyed, encountered the savagery that people bring on each other during war. He says that he hopes that people here never see the destruction that war causes, the misery of poverty and disease following a war like the one that he witnessed. And he says little about himself.

Following the capture of the Philippines, Paul and other seasoned soldiers were sent to occupy Korea, which had been, also, liberated from Japan. He witnessed the creation of the 38th Parallel by which Korea was divided between north and south, pro-Soviet Union in the north , and below it pro-United States.

Paul was discharged from the Army in September 1946. He and Cecilia were married the following April in Velarde. Paul and Cecilia had children: Paul, Larry, Geraldine, James, Anna, Carmela and Barbara.

Cecilia Valdéz Romero died in October 2001; Paul lives in Albuquerque.

Several graduates have performed a great service by perpetuating an Alumni Association. Many of the people mentioned on these pages I would not know about were it not for opportunities to meet them at alumni reunions and similar gatherings of people. Ted Kuntz is one of them.

Ted graduated at the Normal School, Class of '46. He was a boy from Farmington. His father worked on construction projects, and he and his dad were in Canjilón when he met Earl Scarborough, who suggested that he might like the school at El Rito. Ted came to the Normal at age eleven. I have seen Ted's picture with other young men at the Normal in woodworking classes. Those vocational classes were important to a good number of our former students.

Yet, when I asked Ted what he profited from at the Normal, his response was most interesting, probably reflecting a majority opinion among students: "The school taught me how to be independent and to think." I can think of few greater compliments for a student to make about his former school.

After high school, Ted Kuntz went into the US Navy and was on his way to the South Pacific but was told to return home. The war had ended and our boys were no longer needed out in that vast expanse of ocean beyond Hawaii.

Two of the graduating classes members', 1947 and '48, best illustrate how these kids from the Normal stuck together long after their high school days. I've spoken with many of these former students from '47 and '48, wondering, why? Well, they all just simply liked each other, or maybe loved each other is a better way to say it. They also had their leaders, guardian angels maybe, bringing them together, year after year. The two were John Aragon and Anna Mae King.

They were large classes; fifty-one in '47, thirty-five in '48. Yet I knew more than a dozen of them fairly well. I liked them so well that I made a special effort to serve as host for them at the old school a couple of times.

The students of those years cause me to believe that the zenith of that El Rito high school at the Normal was during the late forties and earlier. I also believe that it was an ambient created by the students in a very pretty, idyllic maybe, setting known as the Normal School.

Boarding high schools tended to be more common in England and in New England, USA. As you read what students have to say about their old schools, it is a very mixed reaction. Some of the treatment of students was reportedly inhumane, in a few instances. At the Normal School at El Rito, there seem to have been few complaints by boarding students. Day students, who voice a legitimate concern, are an exception in this case.

Leo Apodaca is one of fellows of the Class of '47 who spoke to me for this book. I had known Leo through our friend John Aragon. Leo spoke about the basic things that a young man needed in his life to maintain interest in school, and be comfortable. The kids felt secure and well fed. Leo was an Albuquerque boy, but he didn't miss the city because the sports program at the Normal kept him plenty busy. There was a lot of use of nicknames at El Rito; somehow "Sluggo" stuck with Leo. He didn't mind. Leo tends to smile and laugh a lot as he recounts days at the Normal.

Danny Englebrecht was another Albuquerque boy. Again, Danny

had a consuming interest in sports. Danny even tried boxing. These were well-conditioned young men. I am writing these memories as Danny speaks, in short bursts.

Danny's mother worked in Albuquerque, and Alonzo Vigil suggested that he might try the boarding school at El Rito. In 1941, at the age of 13, Danny enrolled at the Normal. He tells with an amount of pride that one year he was the state boxing champ in the bantamweight division. He didn't miss home; Albuquerque became a place to get a job in summers.

Leo, Danny and Ted were having a discussion about days at the Normal, what else? Their recollection was that Mr. and Mrs. Grant were parent figures, although they did not see a lot of the Joe Grant. They remembered fondly Charlie Brown and Alonzo Vigil. In their words, "We were one family."

These are men who view their lives as having been successes, and they got their start in life at El Rito. They are happy with themselves and being with each other when   still together.

David Grant was of the Class of '47. He has been deceased a few years, but before his death, he helped me to gather a great deal of information for this book.

I met David in 1997 at his home in Albuquerque, and spoke with him about his father Joe Grant. David spoke mostly about his dad, but I did learn that David was at the top of his class academically. He also had a lot of interest in journalism, edited the school newspaper, *El Aguila*, and he started the student yearbook, *El Chamisal*, in 1947.

In '97, we had planned a high school alumni reunion at Northern New Mexico Community College at El Rito which was to take place the following summer. David gave me biographical information about Joseph Grant, but he did something more. He let me borrow home movies that had been taken by Joe Grant in late 1930s and on through the '40s. They were film footage of the campus and its students, in addition to his family. A talented cinematographer by the name of Roger Salles at our college stitched film from one year to the next, and digitized the new product. The new film opens to music: "Moonlight Serenade," I think it is. The alumni and everyone enjoyed seeing fashions, automobiles, and the campus of the '30s and '40s. David and his brother James came to the reunion in summer of 1998. This is one of my memories of David Grant, Joe Grant's older son.

I have told the story of Joe Grant, in many cases, as told to me by David. David's own memories of his life at the Normal were vivid. He told me about the return from the war of veterans like Lawrence García, whom had David described while in tears with stories, similarly, about guys who had not returned.

David remembered the basketball team of "midgets", coached by Charlie Brown, who were favored to win the state championship in 1947, but were knocked out of the competition by St. Catherine's in Santa Fe. David was on that team, as were Reyes Gonzales, Buzzy Newbern, John Aragón, the elder "Casey" Martínez, Pat Vigil and some younger players. David emphasized that music and dance were as important as sports, and he lauded Pablo Mares's *Orquésta Típica* and the Follies. He related to me that Anna Mae King was as athletic and bright a student as there was on campus. He told me of his love for his teachers, Lena Archuleta and Opel Winfield, and many friends, Charlie López, Gilbert Archuleta, Wallace Archuleta, and, of course, John Aragon and Pat Vigil. Charlie was one of the first to tell me that a young man in school at the time, Norbert Trujillo, "was smarter than all of us."

David left the Normal School after graduation at a young age, attended an additional year of high school in Santa Fe, and went on to the University. He took a degree in political science. One of his first jobs he had prepared for at El Rito, he managed the northern branch of the *Albuquerque Journal.* David Grant represented the Ford Foundation in New Mexico for a number of years, and assisted young scholars in their development. He joined the staff at New Mexico Highlands University during John Aragón's final years with the institution.

The Class of 1948 included two students whom I did not know well, but who each made their mark at the Normal School.

Norbert Trujillo was class valedictorian, but not only was he at the top of his class, his classmates remember him as one of the brightest people whom they have known. Norbert grew up in El Rito. After high school, he attended the university and has been a mathematician or engineer, probably both. He was employed at the White Sands Missile Range during his professional life. He is retired and lives in Las Cruces.

Another fellow of that time whom I never met was Beau Newbern, now deceased. He was from Santa Fe. John Aragon was very fond of Buzzy, as they called him, and remembered him as a fine basketball player. Former students tell me that he was the top player in the district in his final year at El Rito.

I don't know whether Beau Newbern is living. John Aragon, who became a friend, has since passed away.

I remember Chris Jaramillo, also of the Class of '48, who after college returned to teach at El Rito. He was one of my favorite teachers; he taught me the use of a typewriter, a useful skill for sure. What I remember about Chris is that a student was always comfortable with him; he was unusually quiet, gentle as he spoke to the student, and apt to provide direction that the student would follow. I did.

John Aragón was a great favorite of the Class of '48 and one of the better known alumni of the Spanish American Normal School.[16] John has passed on since I started this book. I, and other friends, miss his presence among us.

John prided himself in referring to home as the Barelas district in south Albuquerque. He came to the Normal School at a young age, went on to the University of New Mexico and Highlands University after high school, and returned to Albuquerque in mature adulthood.

I met John Aragón in Tegucigalpa, Honduras in 1963. I was teaching at the National University on a Fulbright scholarship and John was completing a supervisory project for the Ford Foundation, which had several fellows also teaching at the National University of Honduras. Readers may remember the Alliance for Progress in Latin America, initiated during President John F. Kennedy's term of office, which inspired us to go there. We remained friends thereafter, many times at a distance until he came to Highlands University, where I worked.

John Aragón was simultaneously working on a doctoral degree with Dr. Frank Angel, another dear friend, at the University of New Mexico. John completed his doctoral studies in 1966.

In Albuquerque, he became Executive Secretary for the New Mexico School Boards Association, and after completion of the PhD he took a job at the University of New Mexico as director of a Cultural Awareness Center and taught in the College of Education.

It was during these years of the late '60s and early '70s that I got to know John well, and to hear his stories about the Normal School at El Rito. He was a great story teller, and he spoke about people whom I did not know. Some of those names appear on these pages. Others whom he spoke about were Anna Mae King, Buzzy Newbern, Norberto Trujillo, Pat Vigil, Tony García, Richard Malooley, David Grant, Carl Naranjo, Joan Odom, Gillie Lopez, Ernest Dow, Leo Sánchez, Andrés Casey Martínez, Ruben Archuleta and many more whom I have, unfortunately, forgotten. John liked people and these were older, former students of the Normal School whom I did not know at the time.

John told me about their famous "Follies" under the director of Lena Archuleta. And about some of the staff: Lena, Wallace Archuleta, Alonzo Vigil and many more.

Sometime in the mid-1960s, John Aragón was the Chief of Party for the University of New Mexico in a federally funded project in Quito, Ecuador. The University ran a Studies Center in Ecuador of which John was very proud, and his office, with the vast resource of UNM, provided technical services to the Ministry of Education in Ecuador. It was after this that he operated the Cultural Awareness Center at UNM and he invited me to assist in a project or two.

In about 1975, he became president at New Mexico Highlands University, and I got to know John very well. I had been Academic Dean at Highlands when John arrived. I remained the Dean until I resigned in 1979 to come to the Normal School, now called Northern New Mexico Community College.

John and I remained friends and professional associates. After I had come to Northern and John was still president, we worked on projects in Latin America together. The last assignments on which we worked were in Guatemala City and in Quetzaltenango, also in Guatemala. John was a great latin americanist and spoke with enthusiasm about friends and acquaintances in Central and South America.

John was married to Jean Maurice about 1951 during their final year at Highlands University. John and Jean Aragon had four children: John, Jr., Allison, Lisa and Joel.

John's health began to fail in late-1976. The week before he died, a group of friends and I hosted a reunion at the Sheraton Hotel in Albuquerque to pay tribute to a man who had enjoyed a long and prosperous career in education in our state. John died in Albuquerque in February 1997.

The "Follies" had a following as strong as did the boys' athletic teams. Anna Mae King, in the period of around 1947 and '48, comes up in conversation over and over. They were synonymous, of course, with the director, Lena Archuleta. Once in a while former students tell me about their sense of isolation at El Rito, but there is not much question that the campus had the pulse of some of the culture of the rest of the USA. This is a reminder to readers of the famous cast, beginning with Judy Garland and Fred Astair, that constituted the *Ziegfeld Follies* that had one of the longest runs of a musical motion picture in the US. The movie, which debuted in 1946, was inspired by the Broadway show of the same name that ran from 1907 to about 1936. It must have been wonderful to witness the "Follies" in El Rito. The students performed the play at the Lensic Theater in Santa Fe, according to Anna Mae, and other places, by invitation.

Pat Vigil, also Class of '48, was another boy from the *barrio* in Barelas, Albuquerque. He was born there in May 1929 and attended the West San José Elementary School. He met John Aragón there, were friends since elementary school.

Pat followed his older brothers and sister to El Rito; Pat says that his brother Alonzo probably followed their uncle Lencho García, who attended the Spanish American Normal School in an earlier time. Pat and John first attended the Normal School in eighth grade.

Pat has a good memory, appreciation for history and a deep love of the Normal at El Rito and the people who were there. Although basketball was first among sports, Pat remembered the 1946 baseball season, the year the Eagle captured third place in the state play-offs, vividly. Who wouldn't? In '46 large schools and small schools all played in the same pool, and for a small school to excel it had to be unusually strong. I have included a photograph of the '46 Eagles baseball team. Pat was in tenth grade, played right field. Pat started naming standouts on the team to me, and it turned out he thought the world of all his teammates. Charlie Brown was their coach.

I received the impression from Pat first, and several more of the students of the time, that music and art were as important to them as sports. They spoke with the same fervor about the *Orquesta Típica*, the Follies, and northern New Mexico woodwork and furniture that they reserved for sports.

Pat also gave me a photograph of the girls' basketball team that is in this group of pictures from late-forties at the Normal. He also gave me the picture that includes Wallace Archuleta, Joe Grant, Alonzo Vigil and Eloy Abeyta. Pat loved their warmth and camaraderie.

Pat and John, always inseparable, both went to Highlands University after high school. Pat was inducted into the US Army in 1951, and had to return to Highlands to complete his studies.

The Army shipped Pat and a friend and classmate, Juan "Pepino" Vigil, to Hawaii for training. It was the time of the Korean War and they were assigned to the 35th Regimental Combat Team, which were elite fighting forces. I asked Pat about these elite teams and he told me unhesitatingly, "We weren't looking for good conduct metals."

American troops with Pat had the assignment of recapturing South Korea from the Chinese who had overrun the peninsula. All he can remember of the earliest days were those doggone mountains, and that he had to lug a machine-gun on his back. Regretfully, he learned that Juan Vigil had died in battle in Korea. He was the last New Mexican to have seen Juan.

Pat Vigil is a disabled Korean War veteran; I don't know the nature of his wounds. I do know, however, the emotion with which he speaks of others, friend and foe. He told me about a fierce fight against the Chinese against very difficult odds and about the heroics of a Floridian, "hispanic guy", who disobeyed orders and refused to retreat. Pat's orders, about a hundred yards away, were to hold his position; he did. Pat recalled that the hero from Florida kept the sector from collapsing, and he killed about 250 Chinese soldiers. The happy part is that the man was awarded the US Medal of Honor. Pat said to me, "He gave us a sense of hope and dignity."

Pat came home in '53, and married Rosalie Manzanares from La Puente. Rosalie was also of the Class of '48 at the Normal School; she is deceased. Pat has lived in Albuquerque for many years after the war and following his university studies.

Tony García is of the Class of '49. Everyone remembers Tony, but Tony hesitated to say too much about himself, only that he loved the Normal. He told me, "It's the best thing that happened to me. It kept me out of trouble." When we see Tony today, he is a lot other than a guy who would get into trouble. Physically, he is more athletic than fellows forty years his junior. He is a competitive runner, long past age sixty and well into his next decade, and has remained youthful.

Tony went to El Rito with a brother Ralph. An older brother, Ruben García, had attended El Rito for two years. Ruben died at Clark's Field in Oahu in 1941 during the Japanese attack on Pearl Harbor.

What Tony did not tell me I learned from other former students. He attended Highlands University, where he played football. As a running back, he was an all-conference selection.

Tony lives in Albuquerque with his wife Laura, who is also of the Class of '49.

The Class of 1950 had a barely wider geographic distribution among its members than the classes of the Normal School during its first decade, interestingly. I knew some of them, I'll mention: Raymond Rodríguez from Pecos, Leo Sánchez from Albuquerque, Consuelo Trambley from Mora, Ernie Dow from Chilí, Ruben Archuleta from Española, and Indalesio Torres from Black Lake.

Ruben Archuleta graduated at the Northern New Mexico Normal School with the Class of '50, after a stint in the US Army.

If you want to learn about his brother Gilbert, talk with Ruben. If you wish to discuss Ruben, find someone who knows him. Ruben is modest in the extreme.

Ruben went to sixth grade at El Rito in 1942 when Gilbert left to the Navy. Ruben started to show promise as a baseball pitcher as a youngster—I mean like little league and junior league age. Coach Charlie Brown asked Ruben to play ball in eighth grade. By ninth grade, Ruben was a starting pitcher with great confidence in his catcher, Andrés "Casey" Martinez. In spring 1946, at age 15, Ruben pitched a rare no-hitter against Los Alamos High School. Pat Vigil told me about this, Ruben nodded and, finally, opened up to tell me about 1946. Ruben played baseball, football and basketball. The baseball Eagles advanced to the state tournament in baseball; El Rito took third place.

As soon as school was out in '46, Ruben joined the US Army. Don't ask too many questions; Ruben was fifteen. He always was a tall boy, probably looked a couple of years older than his age.

In January 1948, Ruben returned to El Rito, looking forward to playing football, basketball and baseball. If you open up a 1950 *El Chamisal*, here is this photograph of Ruben, the grown boy, extolling his good looks. We don't wish to embarrass him, but the photograph does reveal how the Army would err in inducting the youngster before his time.

Ruben continued building on his local fame as a baseball pitcher by pitching in summer adult leagues in northern New Mexico. He said to me that he had "only a fastball and counted on good control" for his successes. You wonder nowadays how much expert coaching would have done to develop talent of boys like Ruben to achieve beyond anyone's dreams in this sport that he loved.

After high school, Ruben went to work for the Los Alamos Scientific Laboratory, and he worked there from November 1952 to June 1986 when he retired. He and Virginia Montoya married in January 1953. They have four grown children: Larry, Marcella, Carlos and Orlando. Carlos Archuleta worked with us in the metals and machining at Northern New Mexico Community College in the early '80s. Ruben, Virginia and their family reside in Española.

Danny Chavez, Evangeline Manzanares, Evangeline Martinez and Helen Valdez are of the Class of 1951.

Evangeline Martinez has been active with the Alumni Association for a number of years. Evangeline Manzanares was class valedictorian; Danny Chavez was the salutatorian.

Helen Valdez is of the Class of 1951. We read earlier about her father, Sixto Valdez, who received his education at the Normal School in the early 1920s. Helen's brother Eli, who graduated at the Northern New Mexico Normal School in 1955, has been very active in the Normal School Alumni Association throughout his adult life.

Helen was born in 1933; Eli about four years later in '37. They have a brother Ernest whom I have not met; he attended the Normal School briefly.

Helen first went to the Normal School in sixth grade, as a boarding student. She attended sixth, seventh and eighth grades in El Rito, but when her father took a teaching position in Tierra Amarilla she went there with her family during grades 10 and 11. She returned to the Normal School for 11th and 12th grades and graduated at the Normal.

After high school, Helen attended Adams State College in Colorado, transferred to New Mexico Highlands University, where she graduated. She continued graduate work at Highlands during her teaching career. She taught elementary school for 28 years in the Española Public Schools, where she retired in 1986.

Helen returned to the Normal School, Northern New Mexico Community College at El Rito, and learned weaving. She became a very competent weaver, displaying her works throughout New Mexico.

Helen and Ted Bency were married in 1955. Ted is deceased; Helen resides in Los Lunas.

The Class of 1952 was a small class. I'll make special mention of two students whom I got to know many years after they left the Normal School.

Arturo "Casey" Martinez was one of the legends among athletes when I was a student at the Normal School. He was the youngest of three brothers who attended the school. He was a very strong boy who "lettered" in baseball, basketball and football. Baseball was his strong sport, and soon out of high school he was recruited by the San Francisco Giants. Casey was in the US Army at the time, playing ball on the same team as an infielder called Darryl Strickland. Casey could possibly have been a pitcher, but instead he played shortstop, second and third base with Giant farm teams. A back injury suffered while playing in New England put a stop to his promising career with the Giants.

I met Casey in 1974, when we recruited him from a California school to coach basketball and health and physical education at New Mexico Highlands University. I was the Academic Dean. Casey had by then attended universities and acquired a master's degree at Stanford. He had some coaching experience, mostly high school in New Mexico and California, and he became a very successful coach at Highlands. Very soon after he joined Highlands University, he became athletic director.

He resigned at Highlands, eventually, and became superintendent of schools in the Pojoaque school district. He lived near Conchas Lake after retirement; Casey Martinez is deceased.

Regino Salazar, also of the Class of '52, deserves a very special mention. He is one of the individuals who influenced the development of the Normal School after its primary mission had been diverted by the uncontrollable forces of history.

Regino was born in July 1933 in Española. Following the premature death of his mother, Regino began attending at El Rito at age 13 in eighth grade. He was a very popular youngster, known for his intelligence and love of sports. He participated on teams in track, baseball, basketball and football. He was a baseball catcher, and in spite of his small size, he was a blocking back on the football team that played in the old style of a single wing. Regino graduated high school at the Northern New Mexico Normal School in spring 1952; he was the class valedictorian.

After high school, Regino attended New Mexico Highlands University and Northern Arizona University where he obtained a bachelor's degree in business administration. He continued playing football and baseball, the latter sport into his advanced years.

In 1957, Regino joined the US Army and served with his country's occupation forces in South Korea. He continued playing baseball for an armed services team.

Regino's sense of humor is illustrated in a story that I know approximately. Michael Branch was serving in Korea, but did not know the whereabouts of Regino. One day, as Michael was taking photographs of other friends, he stepped back and bumped into someone from whom he asked, "Sorry, excuse me." The other fellow said, "That's the way you guys from El Rito are, pushing your way around." To Michael's surprise, of course, it was old Reggie, as he was know to his buddies from the Normal.

After his hitch in the Army was up, Regino returned to the Española valley to run the family store in El Guache. It was during his adult life that Regino began to make his leadership felt as community organizer and servant. He, naturally, promoted and sponsored local athletic teams. In the early 1970s, as a result of his brother Dennis's appointment to the Normal School's Board of Regents, Regino became interested in the future of the school, which during the early part of the decade was known as the New Mexico Technical Vocational School. He joined forces with people who believed that the Vocational School should also include academic instruction, and thus they founded Northern New Mexico Community College.[17] His brother Dennis has told me that Regino organized members of the community on behalf of this effort, and represented the community in testimony given before the old Board of Educational Finance, the state agency responsible for funding higher education in this state. Thus it was that Regino Salazar contributed to one of the principal efforts historically that advanced the aims of this college.

In a later effort at the turn of the new century, Regino Salazar helped the communities involving northern Española, El Guache and Hernandez to establish a new water system, including a highly productive water well. *Agua Sana*, as the water system is known, will continue to serve its members in this area for a long time to come.

Regino Salazar passed away in November 2005 at age 72.

Students who graduated in spring 1953 left the campus a few months before I arrived for ninth grade, but I later got to know one student with whom I became friends, Charlie Aragon. When I was in tenth grade, Charlie spent one year with us at El Rito in charge of the senior boys's dormitory. He was quiet, extremely polite and soft-spoken, and a good chess player. He spent time with me, teaching me the game of chess.

Later in adult life, I came to know Charlie as John Aragon's brother. That explained some things to me. Namely, Charlie is exceedingly modest, and he would rather spend his time talking about his older brother John. Charlie is still modest, quiet and polite, but he is also thoughtful.

Charlie was preceded at the Normal School by an uncle, Lorenzo "Lencho" García and by John. Lencho was apparently one of the young men who started football at El Rito, in the 1930s.

Charlie was a basketball athlete at El Rito, as you would expect a guy about six foot three to be. He was also a good student, and after high school he went on to the university and became a teacher. He spent his entire career with the Albuquerque Public Schools, where he was also a principal.

Charlie speaks knowledgeably about what the Normal School

did for young people who attended. Since he was there during the Joe Grant years, he had first-hand familiarity with the *esprit-de-corps* that was maintained among both students and teachers, and which he has described to me. He has also described to me what occurred after Joseph B. Grant's departure, which had a profound influence on campus life.

I am indebted to Charlie Aragon for some of my understanding of the Normal School during years prior to my attending as a student.

The Class of 1954 imbued much of the spirit of the old Spanish American Normal School, although I sensed that the students were pleased mightily by the new name, and they sang some words to the "Stars and Stripes Forever" in which they pledged victory and other great things to NNMNS. In a word, this was a group of students who spoke of their school *con sentimiento*, although the English language was beginning to prevail on campus. The *Orquésta Típica*, spanish and mexican music, and even the Follies, were clearly of the past. Rock and roll had not yet displaced popular tunes of Frank Sinatra, Johnny Ray, the Four Lads, the Andrews Sisters, Nat Cole, and Patti Page. Recording artists like Clyde McPhatter, the Dominoes, Muddy Waters, Little Richard, Fats Domino, and the king himself, Elvis Presley, had not made the scene yet, but they would, later in the decade of the '50s. Radio was still "in", but well on the way out. Television would begin to take over the most popular means of keeping in touch with the world, although the latter was seldom a great preoccupation of the vast majority of us. As a popular comedian would say later in the '60s, we lived for the here and now.

Michael Branch was one of the members of the Class of '54. Even I could tell, thirteen in ninth grade, that Michael was youngish, not much fuzz on that face. Because many of us gravitated back to the Normal in adult life, I got to know Michael later on. Michael's mother was the former Anna McGrath from Roy. His dad David Branch, also from Roy, had attended the Normal School in the 1920s. Michael found a home in El Rito, after his father had perished in an automobile accident; Michael was the age ten and in seventh grade.

When I interviewed Michael for this book, he readily offered that he was a kid that needed El Rito, echoing my sentiments. Although he was socially ill-equipped for living with older boys, he immediately felt nurturing care from teachers, staff and students. Lena and Wallace Archuleta immediately came to mind. Later, there were Ruben Rose, Charles Solomon, Facundo Rodriguez, Tom Roybal, Louis Robert Trujillo and many more friends among teachers and staff.

Michael has vivid recollection of the fall of '48, when the typhoid epidemic invaded the school. His best guess is that he must have had plenty of antibodies, acquired on the farm in Dilia, his previous home, because he avoided contracting typhoid fever. If you are unfamiliar with east central New Mexico, the Pecos River flows through Dilia and other farm communities; prior to about 1950, a lot of people drank water directly from the Pecos, as was Michael's experience.

Michael worked for room and board, as did a majority of students. He recalls, as I do, that supervision of boys was lax, which we welcomed. Girls were amply supervised by women in charge of the dormitory; boys self-supervised extremely well. Aside from some hazing by older students, life was pleasant and students felt secure while on campus.

After college, Michael attended the College of Santa Fe and served a hitch in the US Army. He has resided in Santa Fe with his wife Maida and three sons. He is a successful businessman, owner of Branch Realty.

In January 2003, Michael Branch was appointed to the Board of Regents of Northern New Mexico Community College by Governor Bill Richardson. Michael was to guide the Board as Chairman during much of his tenure on the Board, but most certainly during a historic time for Northern New Mexico Community College when it was granted authority by the New Mexico legislature to offer the bachelor's degree to train teachers, as had been stipulated in the purpose of the school in 1909.[18]

Michael Branch was the Chairman of the Board of Regents of Northern New Mexico College.

David Borunda is also a member of the Class of 1954, whom I first knew during the 1953-54 school year at El Rito.

David was born in 1935 in Velarde, which was the first home to several of our alumni, including this author. At a very early age, David moved with his mother to Raton, where he started public school in 1941. David had been orphaned from his father in June 1942, when his father died. He and his brother Archie found their way to El Rito at a very young age; David was in seventh grade, Archie in sixth. David remembers that children his age were housed in dorm 1, in what was called the Junior Building. The boys had very little opportunity for home sickness or for moping about; they immediately began to make friends and to acclimate to close living with other, mostly older, children.

With an amount of sadness, David remembers that Archie contracted typhoid fever in 1948. Archie was one of the children who had to go home, as a result of the epidemic. Archie did not return to El Rito until ninth grade, and decided to stay only one more year. Readers of this would have to imagine how the illness affected these students, and their feeling about the school and environment.

David is one of the students who witnessed the change in campus environment with the departure of Joseph Grant. He was a generally cheerful and outgoing boy, took great pride in participation in football. He also valued his studies and did well academically.

After high school and a service career, David returned to New Mexico and renewed acquaintances with many of the alumni. He took interest in the newer institution, Northern New Mexico Community College, and in I appointed him to the Northern New Mexico College Foundation. David and his wife Chery reside in Albuquerque.

Richard García was an Albuquerque boy who, also, went to the Normal at a young age in 1948 in sixth grade. The boarding school seemed a great atmosphere, although parents had to come for him. He was ill and convalesced a "long time" for a sixth grader.

After he returned, he like the school fine, but thought hazing was brutal. Students were paddled by older kids. Richard voiced the same concern echoed by other students: the school lacked in academic quality. There were teachers whom he appreciated, Reuben Rose being first among them. Summers he and Ted Martinez, his cousin, would return to Albuquerque to work for the City and for Korber's Hardware Store, he remembers.

Richard played football in high school. He, David Borunda and Dennis Salazar were older boys whom I remember as "men about campus."

After high school in 1954, Richard attended UNM for a year, then enlisted in the US Navy. He remained in California and completed a BA degree at the University of Redlands. He spent a career in corporate real estate. Richard resides in Santa Fe.

Dennis Salazar graduated with the Class of '54; he is the proud brother of Regino Salazar, both of whom I have written about in these pages.

When I arrived at El Rito in 1953, Dennis was one of the students who greeted me. He was student proctor in the junior boys' dormitory, as was Lupe Juárez.

Dennis and Regino began attending the Normal School at a very early age; Regino went there in 1946, Dennis in 1947. Their mother had died when they were small children, and although Dennis loved his stepmother, he felt that the campus at El Rito was god-send. He is able to describe the great sense of belonging that kids acquired there, many believing that "students were brothers and sisters." Dennis tended to remain on campus even during summers. Although he remembers vaguely the typhoid epidemic of 1948, neither he nor Regino became ill.

The job as dorm proctor when he was in twelfth grade was a plum; Dennis had worked at more difficult jobs. He remembers fondly Mr. Glenn George who drank lemon juice each morning and advocated cold showers. Glenn George and Frank Byers lived in the Junior Building; Dennis got to know them well.

Dennis was a serious young man and a good student. He played football, basketball and baseball at different times, but football was his sport. He was an all-conference quarterback on a single-wing team, which meant that he was blocking back a great deal of the time.

After high school he attended the University of New Mexico one year. He took and job and married, but was ultimately drafted into the US Army.

After returning from the armed services to Española, he slowly began to reintegrate successfully into the community. He and his brother became successful businessmen, never forgetting their dedication and duty to community. Dennis was elected by voters of Rio Arriba County to the 1969 Constitutional Convention held at the State Capitol in 1969. Bruce King was chairman of the Convention; Dennis got to know him well and in 1971, when Bruce King became Governor, he appointed Dennis to the Board of Regents of the New Mexico Tehnical Vocational School at El Rito.

Dennis's association with the NMTVS was to become long

and fruitful. The change in the NMTVS to Northern New Mexico Community College, owed in great measure to Dennis's efforts, as described in these pages. In addition to being on the founding Board of Northern New Mexico Community College, Dennis was appointed to the Board of Regents again in January 2003 by Governor Bill Richardson. Dennis was a member of the Board in 2004 when the New Mexico legislature finally granted authority to the institution to begin offering the baccalaureate degree. Dennis Salazar has been a mainstay on behalf of Northern New Mexico College, the present institution, and higher education in the North.

Dennis is the proprietor of a liquor establishment in Española, the Saints 'N' Sinners, with his son Kenny. He resides in Española, as he has for many years since his days as an Army soldier.

In 2001, the Board of Regents named the building designed for general eduction on the Española Campus as the Dennis Salazar Building.

We regret the death of Dennis Salazar in November 2020.

Priscilla Trujillo Schafer is a member of the Class of 1954.

Social and cultural history of El Rito are very important, they describe the site and circumstances of our school, the Spanish American Normal School. Priscilla and students of that era share a keen interest in this history.

Priscilla has an excellent memory of times that she was a small child in late '30s and early '40s. She grew up in Placitas in a house her grandparents built. Her relatives were the Trujillos from El Rito, a very fair-skinned people, as she is, and the Ortegas from Vallecitos. Priscilla remembers that her grandfather hauled freight from Denver, CO with the use of oxen and she remembers that the present roadway to El Rito dates from about 1946.

Priscilla started school at the Placitas Elementary School at the age of five; she spoke no English. Max Varoz, a great favorite with many of us, was Principal. She resulted, also, being a young high school student, since she was promoted from seventh to ninth grade, at which time she transferred over to the Normal School. She was age thirteen.

One of the fond memories Priscilla enjoys involve the year 1948. She says her father still owned a horse-drawn wagon, but it was the year that her brother Norberto graduated from the high school at the Normal, first in his class. She remembers that her brother soon departed for the US Air Force. He then returned to New Mexico State University on the GI Bill, and as I have mentioned previously, he had a career at the White Sands Missile Range as a mathematician.

Priscilla loves the Normal School, but as in the case of many youngsters from El Rito, she has mixed feelings about how the school was run. I met her as a ninth grader, she was a high school senior, very friendly and kind to me. It was friendships that the students made at the Normal that were enduring. She also spoke with fondness of teachers, Tom Roybal and Nina Myers. Ms. Myers, particularly, encouraged Priscilla to remain in school and do well. Priscilla, of course, could readily compete with all of her classmates academically. Even today, Priscilla does not understand the indifference of the administration at the Normal toward youngsters from El Rito. Parents had to petition for students to be allowed a place for lunch on campus, since winters are cold at El Rito. She felt that staff were unkind to day students, and would not provide for transportation for after-school activities---ball games, band, and special events.

Priscilla Trujillo graduated from the high school, and did not have many options. In particular, money was scarce for continuation of an education; this was considerably before the era of federal financial aid for students. Parents did not encourage girls, in particular, to continue studying. It was more common to take a job.

Priscilla took a temporary job at the State Department of Education, which was housed at the old St. Michael's College in Santa Fé. In the fall of '54, she remade acquaintance with Joseph Grant, who was State Treasurer, and went to work in the Treasurer's office. She enjoyed those years, but in 1958 she decided to join the Our Lady of Victory Missionary Sisters in Huntington, Indiana, in their convent. She remained one year, but her health failed and she returned to New Mexico a year later. This time she went to work for the State Engineer---Steve Reynolds, at the time.

Following her stay in Indiana, she met Jim Schafer, who would become her husband. She and Jim have three children, Dolores, Michael and Patrick and have resided in Albuquerque. After this move, Priscilla worked for the City of Albuquerque until her retirement.

In January 1995, Priscilla was appointed to the Board of Regents of Northern New Mexico Community College. She and Jim were living part of the time in El Rito where she was assisting with care for an elderly parent. This gave Priscilla opportunity to reacquaint herself with the old Normal School in in its new incarnation, which she loved. She told me that she felt that the "Community College was the best thing that could have happened here, " meaning, of course, northern New Mexico.

Jim took courses in Spanish-colonial furniture making and in weaving, and although they were accomplished weavers, both Jim and Priscilla enjoyed the ambient at El Rito that nurtured these traditional arts.

Priscilla Trujillo Schafer became a member of the 1996 Board of Regents of Northern New Mexico Community College[19], appointed by Governor Gary Johnson. Priscilla was reappointed for a second term to the Board, but she resigned upon moving to Albuquerque again in 2001.

Priscilla was a member of a very good organization and a strong Board member...back at her old school at the Normal.

Joe Martínez, Class of 1954, deserves mention here; we regret that he has passed away.[20]

Joe Martínez as a young man may have been the most talented athlete ever to step on a basketball court in our state. As in most cases involving athletes of past years, this statement may be disputed, but those who were lucky to see him would attest to what I say. In 1954 he led the El Rito Eagles to the District 2B championship, which Frank Byers, the coach, said was a first for the Normal School. But even before the season began, and as school was just starting in fall 1953, you could sense the excitement on campus because Joe was returning for his final year of high school. I went to see him put on a one man exhibition of moves as poetry, and ball through the hoop, almost without fail. This fella was moving as Kobe Bryant would fifty years later. No kidding.

Dennis Salazar, who knew Joe a lot better, told me that Joe handled the ball as though he owned it, as a part of his big hands. He played as power forward on a fairly small team; Joe may have been about five feet eleven (inches, of course.)

The Eagles started out slowly, but they won their last eight games prior to sweeping three games in the district tournament. Joe particularly shone against the big men, usually bigger schools, too. They finished the season with a record of 17 wins 8 losses, losing their final game on the way to the state tournament; the Eagles lost to Maxwell, which finished as the second best team that year. Maxwell had a player who measured 6'8", tall in those days.

Frank Byers was coach of this very successful squad that included Mike Jaramillo, Joe Martinez, Lupe Juarez, Eli Valdez, Oscar Saiz, Estolano Marquez, Eligio Jaramillo, Dennis Branch, Chris Delgado and Sammy Esquibel.

Joe Martinez died in winter 2005; Frank Byers passed away five years later in 2010.

You can tell the passing of an era. The campus was different after 1955. Students of the classes of '54 and '55 were the last group of the Joe Grant period. Teachers left also: Corine Myers and Sam Ortega after spring '54, and then Reuben Rose, Ed Grant, Humberto Gurulé and Frank Byers all departed after graduation in '55. A lot of "institutional memory" was gone, and with it older notions of tradition, things that mattered and those that didn't.

Members of the Class of 1955 seemed a little more accessible to a kid like me in tenth grade, and I got to know many of them rather well. Students with whom I have remained in contact are almost the perfect group, however.

Esperanza Baca is one of the students who graduated in '55. She has a sister Socorro who started ninth grade with me, but she chose to graduate a year early.

Esperanza started school in El Rito in a one-room school. In second grade, she enrolled at the Normal School.

Although she liked some of her teachers, and speaks fondly of John Romero, the director of band, she faults the Normal School for not doing more for students from El Rito. She voices objections to practices at the school which I have described a couple of times in these pages. In summary, the school was a lot less accessible to day students than it was to boarding students.

Esperanza was a very good student and she and a close friend, Arlene Gonzales, were valedictorian and salutatorian, respectively, in 1955. She wished that she had learned to write, but her school had stressed New Mexico history and geography.[21] Esperanza, always serious about scholarship, does not feel that there was a great deal to be learned at the Normal School.

Esperanza is one of the students whom I got to know better after high school than during our stay at the Normal. I did learn from her that she came from a family of very modest means, and she worked summers in Santa Fe at Gene Autry Studios. Upon graduation from high school, she attended New Mexico Highlands University on a music scholarship. She again had to work hard and took a job doing janitorial work at the University. [22] After one semester at Highlands University, Esperanza met her future husband, Nelson Gonzales, originally from Taos, and the couple soon took off for Los Angeles where she enrolled at California State University in Los Angeles. Esperanza also holds a master's degree from Highlands University.

During my early years as president at the Normal School, I got to know Esperanza and Nelson Gonzales. Esperanza was Principal at the El Rito Elementary School, a position for which she gained the respect of the community and area educators. Both she and her husband dedicated entire careers to public education. Nelson was a counselor at the Normal School at one time, but he is primarily known as the Superintendent of the Mesa Vista School District during periods in his career.

Esperanza and Nelson are retired from public education and reside in El Rito. Esperanza has been writing a history of El Rito and the immediate area; she freely shared her historical knowledge with me.

Albert Esparcen is from Trujillo, which is forty miles southeast of Las Vegas where he would have had to travel to high school had he not known about the Normal School at El Rito. Albert is one of the real success stories of the Normal School, in my estimation.[23]

Albert attended elementary school, grades one through eight, at the Ventanas Consolidated Schools. In seventh and eighth grades he had a teacher with who was familiar with with the Northern New Mexico Normal School. Horacio Ulibarrí encouraged Albert to go to El Rito for high school. Ulibarrí spoke with the parents and Albert, and the parents resolved to help their son. It helped to know that another student from Trujillo, Salomon Archuleta, was at El Rito.

During our interview, Albert recalled life at home as a youngster, where his first language became Spanish. His mother spoke English, but conversations at home were in Spanish. Albert felt that life in Trujillo tended to be "socially impoverished" without a lot of outside contact culturally. There was no electricity or water systems in those days. The family had a radio, battery operated, that provided some music in Spanish and English, typically of the Mexican and country-western variety. There was a cistern for water, and it provided a place for some refrigeration, in addition. Albert said, "We were like pioneers; self-sufficient, really."

This self-reliance would be a great help to Albert at El Rito, where his mother accompanied him for his first year. Albert and his mother took the bus from Trujillo to Española, then a mail truck to El Rito. Albert thereafter stayed on campus most of the time, where he worked part time. About the Normal, Albert stated, "I loved it from day one."

Albert was a popular kid; he played football and was on the boxing team. He is one of a small population of athletes who has remained active throughout life, participating in senior olympics even today. He was one of several serious students, but he found time to court his girl friend, Carol Medina, from Abiquiu, whom he would marry years later.

Albert's memories of life at the Normal are pleasant. Although there was some hazing, he felt the idea was to endure it and "fit in." He appreciated that there was little supervision of the boys, although traveling off campus was not easy. Students would hitch-hike to Española (our nearest town), not knowing whether there would be a ride available at the end of the day.

Albert's education at El Rito was adequate. The teacher who stands out in his recollection is Charles Salomon, who taught English. Albert graduated in spring 1955.

Albert enlisted in the US Air Force after high school, was married to Carol, and returned to Santa Fe attend college. He loved the College of Santa Fe and graduated *cum laude*. He subsequently completed a doctoral program in public health and physical rehabilitation at the University of New Mexico. He "tracked down" Horacio Ulibarrí in 1985 to thank him for his interest and support about thirty years back in Trujillo.

Albert had a long and beneficial career with the US Public Health Services from which he is retired. Albert and Carol and their family have lived in Santa Fe. We regret that Carol Medina Esparscen is deceased.

Albert Esparcen succumbed to covid this year (in 2022).

Lupe Juárez, also of the Class of '55, is someone whom I don't see often, although I, and everyone of that time, remembers Lupe for his athleticism. Lupe first went to El Rito in fifth grade, one of the younger boarding students about whom I have known. Lupe has an older brother, Benito Juárez, who also attended the Normal, Class of '52.

For a not-very-big guy, Lupe may be the finest all around athlete of any time at the Normal School. He played football, basketball and baseball, and even tried other sports more casually. He is the school's first genuine "All-American," and it was in football. In his junior year he made the Parade Magazine High School All-American Football Team. He played end on a good team that won a district championship, but lost in the state play-off game to Aztec, which went on to win the state title. Lupe was known as an elusive pass receiver, remembered for his acrobatic catches.

Lupe was a natural leader who seldom had to assert himself. On the basketball court, he could take charge and was a real "money player." I witnessed a tournament game in which the El Rito Eagles played Pojoaque High School. I've related this story many times, but I included the story in *Children of the Normal School* but I shan't do that now. Suffice it to say that Lupe Juárez was a lot of fun to watch.

After high school, it happened that Lupe and I were employed by the same company, ACF Industries in Albuquerque, who did contract work for the Atomic Energy Commission in the early 1960s. I got to know Lupe a bit better then. He has resided in Albuquerque, his home town.

Ted Martínez, also of the Class of 1955, is known today for his contributions to public and higher education in New Mexico. When I first met him at El Rito, I thought perhaps Ted would make his mark in politics; later, it was the military; in fact, he has many talents, but he chose education in which to invest them.

Ted, an Albuquerque boy from the old Martineztown, went to El Rito in sixth grade. He was from a very large family, and welcomed privacy and attention that he received at the Normal School.

He was one of the children who had typhoid fever after a month and one-half on campus. Ted went home and convalesced in quarantine until April of the following year when he was released by the Health Department. He did not return to the Normal School until 10th grade;

Ted remained at the Normal School until the end of first semester of Senior year.

I enjoy telling a couple of stories about Ted Martinez, whom I am fortunate to have known well. First, with regard to politics: as a new student on campus, I was impressed by the social life and how very much there was to do. My first Sunday evening, there was a movie in Cutting Hall, a beautiful building, plain, with hardwood floors and adobe walls. There were sets of rows of chairs, separated by a wide aisle. Girls sat on the right; boys on the left. As I entered, I noticed a hush, deep murmuring by the kids, and, toward the front, a very sunburnt slender kid of about seventeen holding a conference with a couple of elderly women. None of this mattered to me right then, but soon there was an announcement: boys and girls could sit together. There was a roar and applause, and a mad scramble by boys and girls to sit with their friends. The skinny kid with the flat-top haircut, who had negotiated the deal, was, of course, Ted Martínez, the diplomat.

Ted enrolled at UNM for spring semester 1955, rather than remain at El Rito. Opinions about the academic quality of an education at the Normal School vary; Ted feels he was sufficiently prepared for college and he had to take no preparatory courses. While a student, Ted joined the US Marine Reserve, but he was served with a draft notice just the same. He enlisted in the Officer Candidate School and received a commission. Ted retired from the Marine Reserve as Colonel.

After a master's degree at the University, Ted began a career in earnest. He taught at Rio Grande High School, and subsequently entered the employment of the University of New Mexico for some very enjoyable years, as he recalls. He worked in some important student services grant programs, but soon he was given charge of the Student Union. He earned a reputation for his negotiating skill, and when Ferrel Heady became President of the University, Ted was made Assistant to the President. These were difficult years in which there was much student unrest in universities throughout the United States. In New Mexico, issues centered around civil rights, with hispanic students asserting their rights for the first time in the state's history. Ted performed well, both on behalf of the University and to benefit of students.

It was during these years that Ted made a run for a position of the Albuquerque Public Schools' Board of Education. He held a position for several years, during Albuquerque's explosion in growth. Ernest

Stapleton and Frank Sanchez were two superintendents with whom Ted worked as a board member, and whom he admired.

In 1984, Ted was appointed Executive Secretary of the Board of Educational Finance by Governor Toney Anaya. The Governor had appointed a group of us, New Mexico citizens and educators, to assist the old BEF with planning and funding, and to entertain the idea of creating a stronger advocate for higher education. Fred Harris, former senator from Oklahoma and former US presidential candidate, was our chairman. This gave rise to the Commission of Higher Education which Ted served until 1989.

Ted Martínez was appointed President of the Albuquerque Technical-Vocational Institute in July 1989, in which capacity he served for five years until his retirement.

Ted resides in Albuquerque with his wife Dolores. He has daughters Demetria and Elena and a son Dominic; he also has several grandchildren.

Class of 1956 was not a large class. Even with a couple of students in my class who chose to graduate a year early, the class of '56 numbered 33. In spite of this, several of their students were greatly popular among us, Kathy Tafoya who graduated early, and Lydia Jaramillo from Vallecitos were valedictorian and salutatorian of that class, respectively. Kathy was President Clory Tafoya's daughter.

The Class of '56 included a very pleasant, soft-spoken young man from San Ysidro, Estolano Marquez. I noticed him early on when I arrived on campus as he courted a student from my home in Velarde, Olivia Salazar. Estolano was exceptionally friendly; still is.

Estolano was preceded at the Normal School by his sister Cassie of the Class of 1949.

You may well imagine that for a boy with a lot of interest in sports, and residing far from the nearest high school, as Estolano did, the school at El Rito was a haven...for football and basketball, especially. This is a fellow interested in playing ball, not especially interested in the attention he got as a result. Estolano was a good runner, swift as opposed to just fast, a good trackman who loved team sports, also.

I asked Estolano to explain something to me; I knew him as wise in the ways of young men on the ball court or field. I have mentioned previously that, in 1955, Frank Byers resigned as teacher and coach of the basketball Eagles. Who was hired to replace him was Vicente Martínez, his only experience coaching basketball was as an assistant. Yet Vince Martinez, with Estolano Marquez the only senior in 1956, molded a group of youngsters into a formidable team during his very first year as coach, the '55-56 season. The 1956 Eagles posted a record of 17 wins and five losses during the regular season, and breezed to the District 2B finals where they beat a good Pojoaque team 51-47. The Eagles finished third in the state tournament, and this was start of a brief dynasty.

Estolano explained, certainly, this was a team of strong kids, quick and fast, but what mattered was the superb conditioning of Vince Martínez's teams. This was to remain the Eagles' hallmark for another three years.

Estolano, always the wiser member on the team, was surrounded by a group of youngsters on the starting team: David Valdez, Dennis Branch, Ralph Martínez and Porfirio Sánchez. Estolano knew the best was yet to come from this bunch.

Estolano finished high school, married Olivia and moved briefly to his home in San Ysidro. Jobs were in Albuquerque, where they moved. He and Olivia and their family have resided in Albuquerque.

Robert Torres was the first of four brothers to attend the Normal School. The Torres family was from Black Lake, deep in the Sangre de Cristo range of mountains where a good winter for snow produces beautiful lush green grass in summer.

Indalesio had been the first brother to attend; he graduated at the Normal School in 1950. Although I know all of the brothers, I know Indalesio least; he has resided in California.

Manuel followed; he was a graduate of the Class of '54. Manny, as he was called, was affable and good natured. He worked abroad many years. I regret that Manuel is deceased.

The youngest brother, Luis, I have written about in these pages with his Class of '59.

Bob was probably more like the older brothers in that he knew he had to leave Black Lake to go to school. Education was very important in his family; it was imperative that he attend high school, at least. Taos, the nearest large town, was not an option. Off he went to El Rito; Manny was there.

Bob loved the campus, although he realizes today that it was never to seem as beautiful and orderly as it did when Bob arrived there in fall 1953. He liked dormitory life, too, and never felt like just going home. No homesickness. Bob adjusted well to other students, knew whom to avoid and who would become his friends. He knew boarding schools can be special, and it was.

Bob was pleased with his education; it was good. He refers to Reuben Rose as an icon of the school, as he was a favorite with so many students. Although Bob was, later, a better college student than he showed at El Rito, he learned some valuable lessons, like how to get along well with people.

Bob told me the outside world was of no great importance at the time. "We were very secure. Ike was president. Life was so good in El Rito that we really didn't need the world." It is not as though students lived there in isolation. Bob grew to love the music of the '50s and read Somerset Maughm-he got "Of Human Bondage" from Ed Grant-and a biography of Mahatma Ghandi, who impressed Bob with his humility. So, it was only a personal isolation that was felt, not cultural deprivation. Television was not important at the time, and the quality of things seen and heard was excellent, even if quantity was not overwhelming.

Bob enjoys reminiscing about old times at the Normal. Joking was always a good device to allay hostility among students. He has managed to maintain contact through the alumni and its organization.

Bob became a quiet, studious man. He has an architectural degree in planning from California Polytechnical State University in San Luis Obispo, CA; he also has a law degree. He has traveled, and he worked abroad in Saudi Arabia for several years. He is worldly in ways that few Americans tend to be. He has told me in casual conversation about his love for London, and theater in that city.

Bob Torres resides in Taos.

George Luján would have graduated with the Class of '56, had he chosen to stay at the Normal School until the completion of his high school studies. But in August 1954, a month prior to his junior year, George enlisted in the US Navy. George is more like any of us than any single other student whom I knew. For this reason, it is worth examining how one of our schoolmates overcame adversity in order to succeed in life.

George enrolled at El Rito in 1949 for seventh grade. He had been born in 1937, and was orphaned by age five when his mother died; his pop had died when George was four years old. George had two brothers and a sister, but he had to live with an uncle for a while. A bit later he moved in with his mother's mom; she cared for him. George's brothers lived in the house and paid grandma ten bucks a month. After a while, George's brothers rented their own home and George lived with them, but he stated that he "roamed the streets of Santa Fe." George talks about this, not as a hard luck story, but with great humor. He and his brothers lived on West Manhattan (Santa Fe, not New York); it was a friendly neighborhood. George attended St. Francis elementary School. Early in life, George learned how to earn a nickel, even if as a very young boy this is all he did earn.

George's brother Raymond encouraged him to stay in school, which he did, and eventually George made his way to the Normal School at El Rito.

George Luján loved the campus. He speaks highly of the care of students for one another: "You either liked El Rito and got along (with other students), or you did not (and wouldn't like it there.)" A couple of guys named Dennis Salazar and Charlie Aragón were very helpful to George; they were slightly older boys. George remembered fondly his typing teacher, Viola Ulibarrí.

George completed a General Equivalency Diploma (GED) program while in the Navy. The State of New Mexico granted him his diploma. In 1958, George enrolled at the University of New Mexico where he met a former schoolmate, Louise Archuleta from Truchas. George and Louise were married.

Years later, in 1973, George came to El Rito once again, this time to work at the New Mexico Technical Vocational School. He lived on campus, where he was provided housing, and he took his meals in the school cafeteria.

George returned to California to school at the University of California at Irvine, in 1978.

George was the purchasing agent at Northern New Mexico Community College the next time that I saw him in 1979. [24]

George and his wife Kathy lived in Española. Kathy is deceased.

Students of the fifties knew many more kids who attended school in El Rito a year, or more, but who, because of circumstance, simply were not able to finish there. It has always been interesting to listen to the poignancy in their speech as they speak about the old school that they inhabited briefly. There were more kids like George Luján.

Names such as Richard Chávez from Albuquerque, Laura Padilla from Las Vegas, and Lorraine Maestas, a student from Española come to mind for their involvement with the Alumni.

Amarante Sánchez is another Albuquerque boy whom we knew in 1953-54. Students used a nickname for him, "Shadow." He is remembered as a bright kid, energetic, and pleasant.

Amarante was preceded at the Normal School by his brothers Melecio, Leo, and Ray Sánchez. The brothers were student athletes remembered long after their departure from El Rito. In a school in which students took delight in nicknames, the brothers were known as the *Golosos*, each in his turn in the singular.[25]

Amarante became a very successful businessman, after a stint in the armed services and extensive travel. He has been a member of the Alumni Association and one of its supporters. He made special effort to make certain that I conveyed that students of the Normal School were his family.

My classmates were the Class of 1957. In summer 2007, a few of us planned a brief reunion in Albuquerque, since most of our group no longer resided in northern New Mexico. Twelve of our members were able to attend; it was wonderful to see them: Otilia Esquibel, Polly Abeyta, Lydia Archuleta, Cecilia Archuleta, Lee Leyba, Leo García, Olivia Gomez, Ida Montoya, Laura Padilla, Gerald Martínez and Lorraine Maestas. We enjoyed the company of several guests: Celerino Archuleta, Beatrice Martínez, Florence Coriz, Albert Esparcen, Carol Medina, and Ted Martinez. I have listed only the names of former students, which you would recognize here, although all of us were with our spouses or invited guests.

I regret that some of our former classmates were ill, or could not attend for other reasons. I learned that fully twelve of our former classmates were deceased. Nancy Zamora was one of our classmates who is deceased; she and her husband Joe Montoya from Las Vegas were supporters of the organization of Alumni. After her death, Joe visited the campus at El Rito several times to commemorate her passing.

The Class of '57 tended to have fewer ties to the past at the Normal School, without lots of discussion about traditions and intimate friendships the exception rather than the rule. In part, at least, this was beneficial. We all but abolished hazing, which most dictionaries define as the requirement to do work, often humiliating, for someone on penalty of punishment for disobeying an order. The practice did raise its awful head in later years, I am told, but the Class of '57 proudly eschewed such nonsense.

My fondest recollection was the large number of very bright kids in a relatively small class. Sigfredo Maestas was valedictorian; Leo Garcia was salutatorian of the graduating class, but several more were very good students: Cecilia Archuleta, Tillie Esquibel, Connie Valdez, Lydia Archuleta, Lugie Rosanne Martinez, and Nancy Zamora.

Tillie Esquibel Lopez resides in Albuquerque. She has been a strong member of the Alumni Association, helping to keep the group together.[26]

Lee Leyba was a boy from Santa Fe; he didn't complete high school at El Rito. Lee came to the Normal School in ninth grade in 1953, and he stayed through eleventh grade. He then went in the US Coast Guard where he completed the GED program, and became successful in life.

Lee has done more than any single individual to support the Normal School Alumni Association, to promote its reunions, and to bring the children of the Normal together. He speaks with depth of feeling about happiness and content at our school.

Lee and his wife Dolly resided in Albuquerque; Lee is deceased.

The Senior Year was an exceptionally exciting time for each of us as we planned to go out and make our way in the world.[27] For some of us this meant only ratcheting up our studies at a college or university somewhere. The anticipation at times like these is comparable to jumping in frigid waters on a warm day.

Before the year ended, however, we bore witness to one of the most exciting series of events at the Normal School...ever. It was about basketball, of course.

Vince Martinez took a group of (still) young men who had acquitted themselves on the hardwood the previous year by going all the way to "state." This time the boys were a little more mature, and as superbly conditioned as the previous year, and by mid-season 1956-57 the Northern New Mexico Normal School knew this was the year. The Eagles reeled off seven straight wins before suffering their first loss over at West Las Vegas, knowing full well this was but an off-night. They then went on another tear, winning eight in a row before losing to Los Alamos, a Class A school.[28] Along the way, they won the Northern Rio Grande Conference championship by finally breaking a sweat against Española, 64-62, in the final game of the tournament. The Eagles just roared through district and regional tournaments to gain their place at the state tournament. Because the Eagles did not play an easy schedule, even the state tournament was anti-climatic for the most successful basketball season in the high school's thirty-five year history. In the final game of the state tournament, the Eagles beat a team of fairly big kids from Ruidoso by a score of 88 to 44!

During the tournament, the El Rito Normal's likelihood of winning was so great that most of the tourney buzz was about Dennis Branch, who in the semi-final game scored 43 points to set a tournament record, only to be broken the following night by a boy Kim Nash from Hobbs. But we all knew that Dennis was the better player and scorer, and moreover, we had a team we knew around him.

The Eagles in '57 were quick and strong. In addition to being a good shooting team, they could run an entire 32 minutes, which meant that their fast break functioned smoothly.[29] Seldom has their been a better all-around team. The Eagles starting five were David Valdez, Ralph Martínez, Randy Velarde, Porfirio Sánchez and Dennis Branch. Younger boys, Sam Martinez, John Jaramillo, Chris Quintana, Albert Sánchez and Joseph Valdéz, rounded out a squad of ten, the most dominating Class B team to play in New Mexico.[30]

In April 2010, several of the men on this team and invitees, I among them, gathered in Los Lunas for dinner and to pay tribute to their old coach, Vince Martinez.

Vince Martinez brought pride to the boys who played on his teams, and joy to those of us watching them. He is still known as "Marty." No one, colleagues or students, addressed him in any other fashion. He was one tough coach, and is still the same humble, quiet fellow we knew at the Normal School,

Dennis Branch, a boy from Coyote, was the towering figure in New Mexico high school basketball in '56 and '57. A prolific scorer, as a junior he averaged 28 points per game. In the following championship year, Dennis averaged about 30 points per game. He played center—as the biggest man on the team, he was only about five feet eleven inches tall—and mid-post on offense. He had excellent jumping ability, but more than that, he had excellent timing in his jump shot and a great feign to the basket that would fake the opposition out of their shoes. Dennis's point production in 1957 was one of the reasons the Eagles beat the opposition by wide margins. His total point production is still unsurpassed.

The Class of 1958 was interesting in that, for the first time in years, their were almost no students from our larger cities, Santa Fe and Albuquerque. Stanley Sanchez was the only boy from Albuquerque, in fact. There were students from far north central New Mexico; Evila Lobato was from Antonito, CO. She married Henry Serrano after high school.[31]

Juan García grew up almost next door to the Normal School. He is another of our students who did not graduate with their beginning class, but chose to go elsewhere. Juan is the son of Fabián García and Jane Goddard García. You may recall that Jane was one of the earlier graduates of the Normal School.

The elementary school on campus was in the Middle Building when Juan began his school days in El Rito. He remained at the Normal School until end of ninth grade, when he became a boarding student at The Abbey in Canyon City, Colorado. In 1958, the Normal School was short of teachers, as Juan and his parents understood, which made it a good time to transfer to a strong academic high school under the auspices of Benedictine priests.[32]

Juan returned to the Normal School years later, in 1965, after his studies with the College of Santa Fe. He joined the staff during the final years of the high school, and remained with the school as it became New Mexico Technical Vocational School, and then Northern New Mexico

Community College. During the first few years with the school, Juan worked in student financial aid and in the Learning Center.

Juan became better known as the director of the High School Equivalency Program (HEP), which he brought to the campus. For many years, HEP provided assistance to students who had not completed high school for reason of their occupation as migrant workers, or their families' occupation in this line of work. As students, individuals in this program would enter accelerated study in order to take the General Education Diploma (GED) examinations for completion of high school equivalency upon successful completion.

Juan retired as director of HEP, based in El Rito. He has continued to assist his community and Northern New Mexico College in acquiring a water system for the community and College that is a vast improvement on systems in which entities have relied. He has chaired a board of directors of the El Rito Water Users' Association, which now includes the college campus as well.[33] We cannot overemphasize the importance of this effort; for the first time in the hundred-year history of the campus, it has a safe, potable, and abundant supply of water.

Juan and his wife Annette, who is also former staff member of Northern New Mexico College, reside in El Rito.

David Trujillo graduated with the Class of '58. He was a boy from El Rito whose brothers and sisters also attended the Normal School, and I have written about his mother Cloide earlier in these pages.

David started at Placitas Elementary School; Cleo Martinez taught first grade and Margaret Martinez taught second. David moved on to the Normal School for fourth grade. During high school David felt little connection to the school, with the lone exception of the band, in which he excelled and for which he credits John Romero, the band director. Day students' grievances were all similar; I have summarized these elsewhere as a sad commentary on the school's relations with the community of El Rito.

David recalled the music program with comments I had not heard previously. He remembers John and Dora Villa, husband and wife; John Villa directed the *orquesta típica* during David's early years at the the Normal.

Besides Cloide, their mother, the Trujillo children were Olivia, David, Herman, Alfonso, Ben, Eva, Pat, Paula and Anna Marie. Herman was a quiet boy whom I got to know long after high school. Herman became a member of the Board of Regents of the Normal School, after it came to be known as Northern New Mexico Community College.[34]

David attended New Mexico Highlands University after graduation and became a music teacher. He married Priscilla Ceballes from Española. David and Priscilla made their home in Santa Fe, until Priscilla was employed by the New Mexico Technical Vocational School in July 1977.[35]

When I renewed acquaintance with David, he was teaching the music program at Santa Fe Indian School, where he retired. David and Priscilla, surrounded by children and grandchildren, live in Española.

In spring 1958, Robert Archuleta was valedictorian of the graduating class; Ross Martinez, who came from the village of El Guique, was salutatorian.

Robert was a boy from Cuba. His mother, a schoolteacher, wanted Robert to have a better education than was available in the early days within the Cuba school district, and he attended Presbyterian schools at Allison James, Santa Fe, and Menaul in Albuquerque, prior to enrolling at El Rito. Several more youngsters from Cuba had attended El Rito earlier, and they were either related to Robert by family, or he simply knew them.

Robert was a talented musician, played guitar of the 1950s, mostly rock and roll. He also played football, running back.

Robert attended New Mexico Tech[36] and New Mexico State University, where he received a bachelor of science degree. Following college, he worked for the federal government in administering public lands devoted to animal grazing. Robert, an avid fisherman; he and his wife Jean lived in southern Colorado on the banks of the Conejos River. Robert is deceased.

Lucas Trujillo was also a boy from El Rito. Lucas, Class of '58, has a better acquaintance with the Normal School since that time than most of our former students.

Like his brother and sister, Norberto and Priscilla, Lucas started public school in Placitas. Max Varoz was the elementary school principal about whom many fond memories remain in school circles and in the community.

Lucas, an unassuming individual, was a good student throughout high school and he played football during his final three years of the Normal. Lucas's favorite teacher, as he looked back during our interview, was probably Tom Roybal. During his final year, the Eagles won their district and engaged Aztec High School in a bi-district playoff. Lucas recalled playing "under the lights" against a very strong Aztec Tiger team that advanced to the state finals in 1958.

After college, Lucas returned to his home town and taught math at the Normal School from 1964 to 1969 when the high school was discontinued. In his first year, C.H. Robinson was Superintendent and Melvin Cordova was high school Principal. After the Principal and Ruben Lucero left the Normal School, Lucas assisted Coach Vince Martínez with the athletic program.

Lucas remembers that the state dictated the end of the high school which he had attended and where he now taught. He and teachers suspected that the high school in El Rito was to be phased out, but they were not informed until the 1968-69 school year. His recollection is that, "We all voted for the bond issue that authorized the new high school, and knew that henceforth high school students would attend the Mesa Vista campus in Ojo Caliente."

After the closing of the high school, Lucas took a job in the new Mesa Vista School District where he remained until he retired in 1994. He had served Mesa Vista High School for 25 years.

Lucas Trujillo continues to help the community in El Rito and Northern New Mexico College in improving their water system. Lucas has been a member of the board of directors of the El Rito Water Users' Association, whose significance in this effort is described in several places in our book.

Lucas and his family reside in El Rito.

The Eagles had a strong basketball program, and although the '58 version did not capture the state title, they did capture the district championship. From the previous year's state championship team, Ralph Martinez, David Valdez and Randy Velarde returned. During regular season, and an invitational tournament, they won 20 games and lost six. El Rito won the district championship by avenging two regular season losses and beating Pojoaque in the final game. This very good Eagles team was eliminated in bi-district regional play.

The 1959 graduating class included the last group of students whom I would know very well at the Normal School. For this book, I interviewed Louis Torres who knew most kids well; Louis was president of his class from tenth through twelfth grades. He was also preceded by brothers Andalecio, Manuel, and Robert at the Normal, and there was a Torres at the school continuously back to 1947.

Louis grew up in Black Lake, as did his brothers. He attended grades one through six in a one-room schoolhouse, then boarded a bus to Eagle Nest for seventh and eighth grades. The youngest member of his family, Louis suffered a degree of isolation in Black Lake which was remedied when he moved to El Rito for ninth grade. Apart from a few of his relatives in Black Lake, there were no other boys. Some of his Espinoza relatives attended the Normal School earlier: Lourdes, Celedón, and Andrellita.

At El Rito, Louis found happiness in being among many more kids who were like him. "I loved it the day I got there, and the day I left, and I still like to go there," he told me. The outside world had little effect on him, and his teachers were not particularly worldly. Sunday night movies had been discontinued, and most social life centered around athletic events and school dances.

The Normal School served Louis well in many ways, but not academically, which may or may not have been about his own doing. Students were not critical of anything, room or food or any living condition. "We were so happy there, " he observed. Leaving the Normal School upon graduation left him with a sense of loss.

Louis commented that the institution was remiss in not reminding students that they were hosted by the people of El Rito.[37]

Louis Torres's socialization at the Normal School in El Rito is evident today. He assists his community in the pursuit of worthy causes, a true man of the people. He resides in Española.

The Class of 1959 had some very bright and conscientious students. Cecilia Romero, from Peñasco, was valedictorian; Mary Martha Martínez, from El Guique, was salutatorian. [38]

Again in 1959, the Eagles won the state schoolboys' basketball championship, in Class B[39]. A trio of these boys, Ralph Martínez, Randy

Velarde, and Sam Martínez were back for their senior year and very accomplished on the basketball court. Ralph and Randy had been on the starting five of the 1957 champion Eagles. Gilbert Valdéz, Candido Trujillo, Arthur Martínez, Carlos Martínez, Pablo Maestas, Sifredo Martínez, and Gil Valdéz rounded out another fine team coached by Vince Martínez.

The 1959 Eagles breezed through a season, district and regional tournaments, posting a record of 31 wins and two losses on their way to the championship. The El Rito Normal School Eagles beat a good team from San Jon in the state finals by a score of 55-45. El Rito dominated the all-state team with three members, Ralph Martínez, Randy Velarde[40], and Sam Martínez.

The Class of 1960 attended the school that was in a name transition, but was still referred to in *El Chamisal* as the Northern New Mexico Normal School. C.H. Robinson was Superintendent; he was trying to start the college. Jack Flynn had been brought in as Acting Dean to assist. The new administration was interested in a strong academic program.

In 1960, Erlinda Gonzáles, from Roy, was class valedictorian; Lorraine Vigil, a student from El Rito, was salutatorian.

In the first half of the decade of the sixties, the spotlight in sports changed from team sports to individual sports, although the El Rito Eagles garnered plenty of recognition as a team in cross-country competition and in track. This time the coach was Ruben Lucero, who assisted Vicente Martínez with basketball and football, but it was in cross-country, particularly, in which Lucero's teams excelled beginning in 1961.

A part of the following story is told in *Children of the Normal School*. However, parts of this story have to live in the readers of this book. The story bears to be repeated.

I know part of this story from Gerry García,[41] a studious, quiet man from El Rito whose personal accomplishments are nothing short of spectacular, as readers will learn. As a boy, he tended to himself a lot, and ran all over town when he was out and about. He would watch his older brother, Sofío, run on the track team, and he would similarly study the football players practice. Sofío and some of his buddies marveled that Gerry never seemed to tire as he zipped around town and the school. Gerry knew that, as a small boy, he enjoyed some advantage in running full speed downhill, when bigger boys had to hold up to maintain their balance. Gerry always made certain that he didn't beat the older brother, who invited him to run in his first official race.

While in seventh grade, Gerry ran in an invitational meet in Los Lunas where he managed to beat a much older boy who was state champion in the same year, 1960. Gerry began running seriously in eighth grade. As he told me with a quiet little laugh, "Ruben Lucero discovered me." Gerry spoke glowingly about Ruben Lucero and his wife, who encouraged him throughout his high school career and beyond. And what a career it was!

The El Rito Eagles won the state cross-country championship for the first time in 1961. Gerry García ran the course in 11 minutes and six seconds (11:06)[42], fully 36 seconds faster than the state champ had run in the previous year. And Gerry was in eighth grade! He had plenty of competition coming from his own team, however; Sam Archuleta, a young man from Truchas, finished the same course in 11:10. The spirit of fierce competition and joyous camaraderie must have been interesting to watch. The team in 1961 included William Gonzáles, Milnor Branch, Sofío García, Sam Archuleta, Tito Ortíz, and Gerry García; the coach was Ruben Lucero.

The Eagles repeated as state champions in 1962. Coach Lucero led this team composed of Gerry García, Sam Archuleta, William Gonzáles, Billy Trujillo, Tito Ortíz, and Chris Martínez. Gerry repeated as state individual champion; Sam Archuleta placed third. Gerry, this time in ninth grade, posted a time of 10:57.

In 1963, the unprecedented occurred; the El Rito Eagles captured the state championship once again...three in a row. The state champs included once again Gerry García, William Gonzáles, Sam Archuleta, Jerry Billy Trujillo, Chris Martínez, and Alex García. Coach Lucero added Gus Jaramillo, Phillip Branch, Presciliano Archuleta, Jerry Salazar, and Nappy Quintana to round out the squad. Gerry García, as a tenth grader, won the state's top honors with a time identical to the previous year, 10:57.

Part of the story about Gerry García is told in a book devoted to the children of the Normal School. The remainder of the story, after high school at El Rito for Gerry, is told more thoroughly.

María Dolores Gonzáles was with the graduating Class of 1963. She is one of three sisters who attended El Rito. Erlinda, who graduated in '60, and Cecilia, Class of 1962 are the two older sisters. The three sisters were from Roy, out in the *llano* of New Mexico, where local folks speak English as cowboys do, often with a Texas accent. The three girls were close in age, Erlinda having been born in 1942, Cecilia in '44, and María Dolores in '46.

I interviewed María Dolores for several reasons that this will reveal. She is very proud of the accomplishments of her sisters and her own, of course. They tended to follow influence of their mother; she was a teacher in a one-room schoolhouse, while their father moved about in his job. The girls started school in Roy with nuns, but attended grades one to eight in Rosebud.

María Dolores recalled that, when Erlinda completed eighth grade at Rosebud, there was a decision to be made about high school. An uncle, Francis Gonzales, was fresh out of college and was slated to begin his teaching career at the Northern New Mexico Normal School. This gave Erlinda and Cecilia, who was only 11 or 12 years old, reason to think seriously about the boarding school at El Rito, where they subsequently enrolled.

About life at the Normal School, María Dolores is effusive with praise. She said, "Sociologically, it was good to be away from home." The girls had grown up among an amount of racism, and El Rito was so-o-o different. Social life contained activities about which she would grow fond: class initiation, painting the letter "N", dances, and other social events. Initiations were easily tolerated, and the school was good training ground in cooperation and family togetherness.

María Dolores then described for me several parallels in the sisters' activities and successes. All three girls were in band. They all three were cheerleaders in that remarkably schoolish environment of the early sixties. María Dolores was a class vice-president, and in her senior year she edited *El Aguila*, the student newspaper.

Academically, the girls did fine, despite what María Dolores described to me as having been a not-very-strong education. Erlinda, I mentioned earlier, was class valedictorian. Cecilia and María Dolores were both salutatorian during their respective years of graduation.

All three of the girls received scholarships to attend the University of New Mexico. For a while, Erlinda taught in California, but she returned to UNM for her master's and doctoral degrees. She subsequently taught in Indiana and New Mexico State University, before returning to be on the faculty of the University of New Mexico in the Department of Modern Languages. She has resided and been on the faculty in Oregon during the past few years.

Cecilia attended UNM for two years; she transferred to New Mexico Highlands University where she obtained bachelor's and master's degrees in bilingual education. She completed a career in education in Colorado and New Mexico. Cecilia resides in Albuquerque.

María Dolores began studies at the University of New Mexico, became married, and attended Adams State University in Colorado where she acquired a bachelor's degree. She returned to the University of New Mexico where she obtained master's and doctoral degrees in socio-linguistics. She has been on the faculty of UNM. Presently, she is Executive Director of a company, Bilingual Strategies, which offers training for business executives in language translation, mediation, and cultural competency.

In 2010, María Dolores Gonzáles has been elected president of the Normal School Alumni Association. María Dolores resides in Albuquerque.

Sam Archuleta was one of those boys at El Rito from a rural home in Truchas. Sam excelled in track and cross-country, placing in the state cross-country meet two years, as I have recounted. He graduated high school in 1964.

I suspect that Sam was a very good student. He has degrees in law and in business; he operates a business in Albuquerque, offering both services of attorney and as a certified public accountant (CPA).

Sam was president of the Normal School Alumni Association when I met him.

An amazing young man—in 1964, Gerry García was a seasoned veteran athlete in eleventh grade—repeated as state champ in cross-country for the fourth consecutive time. This was a most gratifying year for Gerry. High schools had been divided into three classes: AA, A, and B. El Rito continued in Class B, but Gerry García posted a new time of 9:32 for the same course, faster than boys from Sandia High

School in Albuquerque and Los Lunas High School in Class AA and A, respectively.[43]

The graduating class of 1964 numbered forty. This was a large number for the Normal School; numbers in the few remaining years would get smaller. The class sponsor was a familiar face for many of us out of the past; he was John Romero, the band teacher.

Some of the students were familiar to me also: John Dantis, Mary Agnes Griego, Oliver Vigil, Sam Archuleta, Napoleon Quintana, and Arturo Sisneros, to name a few.

Maxine Gallegos, from La Madera, was class valedictorian; Tom Martin, from El Rito, was salutatorian. Tom is grandson of the school's first president, George J. Martin.

The Normal School enjoyed successes in track, also. A very fine teacher said once that talent is developed, one isn't simply born with it. In these individual sports, one sees the veracity of the statement. In this case, good coaching and hard work by these boys resulted in new track records set for the school. The mile relay team, coached again by Ruben Lucero, won district and conference championships. This four-man team included Sam Archuleta, Billy Trujillo, Billy Jaramillo, and William Gonzales.

The mile medley relay team consisted of Ben Cordova, Dave Padilla, Sam Archuleta, and Gerry García; this team held the school record for a long time.

Pauline Alire graduated with the Class of 1965.

She began school in Placitas in 1954; Max Varoz was principal at the elementary school. Many of her teachers were graduates of the old Normal School.

In 1961, enrolled in high school at the Normal. She remembered, as we spoke, that her favorite teachers were Albert Jenske and Gilbert Vigil.

Following high school, Pauline related to me, it was important to prepare to go work. Parents were unlikely, and couldn't, send their girls to college. Pauline enrolled at the New Mexico Technical Vocational School where she prepared for office work, little realizing fully what the future would hold. She had Priscilla Trujillo, an excellent teacher, for some classes. She also recalled Martha Salazar and Drucilla Duran.

Pauline became the secretary to the president when I came to El Rito and Northern New Mexico Community College in January 1985. She continued on to her retirement as the president's secretary.[44]

In retirement, Pauline has been engaged in a very important project on behalf of her community and the college. She is, along with Juan García and Lucas Trujillo, member of the El Rito Water Users's Association that is consolidating water systems in El Rito. Important to all of us interested in the welfare of the Normal School, this water system includes Northern New Mexico College.

Pauline and her husband, Larry Varoz, resided in El Rito. We regret that Larry is deceased.

The 1965 track team consisted of three very well-tuned young athletes: Gerry García, Billy Trujillo, and Ben Trujillo.

The cross-country team won the District 2B championship and first place in the Northern Rio Grande Conference. The team, still coached by Ruben Lucero, included Pat Romero, Leroy Salazar, Chris Martínez, Rudy Jaramillo, Gerry García, and Alex García.

Ben Trujillo was in the Class of 1965; he was a boy from El Rito.

Ben was the son of Aniceta Trujillo, or Annette, as she was known in El Rito, and the grandson of Jeronimo Jaramillo. Although Venceslao Jaramillo, the founder of the Spanish American Normal School and real hero in this story, did not leave any direct descendants, Ben and Annette and a cousin by the name of Guadalupita Jaramillo were among Venceslao's living relatives when I knew them. This is Ben Trujillo whose name you read as one of three iron men on the 1965 track team. I especially regret that Ben Trujillo is deceased.

Ben started elementary school at the Normal with a pre-first teacher, Lola Valdez, whom everyone in the community still remembers. For second grade, Ben had Mela Leger as his teacher. Ben enjoyed elementary school and had some very good teachers about whom he could only remember last names: Mrs. Chávez and Mrs. Sánchez.

Early on, Ben noticed that a few things at the Normal School were not quite as normal as one would like. Water quality was not good, there being sediments perceptible in each water glass. Substitute facilities had to be sought for an aging Junior Building; the school brought in barracks.

Ben was very complimentary of teachers and staff, including students who worked at the school. As a young boy, he found Dennis Salazar especially helpful.

When he moved to the high school, Melvin Cordova was principal; Ruben Lucero taught and coached track. Ben was very complimentary of Lucero, with whom he ran track. Ben also
played basketball and football. He remembered that he was so grateful for the guidance he received from Ruben Lucero that he gave his coach a western-style belt buckle as a gift.

Ben loved many of his classmates and recalled a few names: Chris Martínez, Leroy Salazar, Juanito Lovato, Angela (Bertha) Trujillo, Gerry García, Florencio Archuleta, Rudy Martínez, and Tito Ortíz.

Ben was pleased about the education that he received at the Normal School. His parents, who were educated, insisted that Ben continue on through high school and college. Ben assumed that this is what he would do, and he did it.

After college, Ben became a businessman and a business consultant. Ben lived and worked in Denver, and commuted to El Rito[45] to visit his mother.

In his later years, Ben Trujillo lived in Santa Fe with his wife until his death in a tragic accident in winter 2010.

Gerry García, Class of 1966, had a long and illustrious athletic career at the Normal School of El Rito, setting indelible records in the process.[46] In fall 1965, Gerry won his fifth consecutive state title for cross-country in a time of 9:41. To top it all off, his time was eight seconds faster than the first place finisher in Class AA, from Hobbs, and 34 seconds faster than the Class A champ, a boy from Silver City.

Gerry had begun elementary school on campus; it was known as El Rito Elementary. Grade seven was part of the high school, which is the reason he enlisted in the track program at this early age. Gerry recalls that teachers lived in portable buildings near the elementary school, and this is how he met Ruben Lucero. He was constantly running everywhere, and "showing off", according to Gerry.

After wonderful high school years, which he feels he owes to Ruben Lucero, the coach and his wife drove Gerry to Portales and Eastern New

Mexico University. Ruben Lucero introduced Gerry to the track coach at ENMU, Carl Babcock, who offered Gerry a scholarship. Gerry did well at Eastern, and he maintains that Ruben and Coach Babcock had furnished him with the structure necessary to succeed. Gerry says that just as "I owe a lot to Ruben. He was my coach for five years," so, too, was Babcock great as his new coach.

Gerry García excelled at ENMU in cross-country, and in 1966 he placed fourth in a field of 320 runners in the National Collegiate Athletic Association (NCAA) meet held in Wheaton, Illinois. He was named All-American in 1966, and won the "Greatest Greyhound Award" at Eastern New Mexico University in 1967, his last year at the school.

For the following school year, Gerry transferred to Lamar University because of the high opinion that he had developed regarding Carl Babcock. He repeated as an All-American at Lamar University, and in the following year he entered the Texas Relays in the 10,000 meter run. That year he finished second to Jack Bachelor and beat Frank Shorter, whom sports enthusiasts will remember as an Olympic champion from Taos. Gerry, one to try to run a mile at blinding speed, nevertheless posted a personal best of 4:18 in an AAU meet in which he led both Bachelor and Shorter, but injured a calf-muscle in the process. As he discusses those days, he emphasizes doing his personal best, and demonstrating loyalty to his former coaches. Carl Babcock died during Gerry's college career, which he thinks about often.

Gerry is married; he and his wife have a daughter. They reside in Albuquerque. Gerry and his wife have both taught with the Albuquerque Public Schools. Still today, Gerry perseveres toward improving himself; he is enrolling in a doctoral program at the University in school administration and special education.

The Class of 1969 knew that it was the last one of the high school, but in spite of outward signs, students did not feel slighted in any way. Their teachers, in particular, made certain that students enjoyed a life as if their school were continuing as usual. The technical vocational school was coming into prominence, however, and even the student yearbook was changed. It was now *El Paisano*, and the younger high schoolers had to share a small portion of their "annual", which constitute much of kids memorabilia.

The graduating class numbered only 19.[47] In addition to seniors, there were 22 students in eleventh grade, 21 sophomores, and 26 in ninth grade. Youngsters who had some years of high school remaining would enroll in the Mesa Vista High School, down the road in Ojo Caliente. There were very few boarding students in the numbers listed.

The teaching staff of the high school supported all of the usual activities for students, who participated in student government, boys basketball, track, cheering squad, and class activities.

Honor students were Greg Martin, Anthony Manzanares, Isabel Vigil, and Richard Romero.

Greg Martin, Class of 1969, was the last of the Martin children to attend high school at the Normal. Greg is Tom Martin's[48] son, and he is grandson to George J. Martin, the school's first president. Tom has a brother Tom and sister Cam who also attended the Normal School. Tom was a music teacher in the Albuquerque Public Schools. Tom resides in Albuquerque; Cam lives in Taos.

Greg was born in 1952 and began school at the El Rito Elementary School on campus. Soon thereafter, he attended St. Thomas Elementary School in Abiquiú in grades two to eight.

Greg Martin came to the Normal School for ninth grade, where he excelled academically and in school athletics. He lettered in four sports: baseball, basketball, football, and track. When he came to the school, Melvin Cordova was still principal, Vincente Martinez and Ruben Lucero coached the sports program, and John Romero was music director. In ninth grade, Anthony Manzanares from Los Ojos and Patrick Barela from Peñasco became his friends.

After high school, Greg enrolled at the University of New Mexico. As his grandfather, his dad, and uncle John Martin, Greg has maintained interest in languages, and he is fluent in Spanish. A student in latin american studies at the University, Greg decided in 1971 to attend UNM's Andean Center in Quito, Ecuador. He furthered his studies in Portuguese and in Quechua, the language among indigenous people of the highlands of South America.

After his studies in Ecuador, Greg had to return to El Rito to assist the family; Tom had become ill.

Greg took over operation of the grocery and dry goods store in January 1974, an establishment started by his grandfather George, as we have described earlier in these pages. Greg closed the store in

August 2009, which tells, more than anything, how the rural nature of communities in northern New Mexico has changed. Communities have become less isolated after almost a century, each year there being more automobiles on more and better roads.

Greg and his wife Josie reside in El Rito.

It is likely that former students of the old high school, and some who attended elementary school on campus in El Rito, will examine these pages, which I chose to call "Sons and Daughters of the Normal School." In telling the stories of these young people, I looked for differences, something unique, in each story, but instead I think I found that early childhood had made us all quite alike one another. Most students were from modest homes, if from a home at all. Ethnic differences were insufficient to set anyone apart. City kids had been denied the isolation, or solitude, that some of us knew as young children. When we arrived at El Rito, however, the isolation that rural kids had known previously existed at our school. Students had only one another, and, if they were lucky, a friend from among staff or teachers.

Why have I tended to emphasize our isolation? Examine some salient facts: until 1946, El Rito did not have a paved road. Electricity came soon thereafter, although the Normal School did have its own small electrical generation plant. Newspapers? A few people on campus purchased *The New Mexican* now and then, but the *Rio Grande Sun*, a local paper down the road in Española was founded in October 1956. Radio station KDCE, the first station in our midst, began broadcasting in October 1963. It isn't useful to lament this cultural isolation, but it is worthwhile contemplating how it affects the minds of young people, their hopes, dreams and aspirations. It is little wonder that for many of us that "sense of loss" that Luis Torres spoke about was more than simply nostalgia. It was the sense that we had created for ourselves privilege where you would least expect it to be found, and which individually we had not known before our days at the Normal School.

There isn't much doubt that old cultures die with the people who constituted them, absent infusion from outside. It is not to say that they may not live, or be resided in, to the fullest. The culture that I describe is unique, and the social milieu is therefore something special. I'm not going to try to explain to you what made them so different. I simply tell the tale, and hope that someone finds it interesting.

Notes:

1. The group of students who have completed the baccalaureate degree are listed in "Graduates" at the end of this book.

2. The photograph of the 1929 first grade class was given to me by John Martin, who is in the picture with Laura Redman and his classmates. It may be found in *Children of the Normal School*.

3. Information about Laura Redman was provided to me by her son and daughter, Larry Parcell and Hyda Marie Dougherty, and her grandson, Colin Dougherty.

4. I met Laura Redman Dougherty on Sunday, April 14, 1985 on the campus in El Rito during the 75th year celebration of the Spanish American Normal School and inauguration of one Sigfredo Maestas as president of then Northern New Mexico Community College. She was age 82 almost. She had been retired several years but she still cared about children, teaching, and the Normal School. I felt that I had just met one of the happiest people I've had the privilege to know.

5. The class of 1923 is listed in the list at the end of this book.

6. I did not meet Lawrence Redman, but I feel as though I know him. I have a tape-recording that was given to me by Meade Martin. He had interviewed Lawrence, who talked about the second and third decades of the 1900s in and around El Rito, and about the Normal School. Much of my information about the Redman family in El Rito is drawn from this interview. About the Normal, Lawrence recalled that George Martin and "a woman" were teaching students in an old red brick building in town because the Normal School's only building had been damaged by fire in 1912. The woman to whom Lawrence referred was Mrs. Bertha Sundt. Lawrence remembered that Joseph Beck, one of the Regents, was a neighbor of Venceslao Jaramillo. Joe Beck owned the first automobile in El Rito. When he left El Rito, he also left the car to John Sargent, George Martin's business associate, and Sargent then sold the car to Lawrence Redman. Lawrence also recalled that the store that later came

to be owned by George Martin and John Sargent had first belonged to an uncle of Joseph Grant.

7. In trying to learn about the lives and times of Laura Redman Dougherty and Lawrence Redman, I contacted Michael, Lawrence's son in Española. Michael is a dentist who has been retired in recent years. He told me how to contact Laura's children and verified some of the information that I had about the Redman family in El Rito. Michael's wife Mary Ellen Montoya Redman taught at the Normal School in the early 1950s.

8. I enjoyed a chance discovery concerning this 1929 photograph. A copy of it was first given to me by Jane Garcia, née Goddard, who lives down the road from the campus in El Rito and whose sister Pauline is in the photo. Soon thereafter, at a reunion of the alumni in Albuquerque, Joe Valdez, himself of the class of 1954, gave me the same picture with the names of all the graduates. José M. Valdez, one of the graduates, is Joe's father. The photograph is in *Children of the Normal School*.

9. I owe thanks to Joe Valdez, Class of '54, for information about his uncle Raymundo Romero.

10. "Only in northern New Mexico," we like to say about incidents like this one involving the 1929 photograph with seven graduates. One day Katie Bateman Allison called me at home to say that she had learned that I was writing this book and that she and her husband Dana had photographs and Normal School memorabilia that I might wish to see. I did not know Katie, but after we three had talked a while she told me that her mother had graduated at the Normal School in the late twenties, she thought 1929. She had a photograph of her mother taken with schoolmates at the Normal. When I saw the picture, I said, "Wait here." I brought out from my office the picture of the 1929 graduating class, and there's Olive Parker. This picture can be found in *Children of the Normal School*.

11. A photograph, likely from 1927, includes both sisters Olive and Marguerite. President John Conway is in the picture, as are Albert Bateman, Ernesto Baca and Ronzo Bateman.

12. A document that I found is a Daily Class Record kept by Mrs. Irene Hickey during the 1927-28 school year. Marguerite was enrolled in English III Literature; brilliant performance.

13. Monero has been a ghost town for thirty to forty years. José Valdéz was my mother Cordelia Rendón's elementary school teacher in mid-1930s in this coal-mining village. I was born in Monero in 1940.

14. A great deal of what I know about Gilbert Archuleta was told to me by his brother Ruben, another great athlete. The younger brother gave me newspaper articles from about seven and as long as twenty years ago when people still remembered Gilbert Archuleta's baseball prowess.

15. Personal information about Gilbert Archuleta I obtained from the *Albuquerque Journal*, Dec 3, 2003, Isabel Sánchez, staff writer.

16. It was in the 47-48 school year that the name of the school was changed to Northern New Mexico Normal School. To avoid confusion about names, I refer to the institution as the Normal School. Changes wrought in 1969, and later, require some further readjustments that are discussed in Chapter Nine and thereafter.

17. The story concerning the establishment of Northern New Mexico Community College is told in some detail in Chapter 10 of this book.

18. I had returned to Northern New Mexico Community College in 1996 and I had opportunity to serve as President with four of our high school alumni, as described in these pages. I am certain that Michael Branch considers the year 2004 as a high point in his career, as I do, in that the ultimate goal for the Spanish American Normal School as a teacher-training college was finally achieved.

19. This is the Board that hired me as President in July 1996, after my absence of seven years from NNMCC.

20. I knew Joe Martinez, but not well. I have known him primarily through his classmates. Many years after high school, I knew Joe in

Española. His wife Mae requested that I deliver a eulogy at funeral services for Joe; I was proud to do this.

21. Public schools in New Mexico generally did not teach New Mexico history during our years in school. This was a serious omission in the curriculum that had to be corrected by the state legislature. Many hispanic people in New Mexico, educators and others, would view what occurred to be deliberate, a result of an odd form of colonialism of the 1800s. The interesting thing to remember is that one writer and historian who wrote "Historical Sketches of New Mexico," in 1883, was none other than L. Bradford Prince, the first acting president of our school.

22. Readers are reminded: this was an era before student federal financial aid. All that existed at public college and universities, typically, were tuition scholarships and various types of employment, not generally what you would call office work.

23. The Normal School had many success stories. One of the enjoyments in writing this chapter is precisely for this reason. In Albert's case, as in the life of many students, the more rural the communities from which they came, the more important the school was to them. This, and the need for a home life, probably sum up students' profound gratitude for their experiences at El Rito.

24. George retired at Northern New Mexico Community College during my presidency. He was an exceptionally strong person in acquisitions and an excellent employee.

25. The dictionary states that *goloso* is used to mean either sweet-toothed or acquisitive. In northern New Mexico it has always been the latter meaning, but with regard to the love of food. At the Normal School, where the diet was steady and adequate, the novelty of scarce or new foods was sufficient for conversation, often in the form of wise-cracks.

26. I make frequent reference to the Alumni Association, which includes students who attended the high school and are the subject of this chapter. The strong contribution, which this loosely held and unaffiliated organization has made in the life of former students, should

not be underestimated. The organization sprung in the sixties and has remained the core of a vast family of students, often bringing former teachers into their group. Not formally sponsored by Northern New Mexico Community College and its present successor, the Northern New Mexico Normal School Alumni Association has nevertheless been a significant contributor to the College's Foundation and its scholarship fund.

27. With the prospects of college, I was happy to leave El Rito on graduation , although I was saddened to leave its people. Glenn C. George and Ed Grant were teachers whom I respected and liked a great deal. My classmates and some of the younger students were dear friends from whom I departed hesitantly. In the community of El Rito I left dozens of friends whom I would see in, what seemed to be, a distant future.

28. There were only two classes of schools then, A and B. The Eagles were by far the strongest school in Class B anywhere in New Mexico, having beaten such Class A powers as St. Michael's, Santa Fe High, Taos High School and the Española Hornets.

29. For anyone who doesn't know, a regular high school game consists of four quarters, eight minutes each.

30. I am quite conscious of the fact that these pages tend to emphasize sports, particularly basketball, and boys' athletics at that. A couple of things you should know: first, school athletics was a large part of student life, and as in modern-day America, they seemed to overshadow academic and intellectual concerns in everyday life. The second matter is that girls' athletic programs were discontinued, for some reason, after late 1940s. To this day, northern New Mexico is simply "nuts about basketball", and the current era does support girls endeavors, as it should.

31. Henry and Evila Serrano are deceased.

32. As has happened in the case of boarding high schools in western US, The Abbey was closed in recent years. I don't know that children of the

Normal School can take consolation in this, but They Abbey is one of several that have ceased to exist.

33. I am pleased to have played a role in this effort. During the final year of my presidency at Northern New Mexico Community College, I worked with the El Rito Water Users' Association in devising a plan by which the college, as owner of a large number of water rights but no suitable water source, could participate with the community of El Rito in a project that would ultimately benefit everyone concerned. When we began, Rudy Maestas chaired the Association, Prudencio Chacón was a valuable member, and Drew Mendez and I assisted on behalf of the College. We presented our plan to the Board of Regents, which approved the project. After I left the College in retirement, new members came on the board for the Water Users' Association, but this past March 2010, the project has come to fruition. Water from a new and abundant source has come to the campus, largely owed to the individuals mentioned.

34. Herman Trujillo was a member of the Board of Regents in fall 1984 when Northern New Mexico Community College conducted a search for a president. It was this Board that employed me as its next president, beginning January 1985. Herman Trujillo was replaced by the incoming Governor of New Mexico that same month.

35. You will learn more about Priscilla Trujillo in the chapter on the community college. She was on the teaching staff of the New Mexico Technical Vocational School during the creation of Northern New Mexico Community College.

36. Robert and I were great friends in high school and following. I was a student at New Mexico Tech when Robert came there in fall 1958. The Tech had a very small choice of programs; Robert transferred to New Mexico State University, which I also attended later.

37. Several former boarding students of the Normal School reminded me of the friendships and hospitality that they enjoyed with other students and residents of El Rito. Louis Torres's comment is to the heart of the matter in attributing cause to a lack of better school and town relationship over the years.

38. Mary Martha Martínez is deceased.

39. To remind you, there were still only Classes A and B, so this was a superb accomplishment.

40. Randy Velarde, an extraordinarily friendly and popular member of the Class of '59, is deceased.

41. Prior to writing this book, I knew Gerry García only from newspaper accounts, and not very many at that. My wife and I were residing in Central America and had almost no news from New Mexico in the early sixties. During Gerry's final years in high school, I was enrolled in the doctoral program at NMSU, and immersed in my work there, unable to pay much attention to news from northern New Mexico. But with some inkling about Gerry's accomplishments, I contacted him in Albuquerque this year, visited, and got him to talk about his years at the Normal School. He shared memorabilia with me; it was fun getting to know him.

42. The course for cross-country in the early 1960s was 2.1 miles. Distances were gradually lengthened, as times got shorter and athletes were bigger and stronger.

43. It's all right to hoop and holler, "Wow!", or whatever suits you. Or you may wish to wait until the next page.

44. I left the community college in July 1989 and was succeeded by Connie Valdez, with whom Pauline continued to work.

45. After 1996 when I returned as president of Northern New Mexico Community College, and I lived in El Rito, my wife Angela and I would see Ben, his wife, and Ben's mother in church on Sundays. Annette had always been very friendly to us, but I did not know that she was a relative of Venceslao Jaramillo. Years later, when I was seeking information and the people of Venceslao Jaramillo, Esperanza Baca, a life-long resident of El Rito and one of my former schoolmates, told me that I should look up Ben Trujillo.

I did as Esperanza suggested, and I was pleased to make the acquaintance of Ben, whom I interviewed in his office in Santa Fe. Until he died, we would occasionally talk on the phone or exchange electronic mail. I liked Ben, as did everyone who knew him.

46. There is an organization that keeps information about meritorious and unusual accomplishments in cross-country and such individual sports, and it posts on the internet. I learned from this web site that Gerry García is only one of seven student athletes throughout the United States who have won the state championship every year of high school... grades nine to twelve. Only seven. But wait a second, and read some more above. Recall also that Gerry won the state title as an eighth grader. Now you may holler and whoop it up.

47. Names are in the list at the end of this book.

48. Not to be confused with Greg's brother Tom, who appeared in these pages earlier. Tom Martin Sr. owned the store in El Rito after George passed on. Tom Sr. was on the Board of Regents of the school in the 1950s, as we have discussed earlier.

PHOTOGRAPHS

Logo drawn by Angela Warneke in about 1985 during the administration of the author. The logo has endured six administrations, including that of Richard J. Bailey, PhD. It shows an eagle, mascot of the College, hovering over the mountains to east and west of both campuses.

Drivers approaching the campus from the south are greeted by solar collectors that serve the campus at El Rito and surrounding communities west of the Rio Grande. The solar collectors are one of the accomplishments of Dr. Bailey on the El Rito campus.

Monument erected by high school students in attendance from 1920 to 1969 standing near the entrance to the campus. It bears plaques of the students in attendance during those years.

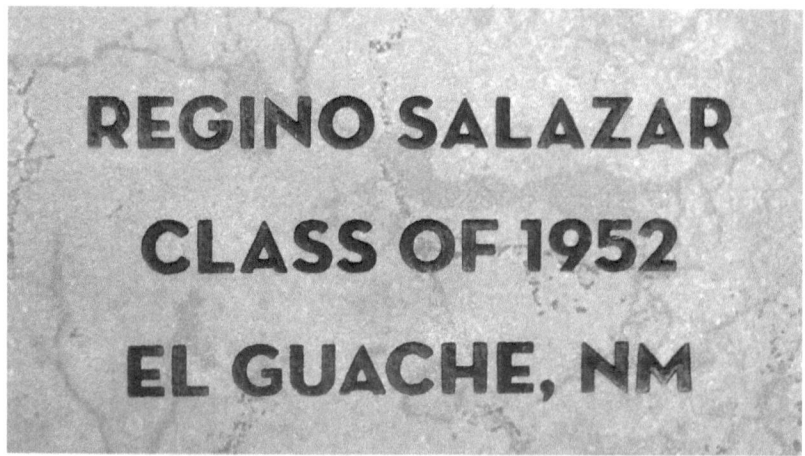

A plaque for Regino Salazar, probably purchased by a brother, Dennis Salazar, who attended school on this campus in the early 1950s, during which time Regino also attended.

GLENN C. GEORGE
FACULTY 1950'S

Plaque for Glenn C. George, a teacher of mathematics during the 1950s. President Sigfredo Maestas was responsible for this commemoration of Mr. George.

Administration has resided in Delgado Hall, named by President Connie A. Valdez and Robert McGeagh, PhD, a member of the faculty, since the early 1990s. Nearby structures include the Joseph B. Grant Gymnasium and Venceslao Jaramillo Hall, a classroom building.

Cutting Hall, one of the buildings prominent on campus, houses the women's dormitories, campus dining room, and a small auditorium. The auditorium has had significant renovations by students and staff under the direction of Drew Mendes.

The North Dormitory was built in the 1930s. It is a series of dormitories for men and women, completed under the direction of Drew Mendes and Michael Valdez. The dorm rooms are attached to an old gymnasium assigned to the high school Alumni Association.

A second campus in Española has received far greater attention to physical facilities in recent years. The logo welcomes visitors to Northern New Mexico College, which is to the foreground of mountains to the east.

The first building on this campus, named in honor of Joseph A. Montoya, Senator from New Mexico. Not shown: Richard Martinez Education Building, Dennis Salazar General Education Building, Celedón Martinez Technical Arts Building, Ben Luján Library, Eagle Memorial Gymnasium, and Sigfredo Maestas High Technology Building.

The Nick L. Salazar Center for the Arts, a prominent building on the Española Campus.

This auditorium seats approximately 350 people.

A performance room, one of several fine rooms in the Center for the Arts.

Bust of Nick L. Salazar, prominent legislator, who was elected in Rio Arriba County numerous times. President José Griego commissioned this work of art by Allison Aragón.

CLASS OF 1909

Top Row—W. Michel, W. Dougherty, E. Dunn, D. McMahon, J. Houlihan.
Middle Row—W. Mulrooney, W. T. Murphy, J. H. Bolton, G. H. Boyd, E. A. Ryan, Robert J. Shea, W. E. Maloney.
Bottom Row—W. J. Foy, T. J. O'Halloran, G. J. Martin, Rev. Bro. Jerome, W. J. Miller, H. A. Donovan, J. F. Tewey.

George J. Martin, first President of the Spanish American Normal School, with his graduating class at Manhattan College. He is bottom row, third from left.

Michael A. Martin, President of the Board of Regents at the time this book was published. Beginning with Mr. Martin's wife Margaret, each generation of the Martin family has shown support for the college by serving on its Board of Regents.

Rosario "Chayo" Garcia, former President of the Board of Regents. Rosario assisted in the selection of Richard J. Bailey, PhD, as President of Northern New Mexico College.

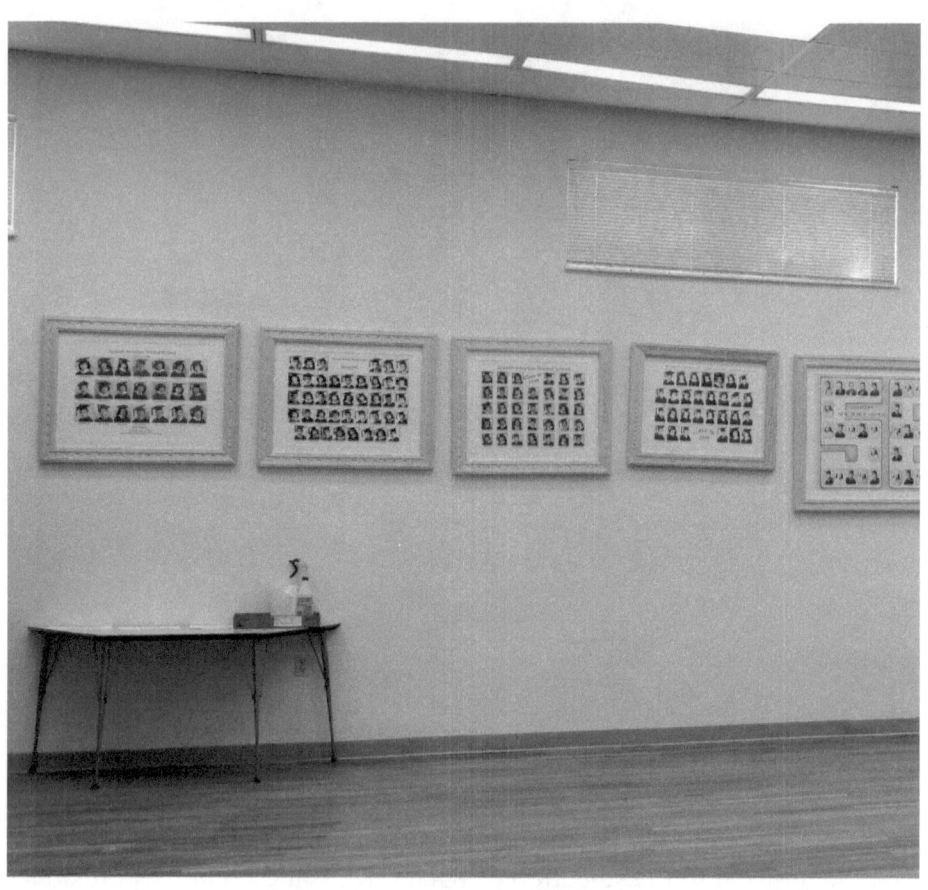

Photographs of each graduating class of the high school hang on the wall inside Alumni Hall.

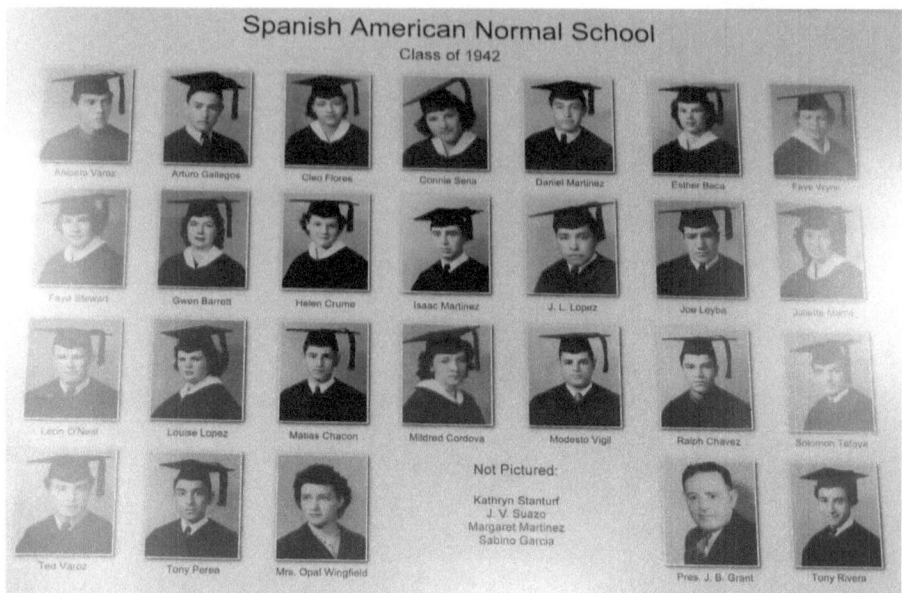

The class of 1942. This class included President Joseph B. Grant, who paid particular attention to students. Aniceto Varoz, show at top left in this picture, was the elementary school principal during the years that the author attended the school.

Cutting Hall, a small but exquisite auditorium, was renovated by staff and students under the direction of Drew Mendes. Bronson Cutting would be proud of the northern New Mexican style of the renovation.

Bust of Bronson Cutting on the west wall of the auditorium. Artist is unknown.

East wall of Cutting Hall. This auditorium is devoted to the history of the college. In addition to the woodwork being northern New Mexican, the original floors were replaced with hardwood flooring, the benches are Honduran mahogany, and the cushions are covered in material from the school's Fiber Arts Program.

Bust of Joseph B. Grant by Allison Aragón.

Painting of Senator Bronson Cutting who donated $50,000 toward the construction of this building. The artist is unknown. An image of this painting is in the *New Mexico Blue Book*, 2020 edition, published by the New Mexico Secretary of State's office.

Bust of George J. Martin by Allison Aragón.

Painting of Venceslao Jaramillo. A younger picture of Mr. Jaramillo appears in *Children of the Normal School* by permission of Rancho de Chimayó. The photograph may be seen at Rancho de Chimayó.

Richard J. Bailey, Jr., PhD, president of Northern New Mexico College.

_____
Diane D. Denish, President
Senate

_____
Margaret Larragoite, Chief Clerk
Senate

_____
Ben Luján, Speaker
House of Representatives

_____
Stephen R. Arias, Chief Clerk
House of Representatives

Approved by me this 5th day of March, 2004

_____
Governor Bill Richardson
State of New Mexico

Signature page of Senate Bill 163.

9
THE NEW MEXICO TECHNICAL VOCATIONAL SCHOOL

The Normal School became a vocational school, absent any trace of a high school that had existed for about fifty years, not at the insistence of the Board of Regents or anyone associated with the school, but in the best example of social engineering that we have seen in this state. Following the inauguration of the Campbell administration in Santa Fe, the administration and Board of the Normal School came under insistent pressure to become a vocational school. Many in northern New Mexico believe that this was another means of "tracking" Hispanics, in particular, into the trades and away from academic studies. Perhaps, but the movement toward vocational schools was state wide, with designated "area" vocational schools in El Rito, Albuquerque, Roswell and Hobbs. Many experiments in social engineering are, of course, successful. A large number fail because of lack of foresight and planning in some measure. In the case of vocational schools, there are none left in New Mexico with a one single, narrow mission.

The first Board of Regents of the vocational school in fall 1969 consisted of five members, in accordance with the state constitution. Frances R. Shipman chaired the Board; other members were Henry Abeyta, Charles López, Louis Saavedra and Luis M. Salazar. Albert Catanach was Superintendent; Paul A. Bell replaced Carl O. Westbrook was Director of Vocational Education. Seledón Martínez continued as Guidance Counselor and Guillermo Jaramillo was Business Manager.

During the 1969 and 1970 years, students in vocational programs published a yearbook which they called *El Paisano*. Roy Gonzales was the first editor of the yearbook; he and the yearbook staff called their school the Northern New Mexico Technical School[1], in the absence of any official action concerning the school's new name. Vocational programs included automotive technology, auto body repair, barbering, business occupations, cosmetology, drafting technology, electrical appliance repair technology, electricity, and nurses' aide training. For the 1970 year, courses in courses in typing and stenography were added.[2] Vocational instructors in the two years included:

    Fred Lopez, Barbering
    Henry Allen, Drafting
    Janice Brown, Nurses' Aide
    Mary Bard, Nurses' Aide
    Bertha Estrada, Home Economics
    Juan García, Communications
    Mildford Tea, Electrical Appliance Repair
    Robert Bal, Auto Mechanics
    Ray Torres, Auto Mechanics
    Tino Lopez, Clerk-Stenography

Other instructors, more readily identifiable with the high school, included, John Romero, band; Lucas Trujillo, social studies, Lucas Trujillo, Jr., mathematics; Bertha Estrada, home economics; Vicente Martínez, physical education; Bertha Estrada, home economics; Al Jenschke, clerk-typists; Gilbert Vigil, human relations; and Amado Valdez, business education.

New instructors were added in the 1970 year in vocational programs, including Perfecto Maestas and Jimmy Gallegos in auto body repair; Louise Harrison, cosmetology; Tino López, stenography; Michael Reynolds, drafting; Rudolph Velarde, electricity; Teresa Ray, nurses' aides; and Toby Lobato, basic studies.

Credit has to be given to Superintendent Albert Catanach, who in summer of 1967 printed "A Report on Developments at Northern New Mexico State School" which laid out, in brief, plans for the vocational school of the late '60s and 1970s. Programs that he mentioned in the report were almost exactly those that came to fruition either at El Rito or in Española. The positions in administration that were outlined as needed were, also, those that came to be at the vocational school.

During the first few years of the vocational school, much of the activity in instructional programs involved the acquisition of new equipment. The addition of the Española Branch, as this off-campus attendance center was known, added a welcome complication in that the school had to avoid duplication of programs between El Rito and Española. The school seldom had sufficient funds to provide for programs, equipment generally being quite expensive. Although the campus at El Rito may have been isolated, that is, away from jobs and possibilities for future employment of students, the Española branch, in contrast, attracted a lot of attention from both state and federal governments interested in helping to grow the economy of Rio Arriba County.

The branch campus in Española grew with the approval of the Board of Educational Finance, the executive branch of government, and the state legislature.

Administrators did a good job of providing services within their available resources. Bussing to the campus at El Rito was provided for students as far away as Questa, Taos, Peñasco and Truchas. Support of the branch campus in Española increased with the assignment of a full-time director, Seledón Martínez, in June 1970.

In June 1970, the name of the institution, New Mexico Technical Vocational School, was officially adopted by the Board of Regents.

Gradual growth of programs in Española resulted in sustainable enrollments by 1971. In spring of that year there were 165 day-time students in Española and 134 enrollees in the evening. In El Rito the total enrollment was 403. The likelihood of sustained evening enrollments in Española is one of the principal advantages that this attendance center enjoyed over the parent campus. Both campuses profited from the support provided to armed-services veterans by the GI Bill and other federal programs such as the Manpower Development Training Act (MDTA).

In spite of the usual, hesitant support by the state, education in New Mexico at a post-secondary level was gaining strength as a result of direct federal support of students' training, and the students own enthusiasm, evident state wide. At the New Mexico Technical Vocational School obviously one important component was missing, an academic one. Progress in the general education of its students would be hindered by the narrow mission of NMTVS for at least eight years, after 1969.

As a result of the school's foray into Española, however, this situation would soon be remedied. This wonderful story constitutes a great deal of the remaining part of this chapter.

A series of events in rapid order would change forever the slow, laid-back approach to change at the Spanish American Normal School.[3]

The first change occurred in the membership of the Board of Regents in March 1971 following the election of Governor Bruce King the previous fall. Governor King named Dennis Salazar and Tony Pacheco, both residents of the Española Valley, to replace Luis M. Salazar and Charles López. Dennis Salazar was aware of, if not fully responsible for, a series of discussions that had been occurring in the Valley about the importance of the New Mexico Technical Vocational School, and drawbacks of its limited mission.

Recall, also, that the vocational school, as early as 1967, was offering courses in Española. Simultaneously, a branch of the University of New Mexico, known as the Northern Branch, was in existence in our communities from Los Alamos to Española to Questa, with offices in Los Alamos and Santa Cruz. Access to higher education in the hinterland was often provided in New Mexico by branches of the University of New Mexico and New Mexico State University. Location of branch campuses of the universities resided in the larger towns, where the universities competed for peoples' favor and attention.[4] Branch campuses served citizens moderately well, providing usually an academic education and little purely vocational training. In the absence of anything resembling a state-wide plan for post-secondary education, the universities proceeded in accordance with their particular devices.

In or about 1970, former students of the Normal School residing in the Española valley, other friends and associates formed a discussion group that constituted, for the most part, what in other places in the world would be referred to as an *intelligentsia*. In Spain and Mexico such groups form *tertulias*, the gathering places requiring no more than a table, anywhere, in a bar or restaurant typically. Thus these fairly young intellectuals[5] began to plan the next step in the evolution of the Normal School. The guru[6] of the group was one Regino Salazar, graduate of the Normal in 1952. Regino was Dennis Salazar's older brother.

Since groups like this one are not exclusive, members will usually simply speak about *la pleve* and what they are up to. The rationale for expanding the mission of the New Mexico Technical Vocational School was evident to them, in ways not clear apparently to state-governmental leaders. A sorely needed academic dimension was missing in the institution, if it were to make a more useful educational contribution in north central New Mexico that was needed. It was not lost to members of the group that in other places in the Nation an institution called the community college encompassed a mission that included academic, vocational and not-for- credit instruction. Continuing education, life-long learning and similar, more modern ideas for increasing the general educational level of the populace were all attractive alternatives to the forward-looking, generally young group of people whose efforts we recount.

Prior to March of 1971 the Vocational School had received notice by the Superintendent that he would resign his position, after having done a thorough job in leading formulation of the vocational-educational plan. Search was conducted to replace Albert Catanach; the employment of Alex Mercure as the new president[7] was announced during the May meeting of the Board.

Thus began a series of informal and formal discussions among everyone concerned that would lead to the expansion of the mission of the New Mexico Technical Vocational Institute to that of a community college. Six years would pass, however, before the establishment of a new institution at El Rito and Española.

The Board of Regents in 1971 included Dennis Salazar as Chairman; Henry Abeyta, Vice Chairman; Tony Pacheco, Secretary-Treasurer; Louis Saavedra and Frances R. Shipman. Teachers and senior staff in El Rito showed little change from the previous two years. New additions included Nelson Gonzales, Counselor; Viola Madrid in Office Education; and Julian Grace in Office Machine Repair.

New teaching staff at the Española Branch were an indication of growth taking place:

Henry Armijo, Accounting
May A. Denton, Cooking and Baking
Martin Lawrence, Electronics
Florentino López, Clerk-Steno
Ronald Peraglio, Welding

Marcel J. Torres, Machine Tool Processes
Lucas Trujillo, Jr., GED
Priscilla Trujillo, Clerk-Typing
Marilyn Gardner, Dental Assistants
Levi Romero, Income Tax and Payroll Accounting
Margaret M. Scott, Medical Secretarial
Willard McCormick, Basic Machine Tool
Robert C. Holland, Electronics
James E. Stone, Salesmanship and Cashiering

Faculty in El Rito remained stable, with the majority of those from the previous year returning. New Hires included Viola Madrid in Office Education and Julian Grace in Office Machine Repair.

During summer 1971 Eugene Ledoux was employed as Vice-President of NMTVS, and the reemployment of Seledón Martínez as Director of Vocational Education with office in Española was reaffirmed. In August, the school received notification of a federal grant for the commencement of an Adult Basic Education program on the branch campus in Española.

Seledón Martínez informed the Board of Regents and President Alex Mercure of his intention to resign his position at the end of October 1971.

By late 1971, the Board had approved plans presented by the president for transfer of the Nurses' Aide program to the Española branch, and initiation of a program in butchering and meat cutting at El Rito.

Nick Salazar; Leo Murphy, Executive Director of the Four Corners Commission; and State Representative Leo Catanach visited with Senator Montoya in Washington, DC, which clinched a grant from the Economic Development Agency (EDA) for the school's first million dollars toward a vocational facility in Española. Nick Salazar took pride in being in the lead on this project. The new acquisition guaranteed that the new attendance center in Española would one day eclipse the parent campus in El Rito in enrollment and breadth of programs. Whereas El Rito was the center of the county, and Española was a scattering of buildings in 1909, the county had gradually grown toward Santa Fé. The matter of causes of the Tierra Amarilla courthouse raid were much in Nick Salazar and other people's mind. The new facility opened in June 1970, with the campus in El Rito still designated the administrative center of the New Mexico Technical Vocational School. Expenditures in Española amounted to $241,253 during the 1970-71 school year; in El Rito expenditures were in the amount of $732,230. This marked the start of reference to the new attendance center as the "Española Campus."

Acquisition of property for the Española branch, and erection of a new building, began to illustrate the interest of state and federal authorities in job creation and economic development in Rio Arriba County and the Española Valley, in particular. The combination classroom and administrative building would later, in 1984, be named after Senator Joseph M. Montoya, who had been the principal proponent for the development of a campus in Española. This was a time that marked, also, the debut of Nick L. Salazar in county and state politics.

The election of Nick L. Salazar as State Representative in 1972 would coincide with steps that were being considered by the Board of Regents under the leadership of Dennis Salazar. President Alex Mercure and his administration, and many friends of the school, evinced a strong tendency to establishing a community college.

During 1972, the Board and administration of NMTVS began to gain confidence that, in spite of its limited mission, the school was gaining in stability and strength of programs being offered. Enrollment on each campus was still relatively small: 243 in El Rito and 170 in Española during Fall term 1972. However, if the Veterans' Administration approved eligible students for attendance, enrollment in El Rito could surpass 300. Enrollment in the building trades continued to be disappointing; office occupations were by far the more popular among students.

A matter has to be pointed out with regard to the success of programs. Priscilla Trujillo, as leader in office occupations, was one of the reasons for the program's success. Many times people will wonder why growth takes place in programs: you may look for leadership among programs that are growing rapidly. Ms. Trujillo was recognized, early in the history of NMTVS, as furnishing the type of leadership necessary for growth.

Stability was reflected in the personnel of the NMTVS from year to year, and in the breadth of services that it was making available for students. The Board of Regents still consisted of the following members: Dennis Salazar, Chairman; Henry Abeyta, Frances R. Shipman, Tony Pacheco, and Louis Saavedra. The administration of President Alex Mercure included Eugene Ledoux as Vice-President; Guillermo Jaramillo, Business Manager; Leota V. Romero, President's Secretary; Nelson Gonzáles, Counselor; and, Pete Ortega, Director of Migrant Program. Later in the year, staff positions were filled: Adrian Ortíz as Director of (Employment) Placement, Anselmo Trujillo to direct Adult Basic Education and evening programs; and, Orlando Stevens as Director of Vocational Education. Jaramillo and Gonzáles resigned during the same year. The teaching staff included:

Robert Bal	Matt Martínez
May Denton	Pete Ortega
Jimmie Gallegos	James Page
Juan García	Manuel Quintana
Marylin Gardner	Cora Salazar
Julian Grace	Milford Tea
Paul Herrera	Raymond Torres
Florentino López	Marcel Torrez
Helen López	Lucas Trujillo
Ross Luján	Pedro Trujillo
Viola Madrid	Priscilla Trujillo
Perfecto Maestas	Drucella Valdez

The matter of approval of attendance for students who could benefit from the GI Bill and students eligible for other financial aid was of increasing concern, and NMTVS was taking steps to alleviate obstacles. NMTVS resolved that, in May 1973, it would file for candidacy for accreditation by the North Central Association of Colleges and Schools, as a technical-vocational school.

NMTVS took steps that would serve it well. In the same year the administration and Board adopted a salary schedule, and although there were questions about sufficiency of funds to meet obligations imposed by the salary schedule, adjustments in expenditures were made to accommodate this commitment to the school's teachers. President Mercure's administration also presented a set of personnel policies that would serve NMTVS well in the years ahead. This was a time in which the school consolidated its gains, in the interest of stability and hoped-for growth, although the mission of the school presented few opportunities for advancement.

Quality of vocational instruction was a concern that was addressed in a couple of ways. The State Department of Education made available courses to instructors that could be applied toward a master's degree, if desired. NMTVS made arrangement with Eastern New Mexico University for a series of courses. This was a time in which the Northern Branch of the University of New Mexico was being planned and NMTVS hoped that the University would make some courses available for vocational instructors. Although opportunities for educational advancement for instructors was scarce, NMTVS persevered with this approach to improvement. The presence of Louis Saavedra on the Board of Regents—Saavedra was President of the Albuquerque Technical-Vocational School—served the Board to remain abreast of statewide efforts that served a similar purpose, improvement of instruction.

The continued presence of Dennis Salazar as Chairman of the Board and Alex Mercure as President inevitably pointed the New Mexico Technical Vocational School in the direction of expansion of its mission. The impetus provided by community members, friends, neighbors and associates was sufficient for the vision of an institution that would combine technical, vocational and academic instruction to remain "front and center." Dennis Salazar credits Alex Mercure to be the "brains" behind this movement, but indeed there were others including Regino Salazar and a number of intellectuals in north central New Mexico. The role of an individual, Frank Serrano III, would ultimately become indispensable in the way in which this bit of history would unfold.

President Alex Mercure and the Board of Regents first employed Frank Serrano in March 1973 with the purpose of preparing candidacy for accreditation of the institution. Serrano had acquired knowledge and experience with a fledgling, distinctly American, institution in the Northwest, the community college. This was just the institution needed for the time and place in north central New Mexico. The popularity of the community college in America was to grow and reach its apex during the Clinton-Gore administration in the White House. Both

President Bill Clinton and Vice-President Al Gore were, during their terms of office, to extoll the ability of the community college in job training. The community college was indeed much more, and Frank Serrano knew this. The community college's dedication and ability in providing, in addition to vocational skills, an academic education and life-long learning for its citizens was becoming known.

During 1975 to 1977, the New Mexico Technical Vocational School was preparing itself well for growth, including the increasing possibility of expanding its mission. All outward signs were that the campus in Española was expanding for this growth. Two new buildings, for construction trades and for metals and machining were erected. An examination of the Catalog for those years indicates concomitant growth in personnel affecting both campuses. In addition to its president, the school numbered 22 full time staff, 15 instructors in daytime programs each in El Rito and Española, and ten evening instructors in Española. As in the case of most vocational schools, NMTVS was on a quarter system that reported instruction per clock hour per course.

After about 1975, the New Mexico Technical Vocational School became the school in transition. Once again, the old Normal School would begin to move closer to its initial purpose, the training of teachers for northern New Mexico, although the road was to be, again, long and slow.

The effort gathered momentum with the naming of a Task Force for Postsecondary Planning in North Central New Mexico, appointed by the Board of Educational Finance. At the first meeting of the Task Force on July 15, Executive Director Robert Huff explained that the task force was "constituted to look at the problem of postsecondary education in the Upper Rio Grande Valley."[8] NMTVS had done its homework; Dennis Salazar, Chairman of the NMTVS Board of Regents, was elected as chairman of a task force that included, in addition, Joe Abeyta, Tony Pacheco and Frances Shipman, also from NMTVS; Alex Mercure, UNM; Adan García, Ojo Caliente Schools; Alex M. Naranjo, Española Schools; Sofío D. Ortega, Questa Schools; and Ginger Welch, Los Alamos Schools. Robert Huff, Bill Witter and Tom Wilson represented the Board of Education Finance. John Aragón was present on behalf of New Mexico Highlands University. Two avid supporters of NMTVS were present, Regino Salazar and Andres Gallegos.

To understand further the reasons and role of the Task Force, it is important to understand that, between 1972 and 1976, new institutional roles had developed in northern New Mexico, individuals' jobs and roles had changed, and, perhaps more important, the political climate in New Mexico had vastly changed, becoming more friendly and useful to NMTVS. First, the Northern Branch of the University of New Mexico was fully established, although it had no permanent facilities. The Northern Branch resided in Los Alamos, Santa Cruz and Questa, approximately, meaning that instruction and a few student services were offered there. NMTVS served the same area, and Peñasco and Truchas, in addition. Chama, Tierra Amarilla and Gallina were served by the same institutions, but with less frequency.

Alex Mercure had resigned as President of the New Mexico Technical Vocational Institute and was, in 1976, Vice-President for continuing education and external programs at the University of New Mexico. Eugene LeDoux was Director of UNM's North Branch.

In the State Capitol, Gerry Apodaca had become Governor of New Mexico in January 1975 and would serve a four-year term. Governor Apodaca appointed a new Executive Secretary of the Board of Educational Finance, Robert Huff.

Although the first meeting of the Task Force was largely organizational, it gave impetus to a well-organized effort on the part of NMTVS, which had its own El Rito/Northern Task Force via which it disseminated institutional information. It informed members of the Task Force of the institution's governance, and its capabilities in assuming a greater role in the region should the Task Force recommend that the New Mexico Technical Vocation School and the Northern Branch of the University be merged.

During the second meeting[9] of the Task Force, on August 25, Robert Huff conveyed a message from Governor Apodaca concerning his interest in recommendations of the Task Force. He made it plain in his remarks that the Task Force need not deliberate too long, that questions concerning the inclusion of Taos and Santa Fe could be examined at a later time as separate items.

Representatives of the Española Public Schools were prepared to state a recommendation, in the form of a motion for consideration by the Task Force that the Northern Branch of the University of New Mexico be merged with the New Mexico Technical Vocational School under the auspices of the Board of Regents of NMTVS. The motion met with a consensus of the Task Force.

The next step, the creation of a community college for north central New Mexico, would require approval by the state legislature and the Governor.

Consensus does not mean, of course, unanimity. Although the University of New Mexico did not object to a motion that would involve the dissolution of the branch campus, there were other questions for which there were no immediate answers. Concerns raised on behalf of Los Alamos, Santa Fe and Taos would be an indication that communities might in the future seek their choice of a different institution for their affiliation. Indeed this occurred, but it is a story for a bit later.

Immediately following, Frank Serrano made a cogent argument in a document, "The Governance of a Comprehensive Community College in North Central New Mexico," that has a date of September 14, 1976, in which he outlines the rationale for merging the Northern Branch of the University of New Mexico with the New Mexico Technical Vocational School for the purposes of creating a community college. The question that would be placed before the legislature was a political one that had the tacit approval of the executive branch, but the document consisted of the basis for an important action to be debated in mid-winter of 1977.

Spring 1977 was the final chapter of the New Mexico Technical School. This somewhat battered iteration of the old Normal School had served a very useful purpose.[10] It had demonstrated to members of the region that career education in technical, vocational and professional fields was needed locally, and that academic offerings would round out a broader, stronger institution of higher education.

Notes:

1. The years 1967 to 1970 were years of transition to a vocational school. The adoption of the new name of the school is discussed a bit later in this chapter.

2. Many times programs were supported with state or federal grant funds and they had to be called by the specific training that was provided. This

gave rise to differing titles given to programs, occasionally giving rise to duplication of existing programs in the curriculum.

3. Spanish American Normal School remains the old, official name of this school and aliases are allowed by the New Mexico legislature to facilitate business at the school in a modern era. This has been the case since about 1950 when the first name-change, to Northern New Mexico Normal School, came to be recognized by the state.

4. This is through no great fault of their own. This happens in a state that has no system of higher education and no central planning with sufficient authority to bring about constructive change. Ours has been a system that stresses control.

5. Most of the members of the group would not consider themselves intellectuals, and may actually scoff at the present description. The discussions that took place among them, however, had an intellectual dimension, no doubt.

6. No derision is intended, certainly. This was a man well respected and esteemed by friends and associates.

7. The chief executive officer of the school was known alternately as president or superintendent, depending on the wishes of the Board of Regents. Since 1971, the position has been designated as the presidency.

8. William E. Sailer, NMTVS, distributed what he called "notes" of the proceedings of meetings of the Task Force. Most of the information about the work of the Task Force is taken from Sailer's documents.

9. I attended this meeting of the Task Force in my capacity of Academic Dean of New Mexico Highlands University. Highlands had an interest in the proceedings of the Task Force for reasons not least of which was its presence in Taos where it maintained an attendance center. The remainder of the story about higher education in Taos is told in these pages in the next chapter.

10. An interview with Representative Nick L. Salazar has been most

helpful. He recalls that legislators from the southeastern part of the state, who had little familiarity with the New Mexico Technical Vocational School, were inclined to close the institution, not advance its mission and purpose. Discussions concerning the community college began in earnest in 1974, according to Representative Salazar's recollection. The struggle to establish Northern New Mexico Community College may have been more protracted than is depicted in these pages, but its establishment owes to the tenacity of leadership, primarily in the person of Frank Serrano, and in the support provided by friends of the new community college, who are mentioned here.

10
NORTHERN NEW MEXICO COMMUNITY COLLEGE: GROWING PAINS AND HALCYON DAYS

Waiting for legislation for the enactment of Northern New Mexico Community College was as exciting as its arrival. In December of 1976, the matter was settled: Representative Nick L. Salazar, a junior member of the House of Representative first elected in 1974, would introduce House Bill 326 which would create a community college by merging the Northern Branch of the University of New Mexico with the New Mexico Technical Vocational School. The latter institution still operated in accordance with provisions of the Constitution of New Mexico, which incorporated assumptions in the creation of the Spanish American Normal School in 1909.

Friends were many who were ready to assist Nick Salazar in his quest to have the old Normal School expand its mission, from a purely vocational school to a "junior college," in the old parlance of previous decades. The Normal School would achieve what had been tried quietly by John V. Conway in the early 1930s and with vigor by Charles H. Robinson in the early 1960s, but to no avail. Nick Salazar credits Frank Serrano for being pivotal in the effort, describing the Technical Vocational School's president as persistent and tough-minded. "He pushed all of us," stated Nick Salazar in reference to Serrano.

Nick Salazar could count on the active support of Senator John Rogers (D-LA), who favored creation of the new college from the outset. Senator Edward Lopez and Representatives Ben Luján, Walter Martínez, David Salman and Richard Carbajal were part of the effort. Many young legislators, Democrats, who were referred to as the "Mama Lucy Gang" were active supporters, many of them from Las Vegas where Mama Lucy's liquor establishment resided. Alex Mercure, now a vice-president at UNM, supported the passage of HB 326, and probably due to his presence, the University of New Mexico did not oppose creation of the college. Robert Huff, Executive Secretary of the Board of Educational Finance, represented Governor Jerry Apodaca's administration, indicating clearly their support for the proposed legislation.

Frank Serrano could count on the active support of the Board of Regents of the NMTVS: Dennis Salazar, Chairman; Frances Shipman, Tony Pacheco, Joe Abeyta and José Roybal. Serrano had, in addition, able administrators in Bob Lutz, Lalo Serna, Bill Sailer, and Connie Valdez, new to the team.

Frank Serrano had taken steps to prepare the New Mexico Technical Vocational School well for the eventuality of the new two-year college replacing NMTVS in July of 1977. One was to apprise the North Central Association of the intention of NMTVS to expand its mission. In the area of finance, one of the reports early in the year from the auditing firm of Henry Armijo reported to the Board that the institution was in good financial condition and that its reporting methods were in line with those required by the Board of Educational Finance. Similarly, reports about vocational instruction, headed by Bob Lutz, were laudable. Connie Valdez had been hired as Director of the Bilingual Programs and Jake Martinez directed Adult Basic Education. Lalo Serna, the chief finance officer, had employed George Luján, a former student of the Normal School, as the person in charge of acquisitions and inventory. Key staff had been hired in preparation for vast changes to come.

The administration employed the services of a consultant, John Greer, to devise a master plan for initiation of the two-year college. This would also serve in support of the institution's application for candidacy for accreditation by the North Central Association of Colleges and Schools that following summer of 1977.

In spite of the excitement of anticipation of July 1, 1977, the official date for the creation of the new institution, deliberations during Board meetings of the first half of the year were remarkably subdued. The NMTVS did examine what it wished to be called after July 1, and in May '77 it resolved that it would be Northern New Mexico Community College.[1] President Serrano informed the Board that the combined budget for the new school would be about six million dollars, resulting from combining of budgets of its two predecessors. He also estimated that enrollment in fall 1977 would be close to 3,000 students.

In July 1977, Northern New Mexico Community College hired Frank Serrano III as its first president, after Serrano's three-year tenure as chief executive officer of the New Mexico Technical School.

The first order of business for Northern New Mexico Community College was to offer instruction throughout northern New Mexico in those communities previously served by the Northern Branch of the University of New Mexico and the New Mexico Technical Vocational Institute. Although the core administrative staff presumably resided at El Rito, expectations on the part of the state and logistical considerations for the new community college, dictated that eventually those services would be located more centrally in the service area, namely in Española. Full time instructors were located in El Rito and Española in vocational programs; full time instructors in academic programs, who continued on with the community college,[2] were located principally in Santa Cruz. Since the (old) Northern Branch of UNM tended to hire part-time instructors, the community college was to consider carefully how many and who, specifically, would join the new school as part of its core teaching faculty.

The Catalog for 1977-79 listed attendance centers that had administrative support at El Rito, Española, Los Alamos and Santa Cruz.

The Board of Regents continued with only one change; Jane Bendt from Los Alamos replaced Tony Pacheco of Española. Dennis Salazar continued as Chairman, along with Joe Abeyta, José Roybal and Frances Shipman.

The Catalog listed only its top administration: Frank Serrano III, President; Lalo Serna, Dean of Finance and Administration; Robert Lutz, Dean of Occupational Services; Dan Simundson, Dean of Academic Services; Guy Trujillo, Dean of Continuing and Community Services; and, Adrian Bustamante, Dean of Student Services. Many instructors in vocational programs continued, and in 1977 there were 19 in El Rito and 33 in Española, including evening programs at the latter location. No fewer than 132 part-time instructors in academic programs were listed, a few of whom would become part of the community college's core of full-time instructors in future years.

Low cost of attendance for students has been emphasized by the Normal School since its founding; we have reviewed costs now and then throughout this history. The year 1978 was no different. Tuition for a full time student was $156.00 per semester and $13.00 per credit for anyone attending part time. Vocational students paid $150.00 per semester. All students paid a lab fee of $20.00, if enrolled in laboratory courses.

Each version or iteration of the Spanish American Normal School has been founded on the same set of constitutional laws under which the institution was founded in 1909. It follows then that although its programs were identical in scope and breadth to those in community colleges in the Nation and in New Mexico, it differed fundamentally in that it is state owned and operated. It is not a "local school" in the sense that local taxation contributes to its funding. The majority of community colleges in the US are funded in part by an assessment of taxes on real property in the immediate surroundings of the community college, known as "the district." A few states have community or junior colleges that are funded by the state in which they reside; Oklahoma is one that comes to mind. Tuition collected from students tends to contribute a small percentage of the college's total budget, typically eight to twenty percent. At one time, some community colleges charged no tuition, but that seems in the distant past.

The control and function of Northern New Mexico Community College rested with a Board of Regents (five members) appointed by the Governor.[3] The Board was responsible for all aspects of the operation of the community college, including its programs. In recent years, the legislature has chosen to include statements affecting programs and offerings at all of its colleges and universities, in part because the legislature appropriates funds for these activities.[4] Following the dissolution of the Northern Branch of the University of New Mexico, in a 1978 Compilation of Laws of New Mexico, Section 21-43 the purpose of Northern New Mexico Community College[5] was described: that the students would receive instruction in occupations and vocations which are useful and necessary in New Mexico's economy and that the community college would be governed by a Board of Regents in a manner similar to previous years. That the Board of Regents would be authorized to board students in a manner that had been done previously.

Everyone associated with Northern New Mexico Community College had cause for optimism, in spite of the fact that matters related to its service area, had been left unresolved.

Even with very careful planning, Northern New Mexico Community College encountered its growing pains. One reason is that each of its constituencies, the different communities, and the state of New Mexico each had expectations of the new institution, some of those expectations in conflict with those of another constituency. For example, the state's Board of Educational Finance had urged the school to move its administrative center, namely the Business Office, from El Rito to the campus in Española. This did not sit well with residents in El Rito.

A second problem arose because the institution's ability to serve Santa Fe was not supported, except as an interim solution to the educational needs of residents of Santa Fe. In fact, Northern New Mexico Community College (NNMCC) continued to serve Santa Fe County and the City until its services were no longer needed *de facto.*

The situation surrounding the attendance center at Los Alamos was to prove more disappointing to Northern New Mexico Community College. Part of the community college's planning strategy included a committee[6] of people assigned to study educational needs in Los Alamos and to report back to the President and the Board of Regents. NNMCC expended great effort in identifying a short and long term future for a campus at Los Alamos. In fact, the present site of the branch college in Los Alamos resulted from planning and acquisition of property that occurred in those early days of NNMCC. Very soon after July 1977, however, activists in Los Alamos began a discussion with the community that would result in secession of the Los Alamos Campus from Northern New Mexico Community College. Simultaneously, administrative changes had occurred at the University of New Mexico in precisely the vice presidency that was in charge of the branches of UNM. Alex Mercure, former president of NMTVS and former vice president at UNM, had been named as Assistant Secretary of Agriculture by President Jimmy Carter. The new vice president at UNM, Alex Sanchez, worked energetically with those at Los Alamos interested in their campus's dissolution of ties with Northern New Mexico Community College.[7] Although NNMCC had strong advocates in the person of Senator John Rogers, and several more friends, differing opinions and any slight weakness on the part of NNMCC were exploited quite readily by those advocating for the creation of a branch college of the University of New Mexico. In October 1979, the Los Alamos School Board resolved to call for a vote of referendum in which citizens could opt for a new branch campus of UNM, in spite of the fact that the Los Alamos School District would have to tax citizens for support of the new branch campus. In January 1980, the people of Los Alamos resolved that it did not want the services of Northern New Mexico Community College and that the University of New Mexico would assume responsibility for educational services in July 1980.[89]

Gradual and persistent growth throughout a thirty year period beginning in about 1980 has helped Northern New Mexico Community College to establish itself among the first rank of sister institutions in New Mexico. All of this growth has been in Española in its academic programs. Vocational programs did moderately well in El Rito. Both campuses have seen considerable improvement in their physical plants, with the addition of new buildings in Española and extensive renovations in El Rito.

Increasing population in Rio Arriba County and northern Santa Fe County have helped to sustain this growth. Earlier notions that Northern New Mexico Community College would become a wider, multi-campus system have not materialized. As much as any other factor, local folks' desire for more local control of their schools eventually led citizens in Los Alamos, Santa Fe, and Taos to exercise their prerogatives about two-year college education in each of their communities. As a result, Los Alamos and Taos have independent branches of the University of New Mexico and the Capitol City has Santa Fe Community College. Educational needs among communities are similar, but they are also unique. In job training, Los Alamos and Taos share a set of similarities with Northern; Santa Fe's requirements are broader, with job training not as important as it has been at Northern New Mexico Community College.

Northern New Mexico Community College's student population fluctuated in number during its first ten years as it added, then lost, portions of its service area. After the early 1990s, however, it started to become clearer whom and where Northern would serve. Rather than to regress as its service area became circumscribed, however, the task of identifying appropriate programs and courses for its students became more purposeful. This, in turn, added a vitality to the campuses that had been slowly building since the emergence of the Community College. Educational needs in its service area were obvious, plain to see; Northern responded and communities, in kind, welcomed its staff and faculty.

The Catalog for 1983-85 shows that Northern New Mexico Community College offered a full complement of programs and courses in academic transfer programs, vocational and technical education, and continuing education. [10] The school was offering associate of arts degrees in banking, fine arts, general studies, liberal arts, and southwest studies. It offered an associate of science degree in (general) science and associate of applied science degrees in agriculture, business administration, computer technology, drafting, electronics technology, laser technology, human care services, human services, marketing management, medical radiography, secretarial administration, and word processing. It offered fully 28 certificate programs in vocational and technical training over a wide field of endeavors.

The institution operated principally on two campuses, El Rito and Española, with the second now eclipsing the former in numbers and, therefore, in importance for those in charge. The Board of Regents included Herman Wisenteiner as Chairman, Mary Agnes Martínez, Herman Trujillo, Tony Pacheco, and Dennis Salazar. Frank Serrano III was President and Ted Trujillo was Vice President of the college.[11]

The community college established bus routes, much as the New Mexico Technical Vocational School had done in the previous decade. They were not large numbers of students using this form of transportation, vehicles were principally fourteen-passenger Ford Econoline vans. The school felt obligated to offer the service; not everyone owned a car.

The character of the school changed immeasurably after the 1960s. Both campuses became commuter campuses, although El Rito continued to offer dormitories for students. In the late seventies and early eighties, construction and growth in Española spurted, primarily through the efforts of the administration and an influential friend of the community college, Representative Nick Salazar. Salazar served on the House Appropriation and Finance Committee, which passed on both institutional budgets and capital outlay (construction) projects.

After the Joseph M. Montoya Building, a Metal Trades Building, and a Vocational Education Building came a new library, a general education building, and an appropriation for a fine arts auditorium. The general education building allowed for consolidation of instruction on the west side campus, no longer dependent on the old facility in Santa Cruz. The campus's enrollment began its steady growth as a result.

The right combination of educational programs, the correct mix of academic and vocational offerings, contributed to growth of the Community College. Selection of programs to meet the educational needs of people in the region was seldom a problem at Northern. Whether with the aid of scant data, or by intimate knowledge of the region by staff, the "right stuff" always seemed to emerge. A great deal of credit belonged to administrative and teaching staff; we'll name a few: Priscilla Trujillo, Robert McGeagh, Dennis Jarrett, Tim Thomas, and Connie Valdez were among the early leaders in developing the school's curriculum. Later on, including the decade of the eighties, you can add the names of Anthony Sena, Larry Tafoya, José Griego, and Tim Roybal to developers and innovators of programs in instruction. In adult basic education and developmental studies, two programs that have been crucial in insuring the success of underprepared students, the Community College has had able leaders in Meredith Machen, Eloy Martinez, Lorenzo Gonzales, and Bernadette Chavira-Merriman, who have been willing to extend services, both on and off campus, to as many students as needed to be served.

The community college throughout America has been a unique institution; Northern New Mexico Community College was like its sister schools in its willingness and ability to serve. These institutions have earned plaudits from high officials in the United States, including its presidents, for their contribution to the economic well-being of the Nation.

Frank Serrano resigned as president in 1984 by which time he, his administration, and Boards of Regents had aided in the development of a school with a strong foundation. If in years past there had been doubt of the Normal School's future, it was now obvious that the college was in north central New Mexico to stay, and that in all likelihood better days remained ahead. The most immediate perspective that one can gain on Northern New Mexico Community College was that the sum of its enrollment, during a brief seven years, would exceed the total number of students served by the Spanish American Normal School and the Northern New Mexico Normal School in the course of their entire history, sixty years.

Connie Valdez, a member of the administration, was named Interim President in July 1984.

Interim presidencies are among the more difficult jobs in a college or university. Governing boards are hoping for stability while they go about searching for the permanent chief executive. Administrative and teaching staff are usually looking for assurances that the future will work out well, and they turn to the temporary head of the school during the interim period. In the interim also, there is a school to run, budgets to look after, supervisory responsibilities to fulfill, staff vacancies to fill, and public relations to maintain on behalf of the College. Connie Valdez proved exceptionally trustworthy in all instances, carrying out her responsibilities in the second half of 1984. She chose not to become a candidate for the presidency, and instead she was chosen by the incoming president, Sigfredo Maestas, as the executive vice-president when he arrived in January 1985.

Northern New Mexico Community College was past most problems dealing with its service area and population as the Community College's tenth year approached.[12] As one would expect, an institution that had been through four name changes had an important problem to solve: the matter of its identity before its public. Because it had last been a technical-vocational school, many people still referred to Northern New Mexico Community College as "the TVI." In fact, the closest institution of this kind was ninety miles away in Albuquerque, enjoying a fine reputation as, precisely, a technical-vocational institute.[13]

The administration and Board of Regents set about solving this problem of the institution's mystique. First was the matter of selecting a short name that everyone could remember readily. It was easy to have people settle on "Northern." Angela Warneke, a graphic artist with the Community College, designed a new logo, with "Northern" in big beautiful letters featuring prominently. The logo, which was chosen by students for its accurate and pleasant impact, still remains the school emblem today. It features, in addition to attractive lettering, an American eagle soaring over juniper and piñon hills of northern New Mexico, reminiscent of El Rito.

During this exciting time, given to growth in its permanent service area, northern Santa Fe and Rio Arriba Counties, the Community College was still guided by Regents Herman Wisenteiner, who chaired the Board, Mary Agnes Martínez, Herman Trujillo, Tony Pacheco, Anthony López, John Bird, and Joseph Figueira. Herman Wisenteiner and Herman Trujillo had terms of office that expired early during this period, but they lent stability to the institution and impetus for new direction. Administration included Sigfredo Maestas as President, Priscilla Trujillo as the newly selected Dean of the College, Max R. Sánchez as Dean of Finance, Connie Valdez in charge of Planning and Development, and Levi Valdez directing Continuing Education. This period of stability signaled that there would be very little change among members of faculty and staff; faculty and staff would likely not wish to leave, and their school wished them to stay.

Construction of new buildings on the campus in Española continued unabated. In El Rito, roadways into and around the campus were paved, and major reconstruction of the North Dorm ensued.[14] A performing arts auditorium, with rooms for studios and art shows, was completed in late 1986 in Española; it is known as the Nick L. Salazar Center for the Arts. The Learning Resource Center was named earlier in honor of State Representative Ben Luján. To be named later in the late 1990s were two existing buildings dedicated to general education and to vocational programs, respectively.

One of the consequences of Northern's status as a state institution means that it does not and may not tax locally for construction projects. During the 1986 legislative session, Northern had sought unsuccessfully funds for construction of a gymnasium, designed, among other sports, for basketball.[15] The legislature was in no mood for funding a gymnasium at a community college. In the waning days of the legislative session, Representative Nick Salazar suggested that he and I visit with Governor Toney Anaya with regard to the requested appropriation for funds to build the gym. Governor Anaya viewed the request with favor, and he was emphatic in his response to the request. We could expect funds to be forthcoming, he stated. The gymnasium was constructed in 1987-88. Upon my return, the administration of Connie Valdez and the Board of Regents had selected the name Eagle Memorial Gymnasium for the facility.

Student population continued to grow at a small, but sustained, pace. Sign of growth has always been touted among educators in New Mexico as a sign of a college or university's vitality, whether or not this is the case. There is an indicator used among community colleges that points to a school's "penetration" in its service area. Generally, an index of two percent, or two citizens per one hundred, is viewed as satisfactory. Northern has always exceeded this expectation by more than a factor of two; its penetration is normally in excess of .05. These are only rough estimates of a school's effectiveness. Northern has the advantage that it is the only institution of its kind, with a full complement of vocational and academic programs, within a twenty-five mile radius or more. Communities in the College's service area are often remote, but Northern has continued to find a way to serve them.

Five individuals, in addition to faculty, department heads, and a number of senior staff members, have been able to guide Northern and to influence its direction. Boards of Regents have encouraged innovation and service by an institution that has not had great sums of money at its disposal. Instead, the Community College had forward-seeing administrators as members of teams of people who were willing to work toward a common goal: more and better educational services for its population. The first of these was Frank Serrano, the first president for ten years, beginning during the time of the New Mexico Technical Vocational School. He was followed by Connie A. Valdez as interim president; Connie Valdez later served as president, from 1989 to 1996. José Griego came as Dean of Instruction during Valdez's presidency; he would become president in 2005. Sigfredo Maestas served two terms as president: 1985 to 1989 and 1996 to 2005. Priscilla Trujillo did not serve as president, but she was Dean of the College in the period 1985 to 1989 and executive vice president during Maestas's second term. Although each served at different times, still they managed to evince a similar vision concerning the need for the Community College in north central New Mexico, and they viewed the same means of providing for its population.

Connie Valdez was one of the most creative administrators in New Mexico and the US. Her first assignment as Interim President may have been for a short period, but as Executive Vice-President and Dean of Planning and Development she showed remarkable skill in organizing and supporting activities in support of bilingual education and the arts. She was one of the organizers of the Española Valley Arts Festival during her tenure as Dean, and promoted the Arts Festival by holding it on campus annually for many years. This led, of course, to increased demand for courses and programs in the arts, including music. During her tenure as President in the early 1990s, she recruited José Griego to be Dean of Instruction. He, in turn, assisted Connie Valdez in expanding the curriculum in the arts, drawing, painting, wood sculpture, pottery, and weaving.

It was Connie Valdez, as President, and Dean Griego who recruited Tim Roybal[16] of Medanales to offer a program in Spanish-Colonial Furniture Making. This program and the program in Fiber Arts, weaving, revived a tradition on the El Rito Campus that was extant in the 1940s and earlier. The furniture making program is now ably led by Rick Gonzales and Dan Tafoya, two of Tim Roybal's former students.

The arts program, in particular the folk arts, have blossomed at Northern New Mexico Community College and it owes primarily to the efforts of Connie Valdez and José Griego. Indeed the program has had many contributors, many of whom will remain unsung. Many are local people who have had an unflagging interest and devotion to carving *santos* and *bultos*, in drawing and constructing *retablos*, and in tin-smithing in Mexican and Spanish styles. Connie Valdez and José Griego promoted and supported these activities, and the latter endure.

Everyone who worked with Connie A. Valdez regrets her passing away in December 2005.

Priscilla Trujillo was never president of the institution, she did not apply for the position, and perhaps, at some point, she should have. She is certainly one of the most able administrators that the author has known. Her capacity for work, deliberate efficiency, and unmatched productivity made her invaluable to Northern. Her own field was in the teaching of students in business and office occupations. She had the longest tenure of the school's administrators, having started as an instructor in 1971. Two years later she became the Chair of departments that were recognized by such names as business and office administration; her start was with the New Mexico Technical Vocational School. She became Dean of Instruction in the early years of Northern New Mexico Community College, then elected to return to her department.

The author recruited Priscilla Trujillo to be Dean of the College in 1985, and she served in this capacity till the President's departure in July 1989. She served as Executive Vice President, again with Maestas, from 1996 to 2004. The title of the position in each case was different; the job was the same. Priscilla Trujillo had executive powers on both campuses and in off-campus programs, and she administered the Española Campus, where her office was located. Her unusual qualifications, having served as teacher, Department Chair, and Dean of Instruction, made it possible for her to maintain supervisory responsibility in all aspects of the Community College. She deferred to the President, primarily in the area of finance, but the Dean of Finance, Max Sanchez in the late 1980s and Loretto García in the 1990s, maintained cordial and cooperative relationships with Priscilla Trujillo throughout their respective tenures.

Sigfredo Maestas had been recruited to the Community College, first in 1979, as I described earlier. He served as President more than thirteen years, first from 1985 to 1989, then from 1996 to 2005. This was the longest tenure of any president of the institution since Joseph B. Grant. Without being too self-serving, we like to view the latter period, in particular, as the halcyon days of the Community College. This arose primarily from the Community College's increased stability, maturity being a prime factor in its favor; by 1996 Northern New Mexico Community College had existed for nineteen years. It had acquired the ability to train people for available jobs in the region, including openings at the Los Alamos National Laboratory. The Community College was also beginning to make its mark as a center of discussion concerning economic development in the valley and Rio Arriba County, in addition to other educational and social issues. Maestas prided himself in being able to engage Boards of Regents and the general public in setting the tone about, and the way for, Northern New Mexico Community College.

José Griego, who shared a similar educational background with President Connie Valdez, has a doctoral degree in bilingual education. He is a former public school principal, which served him well in helping to advance the mission of Northern New Mexico Community College, as will be shown later in these pages.

José Griego loves the arts, and is a musician. During the author's tenure as President of Northern, he helped to recruit Donna Winchell to chair the Art Department. Immediately they made great progress in organizing the curriculum and in enlarging the scope of activities that promoted both classical and folk art.

José Griego, Cathy Berryhill, and Patrick Tate were individuals who organized the curriculum for the Alternative Licensure Program for teachers, and sought and obtained all approvals necessary for the offering. As a result, Northern New Mexico Community College was the first higher educational institution in New Mexico, two-year or four-year, to offer a path for alternative licensure for aspiring teachers.

In winter 2005, upon retirement of Sigfredo Maestas as President, José Griego was selected as fourth President of Northern New Mexico Community College.

By 2005, Northern had approval from the legislature and the Governor of New Mexico, to begin offering the baccalaureate degree. This approval for further expansion of the mission of the institution, is discussed toward end of this chapter.

In addition to contributions of top administrators, NNMCC had faculty and department chairs who were knowledgeable in their fields and adept at development of programs. Among them were Dr. Robert McGeagh in the humanities; Dr. Dennis Jarrett in languages; Dr.Tim Thomas in social science and humanities; Dr. Anthony Sena, in biology and environmental science; Ramona Gonzales, Nancy Schlosser, and Ellen Trabka in nursing; Bruce Smith and Sung Soo Park in technology; Dr. Meredith Machen, Lorenzo Gonzales and Bernadette Chavira-Merriman in Developmental Studies; Priscilla Trujillo, Orlando Roybal, and Drucilla Duran in business and office administration; Catherine Martínez-Berryhill and Patrick Tate in education; Dr. Albert Amador and Ronald Black in mathematics.

Beginning in January 1985, the author's knowledge of affairs involving the Board of Regents of the institution became intimate and much more real. In the first instance, I found working with Boards of Regents profitable for the Community College and enjoyable for me personally. The ability to engage a Board, if it doesn't come naturally, can be learned with a modicum of effort. Although each individual Board has its character and personality as the sum of its five members, in the case of Northern New Mexico Community College Boards were very similar in outlook and goal setting. The outlook was always optimistic, and Boards were usually interested, if not anxious, to know what progress was being made in the numerous efforts the Community College was undertaking because, although mature, the institution was nevertheless in various developmental stages in expanding its mission and horizons.

Rather than to treat of the different Boards who worked with the author and with President Connie Valdez since 1984, it would be best simply to list the names of Board members and to treat of the accomplishments of some of these Board members *as examples* of what many of them did.

Chairman of the Board of Regents was Herman Wisenteiner in 1984 on a Board that included Tony Pacheco, Mary Agnes Martínez, Herman Trujillo, Anthony López, followed soon after by John Bird and Joseph Figueira. Subsequent Boards included Mike Martin, Mary Frances Polanco, Elizabeth Maestas, Elias V. Martínez, Vernon Jaramillo, Priscilla Trujillo-Schafer, Nelson D. Cournoyer, Ted Martínez, Nick J. Vigil, Levi Pesata, Lupe L. García, Rosario (Chayo) García, Dennis Salazar, and Michael Branch.

Any time that there is a change in administration in a college or university, and an interim president as we had at Northern, a brief period of instability ensues. Herman Wisenteiner as Chairman of the Board was helpful to the Interim President and the new President (Maestas) during this period. The Board was strengthened further with the addition of the brilliant minds of Anthony López and Joseph Figueira, and the knowledgeable advice of John Bird and Mary Agnes Martínez, whose intimate knowledge of the valley and Rio Arriba County was useful. Mike Martin is a grandson of George J. Martin, the first President of the Spanish American Normal School, whom you have met. Martin's devotion to Northern remained undiminished and continues to this day. Vernon Jaramillo and Levi Pesata are two former school superintendents whose practical knowledge, in education, administration, and finance, was always evident and helpful. Ted Martínez is a former college president, of then Albuquerque Technical Vocational School, and a person of vast experience in many facets of college and university administration. Nick Vigil is a banking executive, with probably the strongest background in finance possible. Lupe García, Rosario García, and Dennis Salazar are business people in the Española Valley; Michael Branch is similarly in business in Santa Fe. I point out the background of this exceedingly competent team of people because many times governors are criticized about their appointments to these boards. If we were to entertain sports jargon to describe the group, this is certainly and all-star team. We were privileged to work with them.

Herman Wisenteiner, Anthony López, John Bird, Mike Martin, Elías Martínez, Priscilla-Trujillo Schafer, Nick Vigil, Dennis Salazar, and Michael Branch are former chairs of the Board of Regents.

As important as it may be for a president of a college to be satisfied in working with a governing board, and in finding pleasure in his work, so also it seems fair to expect that members of Boards of Regents should enjoy their tenure on the Board, and to view that their work has made real contribution toward the betterment of the institution.

The author interviewed three former Board members for this book. Continuing dialogues are maintained with three other Board members who happen to be alumni of the old Northern New Mexico Normal School.

In the case of Mike Martin, a man from El Rito, born in Santa Fe in 1958, and educated in the local schools, we learned: Martin was educated at St. Thomas Elementary School in Santa Fe. When there came to be insufficient numbers of nuns to teach, the school closed. Mike Martin attended the Mesa Vista High School, which was the successor of Northern New Mexico Normal School for children from El Rito. He attended New Mexico State University after high school and obtained the bachelor of arts degree in Farm and Ranch Management in the school of agricultural economics.

In spring 1987, Mike Martin was appointed to the Board of Regents by Governor Garry Carruthers. Anthony López chaired the Board; other members were Joseph Figueira, and John Bird.

Martin was willing to talk openly about College, its successes and problems. Funding of the college, based on a two-year lag in information, made for difficulties. He felt that short-term programs on the campus at

El Rito "don't cut it long range." He marveled at the success of the Community College Foundation and its growth.

Mike Martin joined the Board at the age of 29, in 1987, and left the Board six years later. During the tenure of Governor Bill Richardson, the Governor inquired of Mike Martin whether he would serve a second time. Martin had to decline; the assignment required more time than he could devote to the Board.

Mike Martin emphasized how much he enjoyed his tenure on the Board. He especially enjoyed its graduation exercises. He felt that when students graduating in the GED Program were added to the commencement program, it made for greater excitement. He also enjoyed the excitement in the Salazar Center for the Arts.

Nick Vigil was appointed to the Board of Regents by Governor Gary Johnson, in winter 1997.

Nick Vigil is a resident of Española, where he grew up and was educated. Always an avid sports fan and sportsman, he played baseball during high school. At the time, he particularly liked and enjoyed one of the coaches at the high school, Casey Martínez. Martínez is one of the alumni of the Normal School whom we featured in Chapter Eight in this book.

Nick Vigil graduated at the Española High School and attended the University of New Mexico. He remembers with fondness his years at UNM and how he worked his way in college. Without him telling you, you can visualize a young man, not spoiled in childhood in the least, working his way confidently toward a degree in business.

He is still a no-nonsense, superbly responsible bank executive that you would expect him to grow to be. An exceptionally good listener, he worked with banks in Santa Fe before becoming Vice President at Valley National Bank in Española.

Soon after coming to the Board of Regents, he was elected its Chair. He worked with Vernon Jaramillo, Priscilla Trujillo-Schafer, Nelson Cournoyer and Ted Martínez on an exceptionally strong Board that offered its president unwavering support. Nick Vigil provided the most thorough financial scrutiny of the College's budgets, expenditures, and accounting during this time, which we at the College found useful and helpful.

Priscilla Trujillo-Schafer was introduced to readers in Chapter Eight, concerning our high school alumni. Suffice it to say that she was extremely supporting to the author as President. During this interview, she reiterated that this was one of the more important and enjoyable times for her as member and Chair of the Board of Regents.

Rosario (Chayo) García was appointed to the Board of Regents in 2002 by Governor Gary Johnson. Rosario García is a businesswoman in Española. Soon after her appointment to the Board, she told me how much she enjoyed her work on the Board. One of the better indicators of a person's dedication to civic duty and public service is her willingness to serve. Rosario García, following her term on the Board of Regents, ran for and became a member of the Española City Council. Her ability to work harmoniously and constructively was evident when she was on the Board of Regents. The Council is fortunate she chose to undertake a new challenge, and those who knew her at Northern are proud that she is on the Council.

John Bird served on the Board of Regents two terms. He was first appointed by Governor Toney Anaya in 1985.

John Bird is a former art teacher in the Española Public Schools, having taught both junior and senior high school. He is also a member of Ohkay Oweenge Pueblo, and he is a former Governor of the Pueblo.

Regent Bird is an example for students who have an interest in how boards operate, and in particular in their harmonious operation. His discussions with the President of the college were always to the point, without any threat implied. His ability to obtain information, and to share it with Board members, is one distinct memory of John Bird that has remained with the author.

Michael Branch, Ted Martínez, and Dennis Salazar have been Board members, seldom simultaneously, but they are friends. Branch and Salazar are of the Normal School Class of 1954; Martínez is of the Class of 1955. They share with the author reasons for their unwavering support of Northern New Mexico College.

The story of Northern New Mexico Community College is one of remarkable success, which owes principally to the dedication of the many people whom I mention in this chapter and to the hard work of its staff and teachers. These elements were always there since the founding of the Community College. Almost magically, however, once the institution came to be recognized as "Northern" and its mission and capability understood by Northern's constituencies, its successes began to mount.

The author's use of the term halcyon days is not exaggerated. Twice in the author/President's memory in late 1990s and early 2000, comments were made by members of the public that bear repeating. C. L. Hunter, former proprietor of the Ford dealership in Española, was reported in the *Rio Grande Sun* to have said that Northern was the best thing that happened in the Española Valley since the Los Alamos National Laboratory.[17]

Although the statement is obviously more flattering than accurate, nevertheless, at a time when Northern New Mexico Community College needed community support, this was strong indication that it was forthcoming.

A few years later, in meetings with representatives of the Los Alamos National Laboratory and its contractors, one of the latter stated that "Northern is an oasis" in northern New Mexico. Of course, he was referring to the absence of higher educational opportunity in the region, and the role that Northern New Mexico Community College was trying to play in bringing this service. Clearly, the situation that Northern had encountered in Los Alamos during the early days of the Community College, was vastly changed by around the period 1998 to 2002. The Los Alamos National Laboratory, under the leadership of Siegfried Hecker, John Browne, and Pete Nanos, had become a helpful friend of Northern New Mexico Community College, as our later discussion illustrates.

How about students? Where are they in this successful story? This is often a question that accrediting agencies ask, but moreover, this is a story that for Northern New Mexico College continues to mount incrementally.

Readers may be unhappy with this book for the paucity of names of students from the days of Northern New Mexico Community College, as we provided from the earlier days of the institution (and as we will provide concerning graduates in the new baccalaureate programs.)

The answer is that there were simply too many. Northern New Mexico Community College has graduated a large number of people annually: associate degrees and certificates. Mike Costello, our former Dean of Students, estimated that Northern averaged 150 to 175 graduating students per year. Graduates of Northern New Mexico Community College would require a book dedicated to them alone.

In contrast, graduates have frequently encountered little difficulty in finding employment. I can recall when Xerox hired one of our first graduates, a woman, in electronics; we were proud.

The Assistant to the President at Northern, Josephine Aguilar, is one of our graduates. She first came to Northern, on the school bus from Peñasco in 1971 and enrolled in Office Administration. Her diligence and hard work has earned her an important position at Northern, but moreover, the esteem of everyone who comes into contact with here. Her experience is more varied than Northern New Mexico Community College. In her early days out of college she worked in Santa Fe for the Construction Industries Division, and then at the National Parks Service for ten years.

Shortly before retiring, I received a telephone call from Johnny Martinez, a young man from Española. He had received a degree in Computer Technology from Northern, and was vice president and co-owner of a computer company in Phoenix, AZ. He was pleased to let me know that Northern had played a vital role in his preparing for a career.

This discussion could continue page after page. The number of graduates of Northern New Mexico Community College is now a few thousand.

Further evidence of Northern's acceptance in the community, and the latter's willingness to support efforts undertaken by the Community College, were evident to me immediately on my arrival as President, my second term, in 1996.

First, response to the Northern New Mexico Community College Foundation was extremely gratifying. Susan Herrera, the present Executive Director of the Los Alamos National Laboratory Foundation, was employed by Northern when I arrived in July. She was employed in one of the College's grant programs, but she wanted to do more to help students and ensure the future of the College. She had experience with fund raising. We immediately got to work in organizing the Foundation, and, in particular, contacting potential members for its board of directors. The purpose of the foundation, in brief, was to raise funds, establish an endowment fund with the money, and award scholarships to students from this permanent fund. We enjoyed two advantages: great enthusiasm on the part of business people of the community and ordinary citizens, and the willingness of the Los Alamos National Laboratory and its contractors to make donations of approximately $10,000...each. Susan suggested that one large annual "event" was all that was necessary to raise funds during the year that would approximate the maximum potential in our community. She was right. The First Annual Endowed Scholarships dinner resulted in a net growth to the scholarship fund of about $85,000. For about another eight years thereafter, the Foundation achieved similar results.

Two other sources of funds materialized. During the year, before and after each gala "event", funds would trickle in from interested donors. The federal government, via its Title V program for developing Hispanic institutions, began to offer a yearly match that may have amounted to close to a half million dollars during a five year period. By the time the author retired as President in 2005, the endowment fund had grown to close to two million dollars.

This has been worth telling because it illustrates that communities in this region, people who work and reside here, are willing and able to support scholarships for students. It is doubtful that fund raising for construction, or some other purpose, would be met with the same enthusiasm that was accorded to the Endowed Scholarship Fund.

Susan Herrera left the Community College soon after the first year of the Foundation. Felicia Casados became the second Director of the NNMCC Foundation. Her good planning, and continued use of the methodology that I have described, ensured the success of the Foundation. By 2004, the Foundation was able to award about 60 scholarships annually and still grow the endowment fund.

The endowment fund and the Foundation seem certain to remain a permanent part of Northern New Mexico College.

Buildings and funds for renovations that were not funded by the state of New Mexico came about by different means.

Representative Nick Salazar, who sought funds for the Community College for more than 25 years, had a working relationship with staff of the

Economic Development Agency (EDA). The Montoya Administration Building had been constructed in the early seventies with EDA funds. In late 1990s, we proposed a high technology manufacturing facility for the training of technicians. We were able to provide smaller amounts from other sources, but EDA provided a majority of funds needed for construction of the building. This building was very popular in its early period for the training of technicians for such industries as Intel, in Albuquerque, with whom the Community College maintained a mutually profitable relationship. A number of Northern's graduates went to work there. In time, the Board of Regents named this facility the Sigfredo Maestas High Technology Manufacturing Facility. One of the Regents, in fact its Chairman, Nick Vigil, was not simply enthusiastic about naming the new facility for the President, but his arguments carried the day at Northern New Mexico Community College. The building now houses programs in Engineering and Information Technology.

Obtaining funds for construction on the campus in El Rito was always more difficult. The southern part of the county in Española has become the population center, and political support for almost any endeavor is easier to acquire, as a result. Readers may cast their eyes to the development of county government, and you will witness that Rio Arriba County is establishing more and more offices in Española, no longer in the northern county seat, Tierra Amarilla.

One of the gems on the El Rito campus has always been Cutting Hall. This auditorium had undergone change, not always designed to make it more attractive. Starting in 1998, for about four years we planned and sought funds for major renovation, especially of the auditorium. The McCune Foundation, in Santa Fe, provided Northern a small grant for designing its renovation, and for planning a theater arts program. In a separate donation, the McCune Foundation's sister office in Pittsburgh, PA awarded an amount of money to the College for the renovation.

Drew Mendez, the Director of Physical Facilities at the time, is an architect and a very creative individual. He designed the renovation, employed local northern New Mexico themes in the auditorium's restoration, and hired local craftsmen to restore ceiling, walls, and floor. The acting stage was restored, and a projection booth for video projection was constructed. Plastered walls and wood throughout predominate in the auditorium, as a result. Much of the wood is carved in a Spanish-colonial style. Heavy wooden benches were constructed of Honduran mahogany. There are few buildings in northern New Mexico to rival the beauty of the interior of Cutting Hall.

The Los Alamos National Laboratory had requested its contractors to assist the region in matters related to economic development and environment. Many seminars related to these were held on the campus of Northern New Mexico Community College in Española.

Among the contractors, and participants during meetings at the College, was Johnson Controls, which had the largest charge among contractors of the Laboratory. Johnson Controls was interested in building a building, perhaps as large as 20,000 square feet, that would invite entrepreneurs in order to help them during their start-up phase in the latter's new business ventures. We got to know Ann Tiernan, a consultant for JCI, as the company was known, and the president of Johnson Controls, Mark Filteau.

After many discussions with Ann Tiernan, she invited an executive team from Johnson Controls to visit with us, the administration, to discuss the possible construction of this building on our campus. JCI liked our proposal, which was that the new building would be used for the purposes stated on the Española campus for ten years rent-free after which Johnson Controls would cede the building to Northern New Mexico Community College.

The experiment with the use of "incubator space" in the JCI Building, as it is called, met some successes. As one would expect, in some instances potential businesses simply closed up and departed the building without realizing any success. In any case, both the Community College and Johnson Controls learned some useful lessons during the experiment.

At end of 2008, Johnson Controls officially ceded the building to Northern New Mexico College.

During this same period, in which the Los Alamos National Laboratory and its contractors, state and county government, and private businesses in the Española Valley became concerned about the further development of the economy, Northern New Mexico Community College was serving as a center for meetings and discussion. Mike Warren, president of Valley National Bank, and the author came on the idea to organize individuals and businesses in the valley to promote development. We organized meetings, provided outside consultants with a broad view of economic developmental efforts in rural United States, and resolved to incorporate as the Greater Española Valley Community Development Corporation.

What started out as a modest effort to promote economic development, soon developed into a forum that entertained economic, educational, social and cultural concerns of its members. Perhaps the most important contribution that these discussions made was toward furthering our understanding of the importance of education of young people in the valley, the county, and throughout Northern's service area.

Other members of the CDC, as the organization came to be known, may have differing views on the import of the various topics and considerations that were explored in meetings. The matter of the education of our young people captured my attention. We, at the Community College, were becoming increasingly alarmed with shrinking high school graduating classes, and and with simultaneously diminishing numbers of teachers in neighboring school districts.

Northern New Mexico Community College had been on sound footing for many years. In 2002, when we observed 25 years of its creation, there was cause for celebration. Connie Valdez, Frank Serrano, and Margaret Mercure, wife of Alex Mercure, joined us in the festivities.

Accreditation visits by the North Central Association, in 1987 and again in 1994, had given Northern assurance that its development was on schedule and on track. Northern New Mexico Community College was a fully functioning, comprehensive community college in tune with similar colleges throughout the nation.

There were ominous signs, however. Because funding for Northern, as throughout higher education in New Mexico, was dependent on enrollment, there was at least mild concern for the future. Graduating classes, particularly at the Española Valley High School, were getting smaller. Other rural high schools in Northern's service area were also getting smaller, but reasons were more connected with changing population of school-age children. In the Española Valley, drop-out rates seemed inordinately high, especially from high school. Teachers in high demand fields, science and mathematics, were becoming more scarce. A view of this panorama indicated that high schools in Northern's service area would be graduating fewer and fewer students, thereby affecting enrollment in the Community College severely. The principal that everyone recognized was that with fewer students, diminished funding would ensue.

For a few years, we tried to attract the attention of the universities in order to offer teacher education programs, or, at the very least, courses on the Española Campus. New Mexico State University seemed interested in providing some assistance, but it was out of their department of Engineering Technology; this didn't quite fill the bill. It seemed unlikely that the University of New Mexico would assist; even their branch colleges in Los Alamos or Taos were not receiving the attention which we were requesting for Northern New Mexico Community College.

New Mexico Highlands University seemed like a likely partner, but administrative and financial instability were afflicting Highlands during almost exactly the same period that we felt north central New Mexico needed help with teacher training programs. Senior administrators at Highlands were cordial, and seemed sympathetic. For a number of reasons, probably owing to commitments in its immediate service area[18], Highlands was unable to respond to our request.

During a discussion that the author held with José Griego, Northern's Dean of Instruction; Carlos Atencio, Executive Director of the Northern Network of public school districts; and Vicente Llamas, former Professor of Physics at Highlands and consultant in science education, we came on the realization that Northern's only option was to seek state authority to offer the baccalaureate degree in teacher education, i.e. in elementary and secondary education. Already the institution had a successful Alternative Licensure Program, and therefore a growing list of courses in the profession. A program in elementary education could be offered almost immediately upon approval by the state and accreditation by the North Central Association. Accreditation visits by the state's public education department could more readily be arranged; New Mexico was coming under the umbrella of the National Council for Accreditation in Teacher Education (NCATE), thereby standardizing accreditation of similar programs.

Secondary education was equally important, and there was perhaps a greater reason for urgency in establish a program for teaching high school, especially language arts, science, and mathematics.

The President and the Dean placed the item for consideration by the Board of Regents. At first, there was moderate hesitancy by the Board, but it consented that we should begin planning a program in teacher education. Soon it became evident that there was support within the Northern Network, which included schools in Northern's service area, and that the Network was contributing to the planning that was occurring. The author attended some of the planning sessions, which occasionally became quite theoretical and philosophical and, as a result, very interesting. Soon thereafter, the Board of Regents and the entire campus, so it seemed, was enthusiastic in knowing that perhaps the original intended mission of the Normal School would be achieved.

11
RETURN TO THE NORMAL SCHOOL'S ORIGINAL MISSION

It was obvious to each of the members present, once we had become familiar with the issue that was before Northern New Mexico Community College, that the only solution to the problem of the state's inability to (1) graduate a sufficient number of teachers in desired fields and (2) ensure that new graduates were applying to local schools for teaching jobs. I knew full well the history of the Spanish American Normal School, and as we discussed the current problem in consideration of this near history, the solution to a vexing problem was to return to the Normal School's original mission.

I should state right at the outset that the presence of José Griego was without a doubt a strength among us. You may say the same about Carlos Atencio. The two scientists in this spring meeting were Dr. Vince Llamas and me; Vince was a physics professor at New Mexico Highlands University, and I had been a chemistry professor at the same institution. Let me review: José Griego had degrees in education. Therefore, he was thoroughly familiar with elementary and secondary education, including the prescribed curricula in New Mexico. And, most importantly, he was very interested in a return to the mission of the Spanish American Normal School. He was the sole source of support that I needed, apart from the Board of Regents, because this body, according to law in the state of New Mexico, Boards determine the offerings at each of the institutions of higher learning.

Venceslao Jaramillo, the founder of the Spanish American Normal School, as I have related this bit of history for our readers, unfortunately left nothing that I have found related to the founding of this institution of higher education. In *Children of the Normal School*, some of which I have unfortunately had to recount here, I provided some biographical information about Mr. Jaramillo which I may have to retell here. I am hesitant to provide the information, not because the source of some of this information Roberta Martin Brosseau, but because the exact information that I found at the time would bear repeating unless correspondence from Venceslao Jaramillo related to the Spanish American Normal School should reappear.

However, I shall reassert that Venceslao Jaramillo is the principal involved in the founding of the Spanish American Normal School. In about 1904, Venceslao had attempted to found a normal school at El Rito, failed, but nevertheless settled for a building on his property and Cleofas's on the outskirts of El Rito. Cleofas and Venceslao had been married in July 1898; New Mexico guarantees that property belonging to one person belongs to the spouse automatically. One of the considerations is that the original building on the campus of the Spanish American Normal School had been associated with a reform school that was not built. The Spanish American Normal School had been planned and built by Venceslao Jaramillo. You do not know the community of El Rito, and therefore Venceslao Jaramillo, as the brilliant man whom he was. Readers may review a book published by Cleofas M. Jaramillo, *Romance of a Little Village Girl*; the copy that I have is published by the University of New Mexico Press in the year 2000.

Venceslao Jaramillo was a lucky man; he had been born in El Rito to Pedro Ygnacio Jaramillo and Ana María Gallegos de Jaramillo on February 27, 1875, but moreover, he'd been born into a family that had had two older sisters. The sisters, in turn, delighted in a brother whom they adored for his brilliance. Venceslao's father had served in the Territory of New Mexico's legislature, when El Rito was a center of some legislative activity that tended to favor north central New Mexico. El Rito had been a sheep-growing community, and prospered until the surrounding area became depleted of grass; people in El Rito gradually switched to growing cattle since that time.

Pedro Ygnacio had married one of the Gallegos sisters; the other was married to Tom Burns further up the road in Park View. Two matters happened in succession to Venceslao Jaramillo: one is that Mr. Burns sent Venceslao to accompany the younger Tom Burns, Jr. to Notre Dame

University (else the campus in which Notre Dame is located.) The second thing that happened is that, following his stay at Notre Dame (Venceslao was 11 years of age), he enrolled in Regis College in Denver and then St. Michael's College in Santa Fé. Following his studies at the latter institution, he was elected to the (Territorial) House of Representatives in 1896. Readers may do the arithmetic as well as I can: however, if you deduct February of 1875 from 1896, you may see that the difference is 21 years, if you are willing to wait for February to come around, in order that Venceslao Jaramillo may enroll in the House of Representatives. I should mention that Venceslao and both Tom Burns were Republican, they belonged to the "party of Lincoln", and thus it was that Venceslao Jaramillo was even allowed to run for office in 1895. Politics in New Mexico were interesting.

Cleofas Jaramillo tells the foregoing story, the political aspect, in a manner that casts admiration on Venceslao Jaramillo emphatically. Roberta Martin Brosseau was Cleofas Jaramillo's friend growing up in El Rito. Many years later, Cleofas would publish a book, *Shadows of the Past*, for which Roberta Martin designed the cover. This book tells the story about growing up in Arroy Hondo, a village north of Taos.

Venceslao sponsored an action in the 1909 legislative session, where he had served in the Territory of New Mexico's Senate, at a time when his friend L. Bradford Prince was senator living in Chamita, County of Rio Arriba. It was clearly Venceslao Jaramillo's bill, reintroduced by L. Bradford Prince, that passed the senate of Territorial New Mexico during its final day.

Each person, a member of the Northern New Mexico Community College, had decided that, if the Board of Regents approved the proposal for NNMCC to develop the bachelor's degree program in elementary and secondary education, it would accomplish what Venceslao Jaramillo had proposed during the 1908 legislative session.

There is a tendency to be repetitive; I hope that readers will forgive this.

Governor L. Bradford Prince, was the bill sponsor and first Chairman of the Board of Regents. Governor Prince had many admirers among us. One of his books I have relied on for a description of biases of the times: *New Mexico's Struggle for Statehood*, the copy is one I have republished by Sunstone Press, 2000. When Bradford Prince was

Governor of New Mexico, he established the Department of Education with its first director as Amado Chávez; he believed firmly that, in order for New Mexico to advance, its populace must be well educated. Each of us who worked for education at all levels would come to admire that characteristic.

During fall 2003, we held discussions with the Commission on Higher Education concerning the need for programs leading to degrees in teacher education in north central New Mexico. The matter of a shortage of teachers, especially in mathematics and science, was very real, but for unknown reasons, the Commission did not propose that another institution could assist on our campus. The Commission merely pointed out that universities were present on one or two other community college campuses, but did not have a concrete solution for the problem that we were discussing. We countered that, in the absence of teacher education programs present in either El Rito or Española, Northern New Mexico Community College was preparing to offer the bachelor's degree in elementary and secondary education, and, possibly, in special education. The Commission was opposed, although we were requesting its support in this effort.

In that late fall and winter, we expressed to the Commission on Higher Education that its support of Northern's efforts to assist northern public school systems with teacher education was not required. We, nevertheless, went on record that we, the institution, desired its approval and support. The fact is that the Board of Regents of Northern New Mexico Community College has the legal right, as authorized by the Constitution of the State of New Mexico, to determine its educational programs. The request was congruent with the original mission of the Spanish American Normal School of 1909, and within the prerogatives of the Board of Regents of said school. What was required was the New Mexico Legislature's approval and the Governor of the State, and their willingness to provide funds for any and all programs of instruction in the College.[19]

Not just parenthetically, it's important to add that this kind of problem, the inability of the state to respond to real need for higher education in any locale, is based on the fact that there is no real system of higher education. Mission, role, and function of higher educational institutions remain a matter for each individual college or university.

At any given time, any consideration of providing for an institution's ability and effectiveness is determined by consideration, primarily, of what exists *today*. In other words, for governing bodies it is as though the institutions were as they are presently, and any change in the manner that they conduct themselves is to be examined in the context of the present. To summarize the explanation further, there is no state plan or social compact by which institutions may be guided.

In the case of the need for teacher education programs locally, our concern and anxiety was born out in about 1996 by the fact that the Española Public School superintendent resorted to recruiting teachers from the Philippine Islands. Other school districts in New Mexico, including the larger ones, have had to recruit teachers from foreign countries.[20]

Student enrollments in community colleges across America have included a large majority of non-traditional students,[21] often including large numbers of women. One of our concerns, that students could not and would not relocate to a university town to complete their studies, arose from the fact that Northern had a vast number of non-traditional students. In the student body, the percentage of women was usually around 65%; a two to one ratio of women to men. Most students commuted to campus for classes; few students lived in the dormitories in El Rito. We speculated that the trend would continue, and we were right. The number of older, independent students continued to increase. Many students had family responsibilities, but we should emphasize, the majority would continue to be women.

Our students need help; they needed programs in which they were interested that were only present at the universities. Teacher education was the prime example of studies that were unavailable in this northern Rio Grande valley.

We learned that the superintendent of the Española Public Schools had begun to recruit students from the Phillipine Islands. Each of the people recruited had to pay a sum of money; their papers, necessary to work in the United States, were presumably set in order as a result. In time, however, students recruited to our shores learned that they could get better jobs in eastern United States, in locations where populations were greater. My wife, who was until retirement a teacher in the Española Public Schools, helped to write letters of recommendation on behalf of a teacher whom she considered exceptional. My wife was sorry to see the person leave the Española Schools, but she felt that it was inevitable that the person would leave. They came to the United States to earn better salaries, after all.

In early 1994, during discussion with Legislative Finance Committee (LFC), we informed this body of the legislature that Northern New Mexico Community College would request specific authority to offer programs in teacher education, as described earlier. The Committee, which has members of both House and Senate, included Representative Nick Salazar of Rio Arriba County and Representative Max Coll of Santa Fe County, among other of its members. During the meeting, Representative Coll expressed to the LFC and to others in the audience, including members of the Commission on Higher Education, that Northern New Mexico Community College had the constitutional authority to offer baccalaureate degree programs, if its Board of Regents approved.

In a meeting with Governor Bill Richardson that included Michael Branch and Dennis Salazar of the Board of Regents, and Ted Martínez, a former Regent, he explained to us that, if the legislature approved our request to expand the mission of Northern New Mexico Community College, he would approve the bill with his signature.

Every indication was that Northern New Mexico Community College's request to add the baccalaureate programs in teacher education would receive a hearing. Chances of approval of a legislative bill that contained financial support of the programs remained unclear, but there was room for optimism.

For reasons that I have explained already, the unexpected occurred first. A House bill that contained our requests was tabled, declared not germane, because during this short session of the legislature only bills needing a legislative appropriation could be introduced. Never mind the fact that the bill was, precisely, a request for present and future legislative funding[22]

The Senate operates by a different set of rules, and immediately Senator Richard Martinez, also from Rio Arriba County, introduced Senate Bill 163, which contained Northern's request for support of the baccalaureate degree in teacher education. As SB 163 progressed through Senate committees, it was modified to state that the Board of

Regents of Northern New Mexico Community College could approve the offering of said programs upon accreditation of program(s) (by its regional accrediting agency.) This would postpone funds for teacher education at Northern, perhaps one year, but it would automatically indicate approval of future formula funds.

Northern's legislative proposal generated much interest and discussion. Legislators from San Miguel County, and other friends of New Mexico Highlands University, expressed a concern, but wished simply for increased cooperation between Highlands and Northern in all matters of higher education. One has to wonder the pressure that was brought to bear on the Office of the Governor by, for example, dissenting members of the Commission on Higher Education. If there was discussion about which we were unaware, it was of small consequence.

The New Mexico State Senate approved Senate Bill 163, with amendments that I have explained, with only one dissenting vote. Senator Martínez was in his first term in the Senate.

Opposition to HB 163 could have been more severe. There is always the occasion in which an unpopular or controversial bill can be tabled in one of several committees. In this case, however, Representative Nick Salazar and the Speaker of the House, Representative Ben Luján of Santa Fe County, made certain that the bill moved along with each hearing. Especially in House Education Committee, the bill could have encountered serious opposition, but it did not, thanks in great measure to vigilance of Representative Salazar and Speaker Luján.

Senate Bill 163 was approved by the House of Representatives, a larger body of people, with three dissenting votes.

After the legislative session in spring 2003, Michael Branch and Dennis Salazar called me by telephone from Albuquerque where they had finished meeting with Governor Bill Richardson. I was convalescing from minor eye-surgery that I had undergone the previous day. Good news. Governor Richardson, true to his word, informed our two regents that he would come to Española to a public signing of Senate Bill 163. Northern New Mexico Community College, the daughter school of the Spanish American Normal School, would again begin training teachers for northern New Mexico as it was intended by educational and political leaders in 1909. [23]

We had been moving rapidly to begin offering the program in teacher education, beginning with a curriculum for elementary education, as explained earlier. The planning effort, after its approval by the Board of Regents, bore fruit quickly. The author had always been inspired by the zeal and enthusiasm for the planned programs by Dean José Griego and Carlos Atencio. The thoroughness in planning and its resultant list and description of courses in each program, also, were of immense satisfaction to me as President, mostly a bystander watching as the product from this effort unfolded.

We were careful not to jump the gun and we therefore invited the Higher Education Commission of the North Central Association to come to Northern New Mexico Community College to review the proposed programs. The people at the Higher Education Commission were enthusiastic about coming to the campus. They had been apprised of efforts by the Community College all along.

Northern had been a member of a select group of institutions[24] that participated in an Academic Quality Improvement Program (AQIP) intended to provide consistent monitoring of progress in achievement of the school's goals and objectives. Expansion of a college's mission is an important event, one that merits particular scrutiny. As a result of Northern's membership in AQIP, the efforts to initiate programs in teacher education were well known.

Governor Bill Richardson came to the campus to sign Senate Bill 163 on March 5, 2004. Legislators, interested citizens, Board members, staff, faculty, and students convened in the Nick Salazar Center for the Arts for this historic occasion.

SB 163 expanded on the authority present in the legal description of Northern New Mexico Community College since 1977. Upon signing the bill, Governor Richardson joked with the audience by pointing to me and saying, "He did it. Sigfredo Maestas made me do it." In fact, Governor Bill Richardson enjoyed great popularity in Rio Arriba County, among other reasons because he was cognizant of its needs. Bill Richardson was former US Congressman from this district, and although he may not have known specific details about Northern New Mexico Community College, he had excellent grasp of needs in the region. The College had hosted him in the past when he convened meetings that addressed sometimes difficult social and economic issues concerning the Española Valley and Rio Arriba County. The Governor, personable man that he is, chose on this occasion to share with others present credit for the new program and to enjoy the occasion with mirthful banter.

The Act itself reads:

> "RELATING TO HIGHER EDUCATION: AUTHORIZING NORTHERN NEW MEXICO STATE SCHOOL TO DEVELOP AND IMPLEMENT A BACCALAUREATE DEGREE PROGRAM IN TEACHER EDUCATION; AMENDING A SECTION OF THE NMSA 1978." amended Section 21-4-3 NMSA 1978 (Laws 1909, Chapter 97, Section 3 as amended) to read:
>
> "21-4-3. NORTHERN NEW MEXICO STATE SCHOOL--PURPOSE OF INSTRUCTION--ACADEMIC STUDENTS--BOARDING OF STUDENTS--"

Rather than repeat the text of HB 163 in its entirety, we will reproduce here the additions to the earlier legislation alluded to above. Changes begin with D. of a four-part section A, B, C, and D. The new language reads as follows:

> "D. The board of regents of northern new mexico state school is authorized to develop, implement and seek accreditation for a baccalaureate degree program in teacher education for the Española campus. The program shall be authorized when the board of regents certifies that the baccalaureate program in teacher education:(1)has been developed and is ready for implementation; and
>
> 2.is ready to receive the accreditation review team from the appropriate accrediting agency. In the development of the program, northern new mexico state school shall engage in a partnership with New Mexico highlands university, an educational institution that is sensitive to the socio-cultural conditions of the region and that is prepared to offer collaborative programs to support the critical higher education needs of students in north central New Mexico."

A copy of the signature page from this historic day is reproduced in the photograph section.[25]

Later in the spring of 2004, the Higher Education Commission (this was a national commission who accredited our programs) sent a site-visit team to Northern New Mexico Community College to review its proposals for *expanding its mission* and including teacher education programs leading to the bachelor of arts degree. The author knew that preparation for offering elementary education was superb, and that accreditation would likely be forthcoming. Our intention was to begin offering the program in elementary education in the August 2004.

After the stipulated period of review, a few days, the site-visit team held an exit interview with me, our administrative staff, and members of Northern's team who had designed the new programs. The site-visitors were effusive in their praise for the thoroughness and quality of Northern's preparation. Much to my surprise, the site-visit team approved not only the degree in elementary education, but granted also approval in secondary education and special education. Of course, staff members were elated. José Griego, the Dean; Patrick Tate, Education Department Chair; department faculty; Carlos Atencio and the many volunteers and consultants whom he and José Griego had recruited to plan the program(s) in teacher education were to be congratulated. Their work was not merely commendable, it was laudable.

Northern New Mexico Community College initiated its first class in a bachelor's degree in elementary education that Fall Term 2004.

Among the President's concerns regarding Northern New Mexico Community College were two that were important to him.

An important problem that needed to be addressed was the water system on the campus in El Rito. I had in-depth knowledge of the problem and hopes for its solution, having lived on that campus longer than I have lived *anywhere*. I have told the story of the many problems that a suitable source of water has caused the institution since it began.

Fortunately, I was assured by Drew Mendez, Director of Physical Facilities, that the El Rito Water Users' Association, its executive committee, continued to work diligently to obtain funds to build an infrastructure. A couple of years before, a well with adequate supply for the community and the College campus had been discovered, and the project was continuing.

A matter of immediate and long-term importance needed to be stressed, and the Board of Regents was most apt to maintain the "institutional memory" required to recognize its importance. The newly-acquired ability of Northern New Mexico Community College would probably tempt future administrations of the College to opt for the creation of a regional college or university, while simultaneously de-emphasizing it community college antecedents and its mission. While adding new baccalaureate degree programs would likely be in the interest of students and the service area, the Community College had achieved many successes. Its services to the region, opportunities for students, assistance to employers and members of the private and public sectors, were vital in the further development of the region, economically, socially, and culturally.

I therefore urged the Board of Regents that it retain the mission and characteristics of a community college, even as Northern developed further its new mission involving teacher education and the bachelor's degree. As a reminder of this, I did not propose a change in name for the institution, although I knew that this would be done in time.

Sigfredo Maestas retired as President of Northern New Mexico Community College in February 2005, after slightly more than thirteen years in this capacity.

Notes:

1. Some of us from afar applauded selection of the new name and its similarity to Northern New Mexico Normal School. What is odd is that the State of New Mexico, and its legislature, insisted that the official name would continue to be Northern New Mexico State School.

2. Some of the core faculty at the Northern Branch had administrative responsibilities. They would move on to the community college and continue many of the same responsibilities, but they viewed themselves as faculty nevertheless. After I came to NNMCC, in fall 1979, we would

institutionalize this practice in line with practices at other colleges (although the practice was not, and is still not, universal.)

3. The same arrangement continues in the case of Northern New Mexico College, owing to the constitutional founding of the original institution.

4. This is an important distinction to make concerning the constitutionality under which the Normal School in its different versions has operated. In each case, the institution may have altered its programs of study with the consent of the state legislature and the governor. In any case, all funds held by the institutions are viewed to be state funds.

5. For many years, the Spanish American Normal School and its successors were known as the Northern New Mexico State School, a name which no one associated with the school liked.

6. The group was known as the Blue Ribbon Committee and its activities were the subject of discussion during several of the meetings of the Board of Regents from October 1977 until late 1979.

7. My knowledge of this period was acquired first hand. In July 1979, Northern New Mexico Community College offered me the job as Dean of Arts and Sciences. My first assignment was in Los Alamos, to try to prevent a dissolution of this part of the community college. Although I enjoyed the job and working at Los Alamos, I discerned very early that cultural differences between the Española valley and other northern communities and Los Alamos were too great. Differences in outlook, especially, were too large to be resolved in a reasonable period of time. The net result was, of course, a loss to both Los Alamos and to other communities in the servicer area of Northern New Mexico Community College.

8. Working relationships among people, specially of differing cultures as I have pointed out these were, have tended to improve over time. One has to wonder whether residents at Los Alamos would view Northern New Mexico Community College in a different light today, In fact, as some of the following pages will show, at least in official quarters at Los

Alamos, friendly and helpful gestures have been extended to Northern New Mexico Community College since the early 1990s.

9. The matter of "differing cultures", which I have stated, deserves explanation. First, Los Alamos is an unusual community in that it is a "company town." It grew as a result of transfer of the old Manhattan Project to this site, and it remains a community of many scientists and engineers. It views itself as a scientific and technological center, which it is. The valley, in contrast, grew from agricultural and pastoral antecedents. How each person views education varies widely, even within communities. Leaderships, not recognizing the veracity of the last statement, often view that our communities are at odds over this important matter, education, when, in fact, the perception is probably false. It is one of the ways that people are sometimes led astray, and I regret that this is indeed what occurred.

10. Community colleges across the United States prided themselves in precisely this broad set of offerings, beginning in the last quarter of the twentieth century, more or less. This vitality was to make community colleges the school of choice for a majority of students after high school. It also made community colleges the training ground for working men and women preparing for jobs in business and industry.

11. The school had grown such as to be unrecognizable from the time of the small, secluded campus in El Rito. With so many more people, the task of listing "who was there" becomes almost impossible. Certainly, students now number in the thousands, rather than the few hundred of the past. Even staff and faculty are a large number. By treating Serrano's tenure in office as one benchmark, I have chosen to list staff and faculty present in 1983; you many find their names in the list at the end of this book.

12. The Taos Public Schools would elect, in early 1990, to sever its relationship with the Community College and, as the community of Los Alamos had done, to request the University of New Mexico to establish a branch campus there.

13. This school is the present Central New Mexico Community College.

14. This building was known by different names during various times. In the late high school period, it was known as the Junior Building. The much needed renovation of this building, which occurred over about a ten-year period of time, is an excellent example of the difficulty of scant resources in an institution. Because it was a dormitory, the state of New Mexico was often unwilling to provide for its maintenance or renovation. By the time we were able to address the problem of years of postponed maintenance, the exterior walls of the building had to be replaced almost in their entirety, in addition to its interior and infrastructure. Northern received some funds from the state to assist with this. We started correcting the problem in 1987, and completed it upon my return as President in the late 1990s. A great deal of credit for completion of the project is owed to Drew Mendez, Director of Physical Facilities, and members of his department, for their resourcefulness.

15. The craze for basketball continues unabated in northern New Mexico, insofar as I can tell. I mentioned that this interest in basketball surpassed all other sports in the region, in Chapter Eight in describing the forties and fifties at the Normal School. Kept in its proper perspective, as an activity for local boys and girls, women and men, it is a healthy activity. Northern New Mexico College has, after thirty years as a higher educational institution, its basketball teams.

16. Tim Roybal is deceased.

17. The name of the Laboratory has changed to Los Alamos National Security.

18. In addition to a brief period of financial crisis, Highlands had commitments in Rio Rancho in instruction. While at first sight surprising, the venture by Highlands University into Rio Rancho was apt to be profitable, ample reason for the institution's presence this far south.

19. The reason for the mixed tenses in these paragraphs is two-fold: first, the requests for approval and support *were made*. The use of the present tense is dictated by the fact that the Board of Regents still maintains, and will as long as the present constitution is in effect, the sole responsibility for the management and control of the original school and its successors.

20. The looming teacher shortage at the start of the 21st century is a complex problem in New Mexico. Analysis of the problem is not within the scope of this book, except to point out that, since 1909, the Spanish American Normal School had as its charge the training of teachers. That the Normal School abdicated this responsibility is a matter that I have tried to explain in some of the early chapters of this book.

21. The vocabulary changes from time to time in higher education, as it does in business, sports, and any other endeavor. Trends seem to dictate how we use catch-all terms to describe what we don't thoroughly understand. The non-traditional student is, or maybe was, that student who was not between the ages of 17 and 22 and who did not reside on campus in the dormitories. This is an approximate, catch-all definition.

22. This is a detail that some may find interesting: funds for programs are generally based on enrollment in classes during the previous year. For new programs, "start-up cost" are occasionally allowed. In this case, if start-up funds were not to be considered, then perhaps the bill could be viewed as not being a "money bill," an awfully fine distinction.

23. Why do I say "again begin training teachers"? This reminds readers that, in the first and second decade of the century, before the state of New Mexico began increasing educational requirements for teachers, the earliest students of the Normal School, whether they graduated or not, sometimes took positions teaching in rural schools.

24. An accurate statement is that there was some amount of self-selection here, actually.

25. This was a historic day for Northern New Mexico Community College and its constituencies, not that bells would ring throughout the state. SB 163 began by affording a means for the Community College to participate vitally in ensuring the education of young people throughout its service area. The bill held out the real possibility that the teacher shortage could be abated. It reaffirmed that the institution had been founded in 1909 based on similar assumptions; and, it assured the Board of Regents that it could continue to guide Northern New Mexico Community College with support of the government of New Mexico.

12
NORTHERN NEW MEXICO COLLEGE

By February 2005, Northern was somewhat different from the institution that it had been the year before. For one thing, it had students enrolled who sought the bachelor of arts degree in elementary education. Also, it needed a president.

The Board of Regents was ready. Maestas had announced his intention to retire back in July, thereby giving the Board ample time to advertise, collect applications, set up a screening committee, interview applicants, and select its president. Board members had joined the Association of Community College Trustees (ACCT) a number of years previously, and they elected to have ACCT assist with their search for a president. After an earnest national search, the Board selected José Griego, the Dean of Instruction, from among more than forty candidates as the President of Northern New Mexico Community College.

José Griego was born in Santa Fe at the Indian Hospital and resided in Embudo during his childhood. At age 12, he moved with his parents to Albuquerque, and he began high school in 1967 at St. Mary's High School. Upon graduation from St. Mary's, he enrolled at the University of Albuquerque, where he received a bachelor of arts degree in theology, history, and Spanish literature. He continued studies in Spanish literature and obtained the master's degree in this discipline. He has a PhD degree in education; the specialty is critical thinking.

Griego's employment history includes three years at the College of Santa Fe, where he taught Spanish literature and bilingual education. He also directed the College's bilingual education program. He worked for a period at the old State Department of Education, and he was executive director of the Guadalupe Historic Foundation, in Santa Fe. He spent twelve years as elementary and junior high school principal with the Peñasco Public Schools, which was to prove valuable to Northern during its planning of programs in teacher education.

Immediately prior to coming to Northern, José Griego was co-curator for the Smithsonian Institute, in 1991-92. Connie Valdez, then President of Northern, hired José Griego, who knew Tim Roybal, participant in the Folk Arts Festival and a wood carver and furniture maker. Even earlier, however, Tim Roybal was associated with *La Escuelita*, a school for wood carvers, where José knew him in the 1980s. José stated that Tim Royal had been hired by Northern New Mexico Community College about 1993, where he immediately brought the wood sculpture and furniture-making program to life.

José Griego brought other wood carvers and artists to the campus: Felipe Ortega, Felix López, Cruz López, and Benjamín López, wood sculptors. He also recruited Karen Martínez, 1998, in weaving and Cipriano Vigil, in music.

José Griego[1] remembered that Connie Valdez was a staunch supporter of vocational education, and she held strong interest in programs involving business and teacher education.

The selection of the new president preceded the start of the 2005 legislative session by barely two weeks. The College was ready, however, since most of its requests for consideration had been submitted months before. This year would provide opportunity for President Griego and the Board of Regents to survey the lay of the land, to examine how legislative and executive branches of government would deal with the College's new mission and issues related to instruction and the College's need for new construction. They were pleasantly surprised, the author discerned from discussions with them.

One of the first orders of business of the administration and the Board of Regents, after the legislative session, was consideration of the name of the institution. The choices were simple, if you wish to think about this. Northern either remained a community college (a while longer) offering the bachelor's degree in teacher education, or else it sought a name change to indicate that it is a regional college or university.[2] In April 2005, by action of the Board of Regents, the school would henceforth be known as Northern New Mexico College.

Northern continues to identify itself by this short-hand name. It has moved rapidly in the past five years to develop baccalaureate degree programs that it has identified as being useful to new students. The 2008-09 Catalog of Northern New Mexico College listed familiar programs leading to the associate degree, and new bachelor's degree programs as follows: a bachelor's degree in music from which students may select either classical guitar or jazz; bachelor's in business administration; bachelor's of engineering programs in Information Engineering Technology, Software Engineering, and Mechanical Engineering; bachelor of arts in elementary education; bachelor's of science in biology, environmental science, and integrative health studies.[3]

The number of students graduating with the bachelor's degree has increased year by year. In 2007, Northern had its first graduate with a bachelor's degree in elementary education. In 2008, there were three graduates, all of them with degrees in elementary education. The following year, 2009, the number of students graduating was 15. In the past year, 2010, there were 46 students who received the bachelor's degree.[4]

Students graduating are almost equally divided among biology, business administration, elementary education, and engineering. There are, of course, more programs in business administration (3) and engineering (3); I have not made a distinction about them as I have tallied these numbers.

Simultaneously, the Northern New Mexico College has been offering associate degree programs that are undistinguishable from those of previous years. One program, Automotive Technology, has been moved to the the campus in Española; one or two other programs have been discontinued, but enrollment in most programs tends to follow historical patterns in the school. Graduation of students with the associate degree, either associate of arts, of science, or applied science remains robust.

The student profile of Northern New Mexico College has not changed significantly during the past five to six years. If anything, its chief characteristics, a wide age-range and more women, have become more obvious on the campuses. Fortunately, graduation rates have increased perhaps slightly, and the number of women graduating is high.

In 2010, Northern's graduation list included about 123 women in a total of 175 graduates. Fully seventy percent of students graduating this past spring were women.

Some interesting observations: an overwhelmingly large percentage of students graduating in nursing and in the new field, elementary education, on this list are women. This is not new, either at Northern or, possibly, across the nation. What is interesting to the author is that women graduating with a bachelor's degree in biology and in engineering are, likewise, in the majority.

Northern New Mexico College continues to serve its students well, in spite of its modest resources, a characteristic that has existed for a hundred years.

Catherine Martínez-Berryhill, the Dean in charge of programs in education, verified that the one baccalaureate program in this college is in elementary education. She reminded the author that the Alternative Licensure Program, offered first by Northern New Mexico Community College in this state, is still in existence at Northern. This past spring, ten students are shown in the list of students graduating. She stated that in the review provided by the state's Professional Education Department, the results for both the baccalaureate degree program and alternative licensure were excellent. This review, as I mentioned earlier, is in accordance with standards dictated by NCATE, the national organization. This is a definite improvement for New Mexico, denoting a further improvement in standards for evaluating teachers and the programs in which they obtain their education and training.

Cathy Martínez-Berryhill returned to the campus after an absence of a few years. She worked in the Student Success Center, during the time that I was President. Following this, she went with the Los Alamos National Laboratory, but she pointed out that she continued to teach for the Community College part time. She reveals a feeling of loyalty and interest in the College in her discussions. She has been back with Northern New Mexico College since 2007.

As one would expect in the fifth year of Northern New Mexico College, with its expanded mission and what has amounted to an ambitious agenda for development of programs in instruction, instructional programs are in a state of flux. The change from Northern

New Mexico Community College to Northern New Mexico College was somewhat similar to the earlier change, in 1977, from vocational school to community college. But it was not as profound a change, and Northern New Mexico College is helped by the fact that its service area is more certain, although the question of Santa Fe still remains. The College has yet to define the role and function for the El Rito Campus, but that will probably be forthcoming soon. There are reasons to be optimistic about this.

Northern New Mexico College has an intercollegiate sports program, in basketball, for the first time. The institution had not sponsored interscholastic sports in about forty years. The Board of Regents is intending their sports programs to be modest, to attract local, in-state, young men and women. Local interest should follow, if Northern persists in its intentions. One should wish them well, and look forward to the College's success in this effort.

Change in leadership can be unsettling for members of a college or university when change occurs at the helm, as I state earlier. In August 2009, José Griego announced his retirement and left it to the Board of Regents to appoint an Interim President while they took their time to go about a careful selection of the new President of the College. The Board selected David F. Trujillo[5] as its Interim President and, again, turned to the Association of Community College Trustees to assist with a national search in selecting a permanent chief executive.

David Trujillo reacted to my question of what he considered most important at Northern with a question about quality. He asked the question as though he were asking himself: Is it good enough? The question immediately elicited empathy of the author. Of course, this is the most important question that can be asked of any educational institution.

David Trujillo then went on to speak about the challenges concerning the transition from a community college to a small college. He pointed to those factors that impinged on success, not always positively. For example, the College was burdened with the implementation of new computer software, for all administrative functions, that was difficult. The attention required took away from AQIP, the Academic Quality Improvement Program, as it did from becoming a four-year school. In addition, the author would add, the College undertook a few too many changes. In everything that he said, David Trujillo implied concurrence with the last statement.

David stated objection to what he called a "statewide perception" of Northern New Mexico College, and lamented resistance (that exists) to what the College has become. He noted that there were always obstacles to what the College was trying to do (to advance its cause.) I let him speak, because it was important that he speak, it was his interview. I was anxious to say to him, however, that his observations, during his relatively brief tenure at Northern New Mexico College, reveal that the history of the institution of the past 100 years repeats itself.[6]

The attitude of the leadership at the Department of Higher Education is that institutions should, "Hold everything." This is in keeping with the Commission's tendency to impinge on prerogatives of Boards of Regents and their individual institutions.

David stated candidly that he felt that growth of Northern New Mexico College as a result of presence in Santa Fe (with baccalaureate programs) was key.

The most immediate reaction to this discussion with David Trujillo concerning these fairly complex matters is that he has been thinking a lot about these issues even as he works overtime.

David Trujillo and Andrés Salazar[7] have made a good team during the interim period, before the leadership of Northern New Mexico College is turned over to its new president. David Trujillo told me about how he had relied on Andrés Salazar during his term as Interim President.

They assured me of the College's commitment to continue the mission of the community college, as an official action of the Board of Regents (November 2005) that insisted that it be maintained. They added that Northern New Mexico Community College stood on two principles: reliance on arts, sciences and teacher education, on the one hand, and technological programs of the community college, as its second pillar.

There is reason to await anxiously the development of a curriculum in secondary education, for example, because programs in engineering have eclipsed progress in teacher education. David and Andrés stated to me that funds would be forthcoming to address the need for teachers in mathematics and science, an effort that should be especially beneficial in secondary education.

In engineering, impetus for programs is derived from two situations: one is the willingness of Los Alamos National Security to hire almost all engineering graduates from Northern. Andrés stated that five were hired by Los Alamos in 2009, and eight more were employed by the firm in 2010.[8]

The two gentlemen were obviously proud of the College's record for hiring. There are now 61 full time faculty, twenty-nine hold PhD degrees, and 20 are hispanic.

Their feeling is that growth for the institution, and therefore needed diversity in programs offered, rests with concomitant growth of the service area. In fact, they view growth of the service area to be imperative in order to maintain growth in enrollment. Growth in diversity of programs is what will ensure opportunity for northern New Mexicans, therefore growth is needed. They suggested that growth of the College depends upon claiming Santa Fe as part of its service area. One could counter that the same is true with regard to Taos County and Los Alamos County. Nevertheless, present law, the institution's governance, and the state's funding methodology for higher education, all seem to support their argument or proposal. Barring any new, artificial restrictions from the state, or a mean, competitive war among institutions, what they propose seems possible.

I would urge anyone who wonders about turf wars to read the first half of Chapter Ten. They are definitely to be avoided, if possible, and I am uncertain that there are any lessons that can be learned from this history, but I'll leave it for readers to judge.

David Trujillo, and his associate and chief finance officer Andrés Salazar, are to be commended for their service to Northern New Mexico College during this interim period in 2010.

Lest anyone forget, the beginning of this story dealt with the state teacher's college that almost was, and either missed or was denied its opportunity to fulfill its originally stated mission. Now it is a teachers' college, although its program is yet to become its "signature program" as was intended in recent past. We are assured, however, that the latter will occur, and we trust that it will. In the meantime, students are graduating in elementary education, which is reason for celebration. Again, readers are urged to turn to the list (at the end of the book) for names of students who graduated.

I interviewed a few students after the program in elementary education began.

Fannie Castillo graduated in 2006 in elementary education. She was born in Gomez Farías, Chihuahua on October 20, 1972.[9] As an elementary school child, Fannie wanted to grow up to work, perhaps for the airlines. Or, she thought perhaps to become a teacher. She attended high school in her home town, Gomez Farías. Math was always her best subject. The parents unfortunately did not have resources for her to continue beyond high school, so she dropped out of high school to marry at age 18.

She began studies toward the high school equivalency by enrolling in the GED Program at Northern New Mexico Community College at age 28.

Fannie was doing housework for Ms. Valerie Fairchild, who encouraged her to attend the Community College. Ms. Fairchild helped Fannie pay for tuition and books. Fannie completed the GED battery of tests and obtained the high school diploma. She enrolled in the Community College to major in education.

Fannie had family living in Española, and children of her own. She could not have continued if the Community College had not had the program in education. Her only option was to move to Las Vegas to attend New Mexico Highlands University, which she could not afford to do.

Fannie enjoyed Northern. Soon the Community College was able to offer the BA degree. Throughout our discussion, Fannie had praise for her teachers: Dr. Gladys Gurulé in English as a Second Language, and Lorenzo Gonzales. She also remembered her classes with Cathy Berryhill as being particularly helpful.

After obtaining her bachelor's degree, she started teaching at Hernandez Elementary School. She had a son, Javier Gonzales, age 11 and in sixth grade at the time of publication of this book. Fannie's daughter, Stephanie Aragón, 17, studies at Northern New Mexico College.

About Northern New Mexico College, she simply said, *"¡Tanto la necesitamos!"*

Please bear in mind that this book took a long time to write and students' circumstances may have changed.

The author had opportunity to interview[10] four of ten graduating students in the Class of 2010. The four students graduated with BA degrees in elementary education. They are Pablita Apodaca, Chrystal Gonzáles, Laura La Rue, and Sandra Valdez.

Students expressed satisfaction with the program, although it tends to be prescribed by the College. There are not very many elective courses in their curriculum.

Pablita Apodaca is from Pojoaque. She was home schooled as a child; she has a young son. Her family situation has encouraged her to teach. In addition, she did not like her previous job in the public defender's office. Being able to attend Northern is helpful in that she has a family of her own. She would find it almost impossible to attend the University of New Mexico, where she would have to commute.

Pablita Apodaca stated that she would seek a position in the Santa Fe schools upon graduation.

Pablita's favorite teacher at the College was Dr. Emily Romero, who taught the course in Educational Foundations. She mentioned Lorenzo Gonzáles as a teacher whom she liked and enjoyed.

Chrystal Gonzáles is from Velarde. She attended Pojoaque High School and graduated there in 2000. She has always wanted to be a teacher. Chrystal lived in Albuquerque after high school, and she mentioned that she would have found it difficult to attend UNM, although more classes seem to be required at Northern New Mexico College. Chrystal will one day move back to Albuquerque and begin a career. Chrystal liked Carol Brown, who teaches Assessment, as her teacher. The author will add a post script: Chrystal Gonzáles graduated in 2010 with highest honors.

Laura LaRue attended Pojoaque High School where she graduated in 2004. After high school, she attended Eastern New Mexico University and considered transferring to the University of New Mexico. Laura will continue her studies in special education. She likes this area and will likely apply to teach in Pojoaque. Laura has a favorite teacher at Northern New Mexico College; she is Pam Picollot, who teaches humanities and social studies. The author has a post script: Laura LaRue graduated in 2010 with honors.

Sandra Valdez is from El Rito. She also attended Pojoaque High School.[11] Sandra comes from a family of educators. She acquired some work experience during a period at the Los Alamos National Laboratory. Upon graduation at Northern, Sandra will seek employment in the region, probably in Pojoaque. Sandra mentioned a number of teachers whom she enjoyed at Northern: Carol Brown, Lorenzo Gonzáles, and Rose Cavalcante.

The Board of Regents selected Nancy "Rusty" Barceló, PhD, as President of Northern New Mexico College during the 100th year of the history of the institution. She becomes President on July 1, 2010.

Nancy Barceló comes to the College from the University of Minnesota where she has been Vice Provost and Vice President for Equity and Diversity.

Dr. Barceló received a Bachelor of Arts degree in Social Work at Chico State University, a Master of Arts degree in Recreational Education at the University of Iowa, and the Doctor of Philosophy degree in Higher Education Administration at the University of Iowa.

The president-select brings a vast wealth of experience that includes thirty years in teaching and university administration. She has served as affiliate faculty, assistant professor, adjunct faculty, including adjunct assistant professor. In the first half of this decade, until 2006, she was Vice President and Vice Provost for Minority Affairs and Diversity at the University of Washington. Prior to this, she had been Associate Vice President for Multicultural and Academic Affairs at the University of Minnesota, in 1996 to 2001.

Dr. Barceló, who is recognized nationally for her excellent professional presentations, developed the infrastructure of a newly formed Office of the Vice Provost and Vice President. She developed and implemented the Faculty Diversity Institute and enhanced U. Minnesota's commitment to diversity.

Dr. Barceló brings experience in fund raising, having established alumni development and led a capital campaign to raise $22 million.

She lists many accomplishments that assisted both the University of Washington and the University of Minnesota.

Nancy Barceló has served on a wide number of campus, community, regional, and national boards. She has written for publication, including *Chicana/Latina Studies: The Journal of Mujeres Activas,* and a chapter in a book by Sylvia Hurtado on diversity and institutional transformation in universities, which is forthcoming.

Northern New Mexico College enters a new era with optimism. Who can safely predict the next ten years, or twenty-five years of the institution, let alone 100 years into what seems a distant future? It is worth the effort nevertheless to lay plans, which the Northern is doing, with a vision as far into the future as common sense permits.

Northern New Mexico College should and will live up to expectations in teacher training. It still needs a program in secondary education, possibly one in special education, also. It has the foundation on which to build. It has already grasped the opportunity to develop its engineering programs, and it has planned a master's degree program in these fields. Northern has yet to do the same in teacher education, but it will.[12]

David Trujillo's observation about difficulties, lack of support, that Northern encounters for some of its efforts, is an indicator of the future for Northern. Those in charge of the institution will persevere, however, as they have for all of these years. At certain times they will be more successful, occasionally less so, but they will persevere. The awakening that has occurred in northern New Mexico since late 1970s, which this author has tried to portray here, will not be lulled in any foreseeable future.

Three factors in particular give me hope. First, with regard to the campus in El Rito, the new water system provides a new day there. Ample and safe water will help transform it into a resident campus. As time goes on, funds will be forthcoming for further renovation of dormitories and for improved student life, and the campus will blossom. Programmatic choices will have to made for El Rito; it is not the purpose of this book to outline them.

Second is the the expanded authority of Northern New Mexico College to offer programs beyond two-years of college. Teacher education has been our focus, as it has for many people, but capabilities of the College in technological fields place it in an enviable position. The presence of Los Alamos National Security, and a new day in cooperation between it and Northern, lend impetus to further development of programs on the campus. I am confident that Northern will rediscover the key in teacher education, and move quickly to become a leading institution in our state.

Not least, cause for hope is instilled by and with people. The arrival of a new president is, also, cause for optimism. Nancy "Rusty" Barceló stands to be successful in leading Northern New Mexico College in new, and some predictable, directions with the assistance of Regents, faculty, staff, and community. I can safely predict that those requisites are forthcoming, this also is cause for optimism.

Notes:

1. I interviewed José Griego in December 2008, in preparation for this book. Information on this page is based largely on the interview.

2. I should add that it was much premature to be thinking "university." The administration and the Board took the logical step in this case.

3. Earlier in the 2009-10 school year, I interviewed Anthony Sena, Provost, and Mike Costello, former Dean of Students and Registrar. Prior to publication, I interviewed Catherine Martínez-Berryhill, Dean of the College of Education. They were able to verify which baccalaureate programs were being offered, and to provide me with their thoughts concerning the future of Northern New Mexico College insofar as its academic and educational offerings are concerned.

4. Readers may wish to consult the list at the end of this book, where the names of graduating students appear by year.

5. I interviewed David Trujillo on two occasions in preparing this book. He was unusually insightful and helpful in the ways that he articulated his views about immediate past, present, and future at Northern New Mexico College.Much of the information, and my own observations, are based on information that I gleaned from his two interviews.

6. I wouldn't say, "merely repeats itself," because the consequences are not trivial. Growth and quality of the institution are most often at stake, and the competitive nature of our higher educational establishment does not help...anyone.

7. During this second interview, which I requested, I asked that Andy Salazar come also in order to continue further the discussion concerning Northern's educational programs. I also wanted to know more about baccalaureate degree programs that had been added, and about plans for the future.

8. This is an astonishingly high placement rate, by any measure.

9. I requested from Fannie Castillo that I be allowed to interview her this past winter. I met her at the Johnson Controls Building, where the College of Education is housed, and, when I saw her, I immediately recognized her as one of my students in a class in chemistry during a summer term. I remember that she, and one other woman, were by far the best students in the class. Fannie's mathematical skill, and her ability to solve problems, made her an outstandingly competent student.

10. The interviews took place in November 2009. Students were in their final year of a four-year course of studies.

11. In late 1990s and early 2000s, there tended to be a large number of students throughout this north central region who elected to attend Pojoaque High School. Some parents drove their children to school in Pojoaque at an earlier age, elementary school. Parents concern about a safe environment seemed to be one factor leading to Pojoaque's popularity. Students seemed to like Pojoaque also. A sociological analysis of this phenomenon would be helpful to educators, one would think. I have not seen one.

12. What gives anyone the right to be optimistic about in this regard? I remember that "Rome was not built in a day," but the day is here, and Northern New Mexico College knows this.

13
NORTHERN NEW MEXICO COLLEGE
ENTERS ITS FIFTH YEAR

The Board of Regents selected Nancy "Rusty" Barceló, PhD, as President of Northern New Mexico College during the 100th year of the history of the institution. She became President on July 1, 2010.

Dr. Barceló came to the College from the University of Minnesota where she has been Vice Provost and Vice President for Equity and Diversity.

Nancy Barceló received the Bachelor of Arts degree in Social Work at Chico State University, a Master of Arts degree in Recreational Education at the University of Iowa, and the Doctor of Philosophy degree in Higher Education Administration from the University of Iowa.

The President-select brought a vast wealth of experience that includes thirty years in teaching and university administration. She served as affiliate faculty, assistant professor, including adjunct assistant professor. In the first half of this decade, until 2006, Dr. Barceló was Vice President and Vice Provost for Minority Affairs and Diversity at the University of Washington. Prior to this Dr. Barceló Associate Vice President for Multicultural and Academic Affairs at the University of Minnesota, in 1996 to 2001.

Dr. Barceló, who is recognized nationally for her excellent professional presentations, developed the infrastructure of a newly formed Office of the Vice Provost and Vice President. She developed and implemented the Faculty Diversity Institute and enhanced U. Minnesota's commitment to diversity.

Similarly, Dr. Barceló brings experience in fund raising, having established alumni development and led a capital campaign to raise $22 million. She lists many accomplishments that assisted both the University of Washington and the University of Minnesota.

Nancy Barceló served on a wide number of campus, community, regional, and national boards. She has written for various publications including *Chicana/Latina Studies: The Journal of Mujeres Activas*, and a chapter in a book by Sylvia Hurtado on diversity and institutional transformation in universities.

Northern New Mexico College enters a new era with optimism. Who can safely predict the next ten years, or twenty-five years of the institution? Let alone 100 years into what seems a distant future. It is nevertheless worth the effort to lay plans, which Northern is doing, with a vision as far into the future as common sense permits.

Northern New Mexico College should and will live up to expectations in teacher training. It needs a program in secondary education, and possibly special education. The public schools need these programs, or programs that their future teachers will need. The College has each foundation on which to build. Similarly, Northern has the ability, and it is in fact planning a master's degree program in engineering fields, although which one will require some study: perhaps in mechanical engineering.

A much smaller investment can be made in secondary education and special education; and the College will eventually do this.

Northern New Mexico College beckoned Dr. Barceló and, conversely, Rusty Barceló, as she prefers to be known, was "captivated" by the Campus at El Rito. It crossed her mind that *this* might be the opportunity for her. The reality, which each and every president has had to learn with which to deal, has been the lack of funds that Dr. Trujillo pointed to in a most pronounced way. Dr. Barceló learned, as each and every president has had to learn, that the "regional" colleges in New Mexico do not receive very much financial support. As I interviewed Dr. Barceló, she revealed to me that she was surprised that the degree of "politicization" that existed was allowed to continue. Nevertheless, it was the funding of the institution that she considered lacking.

Dr. Rusty Barceló, early on, saw that the employment of faculty was the most important thing that she could do for Northern New

Mexico College. Throughout, her primary concern was *maintaining* relationships with faculty and staff were paramount. She felt that on occasion this was simply not possible, although she managed to maintain one set of relationships, and this included the Board of Regents.

She managed to maintain a solid relationship with the Board of Regents. By focussing on accreditation, as a means of survival, Nancy Barceló managed to maintain excellent relations with the Board.

The author of this book managed to interview Dr. Nancy Barceló prior to its publication. Many of the problems with Northern New Mexico College that Dr. Barceló discussed with me were in existence prior to Northern New Mexico Community College becoming the four-year college, but nevertheless the community college gave us opportunity to seek flexibility that we needed in order to operate.

14
NORTHERN NEW MEXICO COLLEGE ENTERS ITS ELEVENTH YEAR

A Board of Regents chaired by Rosario "Chayo" García in 2016 selected a man from Pueblo, Colorado as Northern New Mexico College's fourth president. Dr. Richard J. Bailey Jr. is lately from the state of Colorado where he attended the United States Air Force Academy and received a Bachelor of Science degree in Engineering Sciences. In time, he has earned degrees in International Affairs from Washington University in St. Louis, Missouri and the doctoral degree in Government from Georgetown University in the Nation's Capitol, Washington, DC.

Prior to coming to Northern New Mexico College, Rick Bailey— as he likes to be known—served in the United States Air Force for a period of 24 years. While in the U.S. Air Force, Dr. Bailey served as associate professor of strategy and security studies at the School of Advanced Air and Space Studies at Air University, Maxwell Air Force Base in Alabama. In addition, he served as Air University's first-ever Dean of Students.

While in the U.S. Air Force, Colonel Bailey had an interesting career. Early on, he was an aviator; he flew aeromedical missions, then special operations missions, and finally, world-wide airlift missions. In 2003, the Air Force sent Rick Bailey to Washington, DC to attend Georgetown University at the behest of the U.S. Air Force; this was during the time he earned a PhD in Government. Following this, he worked at the U.S. Department of State in the area of defense trade agreements. He eventually got to work overseas; the assignment was in the Netherlands for the North Atlantic Treaty Organizations within what was then viewed as the Europe and Afghanistan defense system.

Considerably later, he was on this side of the ocean, in Aruba and Curacao. Colonel Bailey served as Commander of two Air Force bases, each in Aruba and Curaçao. Americans may not be familiar with the latter island; it is one of the Netherland Antilles, just off the coast of Venezuela.

Dr. Bailey has familiarity with New Mexico. In a discussion with his wife Diana, she and he had decided that, following a career in the Air Force, they would move to northern New Mexico. After witnessing the ad in the *Chronicle of Higher Education*, Colonel Bailey submitted his application for the president's job at Northern. The rest is history, except that Dr. Bailey would like to state what a pleasure it was to work with Dr. Hugh Prather, during the interviews and, most especially the acquisition of the position. Rick Bailey is married to a woman whose mother and older sister came from Anton Chico, a community south of I-25 and on the Pecos River, the Luceros. Diana Sánchez is her family name; her mother, still living in Pueblo, CO, is Lilly Lucero Sánchez. Through the Baileys I met Fabiola Lucero Mayo, whom I visited in Pueblo and I interviewed for this book; Fabiola is one of the individuals to whom this book is dedicated. Fabiola is presently 96 years of age, and she attended the Spanish American Normal School as a teenager. You have also read about Fabiola in Chapter Eight; Fabiola is Lilly's sister.

(As an aside, I can tell you that one of the reasons to write this book is to relate stories like Fabiola's, and I have grown to love and appreciate their stories as I have known them over the years. Almost every chapter in this volume is a series of stories that I learned first hand, else I knew someone who knew each and every person in the book.)

This story, however, is about Dr. Bailey. One inheritance, of people like Dr. Bailey, is that the person inherits the entire history of this institution of higher education, and we join individuals like Venceslao Jaramillo, who founded the Spanish American Normal School. We contribute to the education of a vast number of people whom we know, because we have opportunity to get to know them, else we do not, and they number at least another few hundred. Dr. Bailey has this sense of urgency…whom we know and whom we do not, become a part of our fold, as they have become for teachers and staff members in all of our history.

Dr. Bailey inherited a large number of problems, big and small, left by each president, who in his or her turn, inherited predecessors's matters relating to the institution. He has dealt with them, and will continue to deal with them, as time and newer problems arise. One of the things that Dr. Bailey knew, because he came to Northern New Mexico College with vast knowledge and experience and semblances of leadership that he had demonstrated in his past. It is obvious, in discussion with him, that he possesses a vast amount of initiative, the gods grant that he will use them well…and thus far, he has.

The following constitute matters, big and small, that he has dealt with and has discussed with the author of this book. The President has crafted with some immediate help, including the Board of Regents, a Strategic Direction document, which the institution will use in the years following the adoption. The institution, following Dr. Bailey's behest, has completed renegotiation with faculty and staff of working agreements for the first time since 2008.

Equally important, Northern New Mexico College has increased enrollment by approximately 20%. Students will be pleased to know that NNMC has also more than doubled its graduation rate. Similarly, students are aware that the College has, in the sum of tuition, fees, etc. the most affordable schedule of costs among High School Equivalency programs in the nation for the past two out of three years. While we are examining student cost performance, it should be noted that the U.S. Department of Education has noted that the default rate, on student loans, has improved more than 50% during the past three years.

Among grants and awards received, Northern New Mexico College has received U.S. Department of Education in the amount of 5.8 million dollars in consideration of Title V awards to schools in the United States; similarly, a 1.5 million dollar Upward Bound grant was received; and, the sum of 1 million dollar workforce agreement was awarded by the Los Alamos National Laboratory to the College. Similarly, smaller grants from National Science Foundation, National Institutes of Health, in addition to similar smaller grants were made to the College.

Dr. Richard Bailey is justifiably proud of the following: as you drive up to the Campus at El Rito, on the west side of State Road 554, you will notice a series of solar collectors that are designed to convert solar power to electricity. Dr. Bailey brokered a partnership between Kit Carson Electric Cooperative and Guzman Energy for this 1.5 million watt solar array on the El Rito Campus which will lower the cost of power for the next thirty years.

In 2019, President Bailey helped to establish the Anna Age Eight Institute on the Española Campus study and prevention of childhood trauma, the first such entity of its kind in the United States at Northern New Mexico College. In 2020, he led the creation of the Northern New Mexico College Eagle Corporation (the first of its kind in the history of the college), allowing the institution to partner with businesses for the purpose of diversifying the College's revenue stream. During his tenure at Northern, Dr. Bailey has helped to form a Sharing Governance Committee with faculty and staff and he has institutionalized a full time Director of Equity and Diversity position.

Northern New Mexico College is the proud recipient of the 2019 Organization of the Year Award and President Bailey was the winner of the Organizational Leader of the Year Award during the same year. NNMC was the New Mexico STEMY award winner as the Science, Technology, Engineering and Mathematics in Higher Education. In 2021, Northern New Mexico College won the Adobe Award for advancements in strategic planning.

Among his busy schedule, he finds time to co-teach the following courses: The Psychology of Gender and Sexuality (PSY 477), Foundations of Integrated Studies (HUMN 2160), Mentoring and Leadership Seminar (ENGR/BIOL 299), and Humanity and Creativity (HUMN 4144).

I had opportunity to interview Rosario García in anticipation of publication of this book. She pointed to Richard J. Bailey's successes of one reason to be optimistic about the future of Northern New Mexico College. Among Dr. Bailey's attributes, Ms. García points to the fact that Dr. Bailey "relates well" with people and, among other attributes, his ability to listen, and to let people know that he is listening, is one of his major attributes.

There can be surprises, but none as certain as your current president resigning to take another job. In late November, 2021, we received notice that President Richard J. Bailey was resigning his position on January 14, 2022.

I called the Chairman of the current Board of Regents and, of course, Dr. Bailey had done such proper things as notifying the Chairman of the Board; just as interesting to me is that the Board was holding a meeting soon after Dr. Bailey had decided to leave Northern New Mexico College. Our local paper, *The Rio Grande Sun*, reported that at a meeting of this august body, Dr. Bailey had informed the Board of his wish to leave the College, and to join Southern Oregon University. The newspaper reported that although no action was immediately provided by the Board, the Chair, Michael A. Martin, decided to take matters into his own hands and provided the motion that the Board could not fathom. Chairman Mike Martin stated a motion to accept Dr. Richard Bailey's retirement.

During our discussion, Mr. Martin reiterated something that he had, perhaps, been thinking about. Mike Martin simply stated the fact that universities stood to lose a president, and that these actions happen, "all the time." Such words from the Chairman of the Board whom in the present circumstance, our young society would, in a word, describe it as "cool." Michael Martin sounded that way to me.

I had to relate this story here, because the words that we can attribute by a young crowd at the College to the Chairman of the Board, Michael A. Martin—without a doubt—are sufficient to describe him.

In the following few months, the Board of Regents of Northern New Mexico College will undertake a search for a president for this wonderful institution within our midst in northern New Mexico. As of 2021, Board of Regents includes the following membership:

President, Michael A. Martin
Vice-President, Erica Rita Velarde, P.E.
Secretary-Treasurer, Porter Swentzell, Ph.D.
Member, Ruben Archuleta
Member, Evelyn Juarez

I note that three members of the Board of Regents are graduates of institutions that we have been describing in this book. The community wishes them well.

15
NORTHERN NEW MEXICO COLLEGE— ENTERING A NEW SAGA

The ability to look far into the future and to predict the future of what seems a good, common-sense name for an institution that began with an idea about what Venceslao Jaramillo envisioned for *his* institution, in the late 1890s, is a notion that I shall forego beginning in this very moment. Certainly, the people who have walked through portals of the Normal School and who have enjoyed the clean air at El Rito have a great deal of people whom to thank. But whom should you thank? I have a good sense of history, having lived 81 years in what seems like a brief lifetime. But...I am serious, whom to thank?

First, there is Venceslao Jaramillo, about whom you have read in the early pages of this book. Following this, there is a gentleman by the name of L. Bradford Prince, who decided to live in northern New Mexico following his retirement from the government of New Mexico. He was state senator, and moreover Venceslao Jaramillo's friend—I have related to you that Venceslao had many friends, in the first chapter of this book.

The Spanish American Normal School failed for the following reasons: none of the children and adults who attended the early Normal School were eligible for the advanced study that was required to be a school teacher, and that was not much. Into its second decade, as I have recounted in the early chapters, students were not ready to study, even high school. In the early 1920s, a man named Filadelfio Baca, whom no one remembers in El Rito, came to the Normal School and founded the high school, and finally, one student finished high school.

Following this, you can count on the family of George J. Martin, his wife Margaret—she served on the Board of Regents as late as the early 1950s. Following this, his son Tom Martin served on the Board when I was a student there in the 1950s. I should be very thankful to the Martin family, a grandson of George Martin, in the person of Mike Martin—if I state his name, Michael Martin, people in his hometown won't recognize his name.

And then there was Joseph B. Grant, whose imprint on the campus is still there today, and yeah so many students attended that school in mid-1930s to the early 1950s, splendid presidency.

In and about 1970, Dennis Salazar became chairman of the Board of Regents, and that Board began to establish programs in Española, just 32 miles away, but which would change the Campus at El Rito markedly. Dennis credited his brother, Regino Salazar for the ideas involving a community college for the north. In a very short period of time, the Normal School became the New Mexico Technical Vocational School, and after a short but turbulent period, the Northern New Mexico Community College was born. Very definitely, Nick L. Salazar, Representative from Rio Arriba County and Frank Serrano III, President of the Technical Vocational School played a role in creating Northern New Mexico Community College.

In recent time, José Griego and I were principally responsible for the creation of Northern New Mexico College. José Griego and I were familiar with the constitution of the State of New Mexico and why it was that a four-year college could hearken back to the days of Venceslao Jaramillo in the late 1890s. José Griego and the Board of Regents at the time, settled on a name that makes perfect sense to me, Northern New Mexico College.

We do not know what the thoughts of Venceslao Jaramillo are with regard to the founding of the Spanish American Normal School. Venceslao Jaramillo left nothing in writing; his wife Cleofes Martínez de Jaramillo did write a couple of brief books; in her second book, *Romance of a Little Village Girl*, Cleofes Jaramillo does describe her marriage to Venceslao and she tells about his ambitions for the Spanish American Normal School. Some of this information I have furnished for you in the first chapter of this book.

Part of the story of why the Spanish American Normal School failed in its name, a normal school is after all is said and done, a teachers' college. One of the reasons is that northern New Mexico, where most of us have lived most of our lives, is a region of vast economic need. One, among many, needs was the need to learn the English language. Venceslao Jaramillo recognized this as a need above all else. He tried to establish the Spanish American Normal School, and failed because other lawmakers, including Governor Miguel Otero, did not concur with Venceslao Jaramillo. New Mexico, as a territory of the United States, had many more needs, and it was many years later that Venceslao Jaramillo would get his wish.

However, there being a fundamental need, for artisans, that later carried the day and, therefore, the Normal School tended early in its history to imbue in its curriculum a largely vocational school. In Spanish we say ¡*Unos proponen, y otros disponen!* Who proposes something as magnificent as the Spanish American Normal School, with that deep understanding that Venceslao Jaramillo possessed, is not necessarily seeing that his dream, in time, would come true. In fact, he may have suffered disappointments near his death in May 1920 in the direction that the Normal School eventually took. But this is before arrival of Filadelfio Baca, who revived a high school, so who knows?

In time, two men arrived at the Normal School, and they had learned that a Normal School was needed, if the present school were to survive, Northern New Mexico Community College. The Community College was experimenting with a teacher-certification program, and it was proving to be successful. The idea of a Normal School, much as Venceslao Jaramillo had imagined it, for north central New Mexico was needed. Sigfredo Maestas, and our heart-felt thanks should go to José Griego, who had appeared several years prior, in Connie Valdez's administration, and helped to establish Northern New Mexico College. This was a case in which the adage Mr. Inside and Mr. Outside worked. José Griego directed a troop inside that included Carlos Atencio, Dr. Vincent Llamas, Donald Tate, and Dr. Katherine Berryhill. This was one of the few times that the politicization of education in New Mexico worked. Who helped with the conversion of Northern New Mexico Community College into Northern New Mexico College was none other than the governor of our state, Bill Richardson.

We had witnessed this phenomenon on two previous occasions.

Governor Jack Campbell had overseen the creation of technical vocational schools in New Mexico, and in the creation of Northern New Mexico Community College there was Governor Gerry Apodaca who strongly supported its creation.

A situation emerged that has to confound demographers and such people who keep track of communities, and its growth, and, in fact, dates from the time of Herodotus, the famed Greek historian. It led Herodotus to say (paraphrasing now) that large communities exist where none existed prior to his time, and that the rich grow, often at the expense of non-existent communities, heretofore.

We have seen the same phenomenon in New Mexico on two occasions. The first, is a contrast between the growth of Las Vegas and Albuquerque. Whereas Las Vegas was on the Santa Fé Trail, had a railroad running through town for much of its history, Albuquerque is much the bigger town at present. Similarly, a contrast may be drawn between El Rito and Española. In the late 1890s, El Rito was a thriving community; it was a center of sheep-growing and, in contrast, Española was a scattering of houses prior to the coming of the Denver-Rio Grande Rail Line to Antonito, Colorado. The rail road, no longer here, was what made the Rio Grande valley blossom as a fertile valley, and hence Rinconada, Embudo, Velarde, Alcalde, Okey-Owinge, Ranchitos grow as did Truchas, Chimayó, Cuarteles, and Santa Cruz de la Cañada.

The presence or absence of water is often the determining factor for growth in our towns in southwestern United States. Have you witnessed more pleasant towns, more salubrious, than El Rito or Las Vegas? Need I say more.

Students Attending the Normal School During the Early Years

Students 1909–1910

José R. López, age 19, El Rito
Manuel Trujillo, age 20, El Rito
Anastacio Trujillo, 21, El Rito
Gilberto Durán, 20, El Rito
Martin Suazo, 19, Tierra Amarilla
Tomas Chávez, 18, Tierra Amarilla
Fidel Jaramillo, 16, Vallecitos
Onesimo Chávez, 16, Vallecitos
Alberto Chávez, 19 Vallecitos
Tomás Martínez, 16, Ranchos de Taos
Albert Miller, 18, Taos
Venceslao Martínez, 20, Taos
Dixie Dixon, 13, El Rito
Carlos Gonzáles, 15, El Rito
Gretchen Dixon, 14, El Rito
Ralph Dixon, 15, El Rito
Mrs. Keller, 23, Monero
May Madole, 17, Venus
Belle Woods, 17, Pagosa Junction, CO
Lenora Woods, 19, Nutrias
Bertha Livesay 20, Golden
Marie Fleming, 28, El Rito
Lida Rowe, 34, Estancia
Lee Rowe, 14, Estancia
Lola Chávez, 17, El Rito
Ana Chávez, 14, El Rito
Bertha Forney, 30, Mountainair
Elizabeth Doane, 28, Roswell
Carmen Martínez, 14, Abiquiu
Amabilís Moya, 17, Coyote
Baselisa Márquez, 15, El Rito
Cleofas Martínez, 18, La Madera

Jesus M. Jaramillo, 59, El Rito
Juan García, 19, Ojo Caliente
Geronimo Archuleta, 17, El Rito
Socorro Chacón, 16, El Rito
Oscar Hoskins, 20, Frankfort, KY
Alfredo Salazar, 14, Chamita
Refugio Guillén, 24, Alcalde
Guadalupe Trujillo, 20, Ojo Caliente
Celestino Jaramillo, 17, El Rito
Pedro Martínez, 16, Alcalde
Amalia Martínez, 25, Velarde
Eli Martínez, 18, Tierra Amarilla
Marie Ferran, 24, Gallina
Clotilde Ortíz, 25, Alcalde

Students 1910–1911

Alfredo Salazar, 15, Chamita
Ralph Dixon, 16, El Rito
Gretchen Dixon, 15, El Rito
Dixie Dixon, 15, El Rito
Manuel S. Trujillo, 18, El Rito
Carlos Gonzáles, 15, El Rito
Jose R. López, 19, El Rito
Lenora Woods, 19, Venus
Belle Woods, 17, Venus
Sarah Keller, 23, Venus
Julian Trujillo, 17, Ojo Caliente
Martin J. Suazo, 20, Park View
Amalia M. Rodríguez, 27, Velarde
Amalia Chávez, 15, Vallecitos
Onesimo Chávez, 17, Vallecitos
Nettie Wartembe, 47, Springer
Tomás Rivera, 25, El Rito
Celestino Jaramillo, 18, El Rito
Cleofes Martínez, 20, Ojo Caliente
Pablo Gallegos, 18, Ojo Caliente
William Gallegos, 16, Ojo Caliente

Alberto Chávez 17, Vallecitos
Miguel A.Gallegos, 19, El Rito
Cristóbal Quintana, 17, Taos
José M. Quintana, 16, Taos
Sadie Pippin, 24, Santa Fe
Fidel Jaramillo, 16, Vallecitos
Marína Jaramillo, 14, Vallecitos
Anastacio Trujillo, 20, El Rito
Lorenzo Herrera, 17, Chamita
Tomas Martinez 18, Ranchos de Taos
Celso E. Martínez, 23, Ranchos de Taos
Gilberto Durán, 23, El Rito
Emilio Salazar, 16, Park View
Clotilde Trujillo, 23, El Rito
Flavio Montoya, 28, Española
Ursulo Ortíz, 21, Chimayó
Bonifacio R. Martínez, 22, Chimayo
Ramon R. Quintana, 22, Santa Cruz
Juan B. García, 21, Ojo Caliente
Juan S. Rael, 20, Questa
J. Enrique Rael, 19, Questa
Praxedes Rael, 15, Questa
Epifanio Rivera, 14, Ojo Caliente
Preciliano Moya, 15, Abiquiu
Baselisa Márquez, 17, El Rito
Francisco Rivera, 19, El Rito
Francisco Vigil, 17, El Rito
Jose D. Trujillo, 16, El Rito
Eduardo Baros, 15, El Rito
Amalia Chávez, 25, Abiquiu
Refugio Guillén, 27, Alcalde
Senaidita Guillén, 16, Alcalde

Students 1911–1912

Ralph Dixon, 17, El Rito
Gretchen Dixon, 16, El Rito
Dixie Dixon, 15, El Rito

Rudy Jaramillo, 12, El Rito
Ciria Martínez, 15, El Rito
Clotilde Trujillo, 24, El Rito
Preciliano López, 18, El Rito
Gusman Martínez, 14, El Rito
Fabián Gonzáles, 20, El Rito
Jose R. López, 20, El Rito
Gerónimo Archuleta, 19, El Rito
Miguel Gallegos, 20, El Rito
Carlos Gonzáles, 15, El Rito
Sadie Pippin, 25, Santa Fe
Julian Trujillo, 18, Ojo Caliente
Pablo Gallegos, 19, Ojo Caliente
Cleofes Martínez, 21, Ojo Caliente
William Gallegos, 17, Ojo Caliente
Dionicio Sánchez, 16, Ojo Caliente
Manuel Griego, 17, Ojo Caliente
Guadalupe Trujillo, 22, Ojo Caliente
Juan Espinoza, 22, Chamita
Maximiliano Salazar, 18, Chamita
Alfredo Salazar, 15, Chamita
Serapio Herrera, 11, Chamita
Lorenzo Herrera, 18, Chamita
Agustin García, 21, Chamita
German Gallegos, 18, Chamita
Canuto Trujillo, 16, Chimayó
Nemecio Martínez, 21, Chimayó
Joseph McWilliams, 20, Tierra Amarilla
Katherine Martínez, 14, Tierra Amarilla
Jose M. Quintana, 18, Taos
Cristóbal Quintana, 17, Taos
Antonio Montoya, 22, Taos
Juan Cisneros, 19, Taos
Fares Martínez, 22, Taos
Eusebio Vigil, 19, Taos
Nepomuceno Vigil, 20, Taos
Marcos Pacheco, 16, Arroyo Seco
Onesimo Torres, 19, Arroyo Seco

Alberto Chávez, 18, Vallecitos
Fidel Jaramillo, 17, Vallecitos
Quirino Vargas, 12, Vallecitos
Onesimo Chávez, 18, Vallecitos
Amalia Chávez, 16, Vallecitos
Lucia Chávez, 13, Vallecitos
Josefina Chávez, 10, Vallecitos
Jose R. P. Martínez, 12, Cebolla
Joe T. Montaño, 22, Cebolla
Juan Rael, 21, Questa
J. Enrique Rael, 21, Questa
Esequiel Rael, 18, Questa
Praxedes Rael, 18, Questa
Bailon B. Montaño, 19, Pastura
Amado Martínez, 17, Velarde
José D. Velarde, 18, Velarde
Juan López, 17, Santa Cruz
Josefina López, 18, Santa Cruz
Regina López, 15, Santa Cruz
Matilde Martínez, 15, El Rito
Jesusita Gallegos, 18, Abiquiu

Graduates of the Normal School (as high school)

Graduating Class of 1922

Laura Redman

Graduating Class of 1923

Glenn Redman
Sixto Valdez
Sarah Vargas

Graduating Class of 1924

Anita Arellano
Pablo Flores
Bolivar Martínez
Lawrence Redman
José B. Trujillo
Lafayette Varela
Cornelio Vigil

Graduating Class of 1929

Raymond Romero (Vadito)
Pauline Goddard (El Rito)
Richard Ortega (Chimayó)
Olive Parker (El Rito)
José M. Valdez (Lyden)
Simmie Atencio (Santa Cruz)
Cruz Trujillo (Chimayó)

Graduating Class of 1932

Lorencíta Chávez
Manuelita Herrera
Fernando Cruz
Trinidad López
Casimira Gonzáles
Pedro Maestas
E. Otila Gonzáles
Frederick Martínez
Hernando J. Gonzáles
Guillermo Martínez
Calicia Griego
Nellie Miranda
Faustina Gurulé
J. Amado Trujillo
Fay Marie Hembree
Samuel Trujllo

Graduating Class of 1933

Margarita Abeyta
Pedro Tomás Lucero
Presciliano Alire
Thomas Allen Martin
Branche Viola Bull
Elena Estella Martínez
Nicholas Candelaria
José Elías Romero
Martinianeau Felix
Juan Pedro Romero
Edward Earl Goodwin
Lydia Valdéz
Isaac Gurulé
Mati Anita Vigil
Juan Francisco Lobato
Harriet Eluisa Weaver
Alberto López
Haskell Ward Weaver
Stella López

Graduating Class of 1934

María Florentine Archuleta
Gilberto Archuleta
Natividad Atencio
Margaret Alice DesGeorges
José Isaac Dominguez
Ernestina F. Durán
Juan Antonio García
Salomon García
Michael Garner
Herbert Doyle Johnson
José Abbot Jaramillo
David Jaramillo
George A. Lobato
Pedro López
Isidoro Lucero, Jr.
Juan Francisco Manzanares
Carlos Martínez, Jr.
Elisa Ortíz
Beatrice Mae McKinnrey
María Cordelia Ortíz
Rosa Cecilia Ortíz
María Dolores Montoya
Amadeo Romero
Agneda Sánchez
María Irene Sánchez
Juan Ray Sena
José Lucas Trujillo
Cruz U. Valdéz

Graduating Class of 1938

Ernestine Cora Alarid
Eugene Chacón
Mike A. Chacón
Ramona Chávez
Cordilia Córdova
Mary Emalyn Daggett
Dan G. García
William Fred Gilliam
Joe A. Gonzáles
Ida Herrera
Joseph A. Luchetti
Dilia Manzanares
Fermín Presiliano Manzanares
Magdalena Manzanares
Severo Martínez
Manuel Eustaquio Medina
Preddie Medina
María L. Montoya
Joe F. Ortíz
Úrsula Ortíz
Ernest Quintana
Grace Sånchez
Manuel D. Sánchez
Victor F. Sánchez
María Eloisa Santistevan
Albert Curtis Thatcher
Amelia Trujillo
Cleofas L. Trujillo
Waldo Velásquez
Alonzo Henry Vigil
Mary Laura Vigil
Paul R. Vigil

Graduating Class of 1939

Eduvigen Archuletas
Rosinda Cordilia Rivera
Sam Jaramillo
Eliseo G. Vigil
Marcelino M. Sánchez
Lucas Jaramillo
Magin Rosina Chavez
Jimmie J. Billia
Eleno Candelaria
Flora Montoya
Cardenio Ramirez Montoya, Jr.
Jose Eduardo Vigil
John Scarborough
Onesimo Guillermo Martínez, Jr.
Salomon Mascareñas
Patrocino Martínez, Jr.
Julia Chacón
Juan M. Martínez
Malaquías Martínez
Marie Celina Martínez
James T. Cage, Jr.
Albert J. Villareal
Margarito Alex Archuleta
John A. Martin
Jewell Irene Allison
Celestine Jaramillo
Edward Varoz, Jr.

Graduating Class of 1941

Adela Pacheco
Clorinda Manzanares
Antonia Herrera
Elaiza Gonzáles
Regina Manzanares
Mary Frances Sánchez
Dora Atencio
Emma Jo Ball
Lawrence Velásquez
Abedón Varoz
Benito Valdéz
Ross Roybal
Robert Herrera
Antonio Chávez
Reducindo Chávez
Tony Manzanares
Sarah Jácquez
Stella Norris
Helen Espinoza
Lucille Wasson
Alma Banowsky
Eloisa Casados
Ernestine Lucero
Liberato Quintana
Fred Sandoval
Fiore Luchetti
Tommy Foster
Jack Roberson
Berny Valdéz
Billy Hartwell
Jane Goddard
Cristobal Lavadie
Lawrence García

Graduating Class of 1942

Helen Crume
Daniel Martínez
Arturo Gallegos
Aniceto Varoz
Matías Chacón
Tony Rivera
J. L. López
Kathryn Stanturf
Ted Varoz
Mildred Córdova
Modesto Vigil
Gwen Barrett
Esther Baca
Joseph Martínez
Louise López
V. Suazo
Cleo Flores
Leon O'Neal
Ralph Chávez
Faye Stewart
Juliette Mente
Salomon Tafoya
Tony Perea
Margaret Martínez
Joe Leyba
Connie Sena
Faye Wynn
Sabino García
Mack Scarborough

Graduating Class of 1943

Donald Evans
Della Mente
Leopoldo Trujillo
Cruzita Olguín
I. B. Pickett, Jr.
Cleo Archuleta
Bernice Domínguez
Epimenio Baca
Wanda Harris
Fred Jácquez
Maria D. Gonzáles
Martín Jaramillo
Tina Córdova
Dan Lovato
Martin Chase
Ofelia Ortega
Alex Salazar
Alice Varoz
Louise Vigil
Polly C. García
Nick García
Margaret Luján
Rubén Miera
Gordon Darling
Billie B. Johnson
Pat Martin
Alfredo Aguirre
Manuel García
Trinidad Griego
Lizzie Le Doux
Mary Sánchez
Ubaldo Vigil
Ida Johnson
Ambrosio Martínez
Cecilia Sena

Graduating Class of 1944

Paul Romero
Helen Jo Medina
Teofila Jácquez
Jeanne Belknap
Angela Velarde
Tony Griego
Leonor Torres
Johnny Manzanares
Isabel Jaramillo
Mela Baca
Joe Trujillo
Ramona Martínez
Antonio Herrera
Dulcinea Girón
Alfonso Luján
Carmen Lucero
Martha Archuleta
José Fernández
Eva Dean Roberson
Neva Jean Roberson
Isabel G. Trujillo
Joe R. Gonzáles

Graduating Class of 1945

Filemon Lovato
Julia Jaramillo
Rubén Manzanares
Irma Sisneros
Rufina Gallegos
Carlos López
Priscilla Rael
Manuela Vigil
Olivia Luján
Cora Martínez
Consuelo Manzanares
Gloria Vouterin
Ralph García
Margaret Atencio
Carroll Walsh
Lawrence Martínez
Clorinda Suazo
Elías Quintana

Graduating Class of 1946

Elsie Rael
Louise Abeyta
Helen Mendoza
Albinita Maestas
Frances Sánchez
Pearl Bacalski
Aurora Cisneros
Lorencita Barela
Camilo E. Medina, Jr.
Gilbert Martínez
Antonia Vigil
Malaquías Rael
Loretta Martínez
Orlinda Trujillo
Theodore Kuntz
Thomas Lavadie
Leona Adams
Louise Naranjo
Veroniz Lucero
Michael García
Loyola Aragón
Candelaria Martínez
Rumaldo Miera
José M. Herrera
Rudolfo Jaramillo
Ernesto Martínez
William Scarborough
Bernie Jaramillo

Graduating Class of 1947

Leo Apodaca
Fabiola Jaramillo
Leo Montoya
Elfego Aranda
Gilbert Jaramillo
Margaret Ortíz
Lupe Chávez
Ross López
Concy Romero
Lena Cisneros
Richard Malooly
Sam Romero
Albert Dominguez
Pauline Manzanares
Francis Roybal
Cora I. Eichtle
Juanita Márquez
Edward Salazar
Lloyd Englebrecht
Andrés Martínez
Helen Sánchez
Leo Fernández
Anita E. Martínez
Isabel Sánchez
Frankie Gallegos
Annie Martínez

George Sandoval
Mike Gallegos
Atanacio Martínez
Alice Trujillo
Dolores Gómez
Chris Martínez
Marcia Trujillo
Reyes Gonzáles
Rosella Martínez
Ramona Trujillo
David Grant
Rosina Mendoza
Eleanor Vigil
Ernest Gurulé
Mary Jean Mondragón

Graduating Class of 1948

Eva Aragón
Rose Gallegos
Lillian Mondragón
John Aragón
Ramona Gonzáles
Beau Newbern
Cliseria Archuleta
Hilda Gutiérrez
Annie Ocaña
Amelia Baca
Cristóbal Jaramillo
Dolores Rodríguez
Geneva Baca
Anna Mae King
Genaro Roybal
Edward Birmingham
Juanita Lucero
Dorothea Russ
Audoro Campos
Gilbert Maestas
Hannah Suazo
Roy Carrejo
Rosalie Manzanares
Norbert Trujillo
Carmen Chacón
Gonzalo Martínez
Mary A. Valdéz
Belen Espinoza
Orlando Martínez
Adelia Vigil
Porfirio Frésquez
Mary Macareñas
Pat Vigil
Flora Gallegos
Jean McCoy

Graduating Class of 1949

Lucy Archuleta
Billy Gonzáles
Lourdes Pacheco
Madge Baca
Irene Herrera
Fred Rael
Nick G. Baca
Delourdes Jácquez
Ermelina Romero
Betty Jo Carnes
Anastacio Lobato
Tillie Sisneros
Elsie García
Cassie Márquez
Leo R. Suazo
Filemon García
Eduardo Martínez
Mary Trujillo
Lila García
Isabella Martiínez
Susie Trujillo
Preciliano García
Robert Mascareñas
Lila Valdéz
Tony García
Carl Naranjo
Theresa Vigil
Berniece Gonzáles
Joan Odom

Graduating Class of 1950

Ruben Archuleta
Leo Sánchez
Consuelo Trambley
Wanda Adams
Clotario Archuleta
Orlando Arellano
Ernie Dow
Laura Branch
Rosalie Chávez
Charlie García
Ralph Gallegos
Marcella Durán
Bernie Gallegos
Elias Hurtado
Eloise Gallegos
Albiar Jaramillo
Tony Lucero
Eva Gallegos
Frances García
Salomon Martínez
Sally García
Elizario Montoya
Ben Roybal
Stella O. Gallegos
Marcia Hurtado
David Thatcher
Soraida Lucero
Indalesio Torres
Luis J. Trujillo
Helen Madrid
Fabiola Manzanares
Ernie Vigil
Mary Gloria Márquez
Mary Martínez
Olivia Martínez
Virginia Mondragón
Frances Moya
Kathie Price
Florence Quintana
Lucy Roybal
Rosina Salazar
Celia Sisneros
Angie Varela
Gilbert Vigil
Isidore Vigil
Juan Vigil
Richard Rael
Ernestine Rael
Raymond Rodriguez

Graduating Class of 1951

Evangeline Martínez
Laurence Smith
Eremita Salazar
Tony Montoya
Beva Manzanares
Danny Chávez
Joe Fernández
Orilia Vigil
Donald Hatch
Evangeline Manzanares
Horacio Jaramillo
Marie Sánchez
Rose Lucero
Luis Baca
Consuelo Moya
Azucena Lobato
Steve Archuleta
Abel Gómez
Stella Manzanares
Joe Jaramillo
Corine Sánchez
Rose Rivera
Susan McCoskey
David Smith
Helen L. Valdez
Leonard Trujillo
Claudina Manzanares
Arcelia Vigil
Orlando Peña
Lisbeth Giddings

Graduating Class of 1952

Theresa Baca
Roman Chacón
Pete Chávez
Terry Crider
Irene Delgado
Fern Harris
Alfonso Jaramillo
Benito Juárez
Mary Margaret Lobato
Libradita Lucero
Fred Mares
Johnny Molina
Johnny Molina
Roman Mondragón
Celina Ortíz
Saby Rimbert
Ruby Rivera
Lucy Trujillo
Mary Valencia
Arturo "Casey" Martínez
Regino Salazar

Graduating Class of 1953

Charlie Aragón
Joella Archuleta
Lorraine Archuleta
Lawrence Barone
Katie Bateman
Flora Dominguez
Archie Dow
Carmen Durán
Amalia Espinoza
Elizabeth Lobato
Pete Lobato
Maxine Lucero
Rosina Lucero
Ruben Lucero
Josephine Maes
Marie Maes
Angelina Martinez
Beatrice Martínez
Florence Mondragón
Tony Montoya
Raul Martínez
Albert Romero
Eddie Sisneros
Adelia Trujillo
Sencionita Varoz
Ermelinda Trujillo

Graduating Class of 1954

Julia Archuleta
Salomon Archuleta
Oralia Vigil
Mary Baros
Dorothy Bateman
David Borunda
Michael Branch
Jimmy Chávez
Lourdes Espinoza
Sammy Esquibel
Reyna Gonzáles
Richard García
Elva Jaramillo
Mike Jaramillo
Mel Lobato
Delfinia Lucero
Delia López
Ernestine Lucero
Urcinia Lucero
Betty Maes
Toribio Manzanares
Joe Martínez
Rafaelita Martínez
Gloria Ortíz
Simmie Romero
Dennis Salazar
Tim Sánchez
Theresa Sandoval
Manuel Torres
Aurelia Trujillo
Prescilla Trujillo
Barbara Valdez
Joe Valdez
Helen N. Valdez
Mary Vigil

Graduating Class of 1955

Alfonso Archuleta
Louise Archuleta
Mary Atencio
Viola Ávila
Esperanza Baca
Arnold Boggus
Emma Duran
Jo Ann Durán
Albert Esparcen
Manuel Ferran
Arlene Gonzáles
Lupe Juárez
Horacio Archuleta
Lorraine Gonzáles
Roman López
Felix López
Denny Lucero
Savino Lucero
Sylvia Lucero
Laura Lucero
Ted Martínez
Ida Peña
Rosemary Romero
Lee Sisneros
Leroy Martínez
Ernestine Trujillo
Olivia Trujillo
Mary Lou Trujillo
Patsy Trujillo
Peggy Trujillo
Viola Trujillo
Eli Valdez
Amarante Varoz

Graduating Class of 1956

Leo Archuleta
Socorro Baca
Chris Delgado
Orlando Dow
Ray Esquibel
Vangie Frésquez
Gerald Garcia
Eliseo Griego
Lydia Jaramillo
Sabine Griego
Santiago Jaramillo
Gerald Lewis
Horace López
Agustina Lucero
Josie Lucero
Isaura Maes
George Maestas
Dora Maestas
Orlando Manzanares
Estolano Márquez
Tito Martínez
Josie Ocaña
Norma Ordoñez
Florence Ruiz
Johnny Sánchez
Olivia Salazar
Katherine Tafoya
Sylvia Tafoya
Robert Torres
Abedon Trujillo
Eloy Trujillo
Reyna Velarde
Nancy Lee Vigil

Graduating Class of 1957

Vivian Manzanares
Sigfredo Maestas
Phil Miera
Gilbert Maestas
Florida Archuleta
Arthur Sanchez
David Baca
Tito Valdez
Otilia Esquibel
Connie Valdez
Joe Ortega
Polly Abeyta
Pete Romero
Cecilia Archuleta
Virginia Archuleta
Armida Velarde
Josie Lucero
Ida Montoya
Dennis Branch
Richard Manzanares
Leo Garcia
Cecilia Archuleta
Louie Sanchez
Sara Mary Chavez

Celedon Espinoza
Lydia Archuleta
Lugie R. Martinez
Nancy Zamora
Dorothy Trujillo
Erlinda Baca
Susie Martínez
Pete Manzanares
Janet Boggus
Gloria Baca
Porfirio Sánchez
Tom Bachicha
Eligio Jaramillo
Lee Leyba

Graduating Class of 1958

Celerino Archuleta
Rey Sisneros
Rosalie Montoya
Joe Stanley Sanchez
Drucella Trujillo
Viola López
David Trujillo
Mary Katherine Romero
Henry Serrano
Catherine Manzanares
Dulcie Peña
Mel Archuleta
Virginia Garcia
Olivia Gonzáles
Gilbert Varoz
Cora Ortega
Servilia Baca
Richard Martínez
Ross Martinez
Evila Lobato
Robert Trujillo
Lucille Trujillo
Helen Medina
Lucas Trujillo
Chris Quintana
Augustine H. Martínez
Ramon Baca, Jr.
Patricia Esquibel
Rudy Cornay
Robert Archuleta
Nila Jaramillo

Graduating Class of 1959

Luis Torres
Grace Márquez
Carlos Ortega
Louis Velarde
Criselda Archuleta
Rubén Lovato
Rudy Sisneros
Carmen Manzanares
Leroy Mondragón
Gilbert García
Ralph Martínez
Frances Vigil
Adán García
Mary Branch
Gilbert Sisneros
Gloria Bustos
Cecilia Romero
Mae Rose Maestas
Arthur C. de Baca
Elvira Vigil
Frido Martínez
Mary Martha Martínez
Adolfo Manzanares
Lía Ortega
Johnny Jaramillo
Randy Velarde
Cándido Trujillo
Sammy Martínez
Lucille Gonzáles
Alex Loomis
Mike Trujillo
Eloisa Jaramillo
Rudy Jaramillo
Elizaida Campos
Rudy Archuleta
Eloisa Manzanares

Graduating Class of 1960

Cleo G. Chávez
Manuel Corrales
Raymond Lobato
Rebecca Trujillo
Judy Martínez
John David Sánchez
Raymond Sánchez
Marie Trujillo
Erlinda Gonzáles
Ralph Herrera
Mary Frances Apodaca
Leroy Silva
Odelia Lucero
Roberta Lucero
Isaac Serrano
Robert Vigil
Mary Alice Cornay
Florinda Campos
Esmael Valerio
Betty Varoz
Bertina Archuleta
Leon Baca
Herman Trujillo
Lorraine Vigil
Fabiola Lucero
Ninfa Griego
Criselda Ortíz
Robert Romero
Dora C. Martinez
Gilbert Mascareñas
Priscilla Jaramillo
Joseph Valdez
Pete García
Johnny Atencio
Phil Flores

Graduating Class of 1961

Liova Archuleta
Marie Archuleta
Sally Archuleta
Patricia Baca
Alfred Barboa
Larry Barela
Priscilla Carrillo
Freddie Chávez
Robert Córdova
Leo Estrada
Arthur Griego
Alice Gutiérrez
Helen Gutiérrez
Theresa Lobato
Susie López
Pablo Maestas
Patricia Nieto
Dillio Ocaña
Sulema Ortega
Julian Padilla
Robert Romero
Ernest Santistevan
Jack Sena
Barry Stewart
Joan Trujillo
Joe Trujillo
Gilbert Valdez
Gene Varoz
Sifredo Martínez
Ruben Varela

Graduating Class of 1962

Diana Archuleta
Bertha Baca
Milnor Branch
Beva García
Juliet García
Amabel Gonzáles
Cecilia Gonzáles
Joe Gilbert Gonzáles
Lawrence Gutiérrez
Janet Klimka
Stella Candelaria
Annabell López
Mary Manzanares
Catherine Ann (Cam) Martin
Cora Martínez
Fredy Martínez
Bertram Peña
Ernest Peña
Rosie Quintana
Virginia Rimbert
Johnny Romero
Robert Rosales
Raymond Valdez
Peter Valdez
Amelia M. Vigil
Louise Dominguez
Douglas Mahaney

Graduating Class of 1963

Betty Atencio
James Baca
Johnell Carson
Oralia Chávez
Archie Crump
Benny Córdova
Helen Ferran
Beverly Gallegos
Dolores Gonzáles
Billy Jaramillo
Loretta Maes
Gloria Manzanares
Tony Marquez
Cecilia Martínez
Rosabel Martínez
Flora Moya
Allen Nickelson
Robert Rivera
Marian Sánchez
Marcia Valdez
Sue Ann Valencia
Cordy Varoz
Richard Velásquez

Graduating Class of 1964

Barbara Ann García
Johnny Baca
Jane Gómez
Teofilo Madrid
Tommy Martin
Sandra Gonzáles
John Esquivel
Roger Valdez
David Padilla
Stella Holmes
Marianne Valdez
Bob Couch
David Valdez
Nick Dantis
Gladys Archuleta
Mary Agnes Griego
Oliver Vigil, Jr.
Sam Archuleta
Maxine Gallegos
Napoleon Quintana
Milfred Martínez
Mercy Sandoval
Joe Martínez
Simmie García
Arturo Sisneros
Gilbert López
George Ann Vigil
Henry Baca
Mike Salazar
Esther Sánchez
William Gonzales
Ruth Salazar
John Dantis
Nancy Martínez
Alonzo García
Mary Ortíz
Silviano Archuleta
Dolores Martínez
Roger Davis
Sherry Fribley
José Rosario López

Graduating Class of 1965

Sam García
Mary Jane López
Carlos Martínez
Corine Archuleta
Clarence Jaramillo
Severo Padilla
Joe Córdova
Lawrence Baca
Joseph Baca
Billy A. Trujillo
Leo Griego
Palmeria Quintana
Albert Carrillo
Marcella Valdez
Sandra Vigil
Bobby Joe Gonzáles
Joann Martínez
Toby Lucero
Helen Harman
Ben Trujillo
Adelina García
Ernest Yanez

Roger Martínez
Cordy Lucero
Danny Trujillo
Barbara Valdez
Alfonso Trujillo
Pauline Alire
Cindy Hernandez
Fabian Martínez
Bertha Lucero
Jimmy Atencio
Ricky Martínez
Johnny Griego
Sam Salazar
Bertha Angela Trujillo
Tito Ortíz
Frances Romero
Larry Rogers
Peter Archuleta
Rudy Martínez

Graduating Class of 1966

Arnold Gallegos
Gerry García
Andy Archuleta
Florencio Archuleta
Leroy Salazar
Cecilia García
Rudy Jaramillo
Bertha Archuleta
Leo Valdez
Dorothy Martínez
Chris Martínez
Mary Toni Martínez
Juanito Lovato
Lucy Varoz
Sonny Maes
Marcella Martínez
Edith Valdez
Michael Ortíz
Alfred Gonzáles
Dolores García
Alice Lovato
Cruz Martínez
Tony Mauro
Sonny Ford
Mary Márquez
Alfonso Lucero
Juanita Ocaña
David Varoz

Graduating Class of 1967

Herman Abeyta
Susie G. Alire
Hilbert Archuleta
Presciliano Archuleta
Toby Archuleta
Phillip Branch
Diane Brewster
Roberta Campos
Georgina S. Chávez
Leo G. Cisneros
Fred DeVargas
Mabel Díaz
Rosemary Díaz
Donna Ellen Gallegos
Eileen Dorothy Gallegos
Joe García
Lawrence J. García
Janet Goddard
Eddie Gutiérrez
Ricky Gutiérrez
Josie López
Ponciano Madrid
Joseph Emery Maes
Tito Maestas
Steve Mantel
Barnie Martínez
Lito Montoya
Michael J. Ortíz
Serafin Padilla
Arthur Rodarte
Anthony Sandoval
Richard Sisneros
Jo Ann Trujillo
Richard Trujillo
Robert Valdez
Kathleen Vigil
Bud Vizcaíno

Graduating Class of 1968

Prescilla Alire
Charlene Archuleta
Donald Archuleta
Ruben Archuleta
Pamela Atencio
Yolanda Atencio
Lorraine Blea
Anthony Chacón
Chris Chávez
Alex García
Robert Goddard
Dolores Gonzáles
Johnny Gonzáles
Stanley Griego
Christine Gutiérrez
Gloria Herrera
Guzman Jaramillo
Cornelio López
Josephine Ybarra
Elma López
David Lucero
Raymond Lucero
Ralph Maes
Veronica Maes
Pauline Martínez
Phyllis Martínez
Prescilla Moya
George Peña
Arthur Romero
Marquita Sena
Jerome Torres
Catherine Valdez
Michael Valdez
Ramona Valdez

Graduating Class of 1969

Victor Chávez
Pamela García
Lydia Gutiérrez
David Jaramillo
Corine Lucero
Irene López
Anthony Manzanares
Greg Martin
JoAnne Martínez
Theresa Martínez
Judy Morales
Richard Romero
Benjie Trujillo
Eva Trujillo
Melva J. Trujillo
Steven Valdez
Isabel Vigil
John Wilkins
Linda Wilkins

INDEX OF PRINCIPAL NAMES

A

Eloy Abeyta, Bursar and Registrar during Joseph B. Grant years.

Frederick Lewis Allen, author, *Only Yesterday: An Informal History of the 1920s,* Perennial Classics, 1931.

Toney Anaya, Governor of New Mexico, 1983–1987.

Gerry Apodaca, Governor of New Mexico, 1975–1979.

Allison Aragón, artist, daughter of John A. Aragón.

John Aragón, President of New Mexico Highlands University.

Lena Archuleta, teacher during Joseph B. Grant years.

Gilbert Archuleta, staff member during Joseph B. Grant years.

Ruben Archuleta, like his older brother, an outstanding baseball player.

Carlos Atencio, member of a committee that created Northern New Mexico College.

Roman Atencio, Board of Regents; from Dixon, New Mexico.

B

Joe and Sue Baca, descendants of Filadelfio Baca; alumni guests from California.

Filadelfio Baca, sixth President of the Spanish American Normal School; founder of the high school.

Roman Baca, member, Board of Regents.

Richard J. Bailey, third President of Northern New Mexico College.

Nancy Barceló, second President of Northern New Mexico College.

Helen Valdez Bencey, daughter of Tito Valdez who was Assistant Superintendent of the Rio Arriba County schools.

John Bird, Governor, San Juan Pueblo and member, Board of Regents.

Michael Branch, member, Board of Regents.

Charles Brown, boys' Advisor and Coach, Joseph F. Grant years.

Frank Byers, coach in the early 1950s.

T. D. Burns, rancher, Chairman of the Rio Arriba County Commission, and uncle by marriage to Venceslao Jaramillo.

Tom Burns, lawyer, first cousin of Venceslao Jaramillo.

C

Mrs. E. C. Cabot, member, Board of Regents.

Amado Chavez, the first State School Superintendent appointed by Territorial Governor L. Bradford Prince.

Dennis Chavez, challenged Bronson Cutting for the governor's seat in

1934 and succeeded Bronson Cutting in the United States Senate.

W. D. Caster, Director, Academic Work.

John V. Conway, eighth President of the Spanish American Normal School; made a valiant effort to have the Normal School declared a junior college.

John W. Conway, John V. Conway's father.

María Paz Valdez Conway, John V. Conway's mother.

Ray Crider, Principal, 1951.

George Curry, Governor, 1907–1910.

D

Horace DeVargas, New Mexico State Senate; Chairman, Senate Education Committee.

Mrs. George Dixon, Assistant Principal, prior to appointment of George J. Martin as president.

E

Elizabeth L. Eckles, member, Board of Regents.

Stephen Elkins, Governor's designee to the House of Representatives; statehood was the issue.

G

Eloisa Gallegos, married to Facundo Rodriguez, Principal; staff member early 1950s.

Lawrence García, architect of record, Grant Gymnasium; a graduate of the Spanish American Normal School.

Rosario "Chayo" García, member, Board of Regents.

Glenn C. George, mathematics teacher, 1950s.

Edward H. Grant, science teacher, 1950s.

Joseph F. Grant, President of the Spanish American Normal School, 1934–1951.

José Griego, first President of Northern New Mexico College.

J

Cleofas M. Jaramillo, author of two books: *Shadows of the Past: Sombras del Pasado,* Ancient City Press, 1944; and, *Romance of a Little Village Girl* with an introduction by Tey Diana Rebodello, published in 2000 by The University of New Mexico Press. Readers will find it interesting that, apart from the second book cited above, Venceslao Jaramillo left little in writing. Letters that are left and archived in Santa Fé, New Mexico.

Venceslao Jaramillo, Founder of the Spanish American Normal School.

Willie Jaramillo, Bursar, early 1950s and 1960s.

José Jordi, seventh President of the Spanish American Normal School.

K

David E. Kyvig, author, *Daily Life in the United States, 1920–1940,* published in 2002, 2004; Ivan R. Dee, publisher, Chicago.

L

Ray and Mela Leger, he in the New Mexico Senate; they both taught at El Rito in the early 1950s.

Andrés Lucero, father of Fabiola Lucero Mayo.
Fabiola Lucero Mayo, class of 1944.

Felicita Bachicha Lucero, mother of Fabiola Lucero Mayo.

Dr. Guillermo Lux, author, *Politics and Education in Hispanic New Mexico: From Spanish American Normal School to Northern New Mexico Community College.*

M

Elizabeth Maestas, member, Board of Regents.

Filiberto Maestas, appointed member of the Board of Regents, 1951.

Sigfredo Maestas, third President of Northern New Mexico Community College; founder of the present institution, Northern New Mexico College, in order to fulfill its constitutional mandate: to train more teachers for public schools of this region.

Octaviano Manzanares, member, Board of Regents.

Pablo Mares, founder of the *Orquesta Típica* on the Spanish American Normal School campus.

George J. Martin, first President of the Spanish American Normal School.

Margaret Allen Martin, member, Board of Regents.

Michael A. Martin, member (twice), Board of Regents

Tom A. Martin, member, Board of Regents.

Louis F. "Lito" Martínez, Superintendent of the New Mexico Technical Vocational School, 1964.

Ted F. Martínez, member, Board of Regents. Ted's wife is Dolores; they have three children: Demetria, Elena Gallegos, and Dominic. Ted and Dolores have three grandchildren.

Vincent Martínez, Coach and teacher, 1950s and 1960s.

Robert McGeagh, PhD, provided documents for the naming of Delgado Hall on the campus in El Rito.

Edwin L. Mechem, Governor, 1951–1955, 1957–1959, 1961–1962; U.S. Senator; presided over the dedication of Venceslao Jaramillo Hall.

Juan E. Medina, member, Board of Regents; d. 1956.

Del Miera, member, Board of Regents.

John E. Miles, Governor, 1939–1943; U.S. House of Representatives.

Mary Ellen Montoya, teacher in 1949, 1950, and 1951, the final years of Joseph F. Grant.

Corinne L. Myers, Spanish teacher, early 1950s.

O

Emma T. Oakley, member, Board of Regents.

Miguel A. Otero, Governor, 1897–1906.

P

Herbert W. Prather, Principal and instructor, Joseph F. Grant years.

L. Bradford Prince, Territorial Governor, 1889–1893. Appointed by President Benjamin Harrison. Served in the New Mexico State Senate.

R

Celia DeBaca Redman, teacher from Las Vegas, New Mexico; member, Board of Regents.
Laura Redman, first graduate of the high school, Spanish American Normal School.

Lawrence Redman, brother of Laura Redman.

Michael Redman, dentist in Española, New Mexico; son of Lawrence Redman. Married to Mary Ellen Montoya, a teacher at El Rito during the final Joseph F. Grant years.

S

Priscilla Trujillo Schafer, graduate of Northern New Mexico Normal School; member of the Board of Regents. Married to James C. Schafer with whom they had three children: Michael Schafer, who died in February, 2019; Patrick Schafer, who is a Franciscan priest in Albuquerque; and Dolores Thompson, who is an engineer and lives in Portland, Oregon.

T

Priscilla C. Trujillo, Dean of the College; the most capable administrator in either of three institutions that I was associated with during 30 years of service.

V

Connie A. Valdez, second (interim) and fourth President of Northern New Mexico Community College.

Nick J. Vigil, member, Board of Regents.

W

Tom Wiley, author, *Public School Education in New Mexico,* 1965; Division of Government Research, The University of New Mexico, publisher.

Z

Mrs. O. C. Zingg.

O. C. Zingg, President of the Spanish American Normal School.

www.ingramcontent.com/pod-product-compliance
Lightning Source LLC
Chambersburg PA
CBHW030521230426
43665CB00010B/710